ArtScroll Mesorah Series®

Rabbi Nosson Scherman / Rabbi Meir Zlotowitz

General Editors

Published by
Mesorah Publications, ltd.

**Stories for all year,
from the life of the
Bostoner Rebbe, shlita,
of Boston and Jerusalem**

FIRST EDITION
First Impression . . . August 1997

Published and Distributed by
MESORAH PUBLICATIONS, Ltd.
4401 Second Avenue
Brooklyn, New York 11232

Distributed in Europe by
J. LEHMANN HEBREW BOOKSELLERS
20 Cambridge Terrace
Gateshead, Tyne and Wear
England NE8 1RP

Distributed in Israel by
SIFRIATI / A. GITLER — BOOKS
10 Hashomer Street
Bnei Brak 51361

Distributed in Australia & New Zealand by
GOLDS BOOK & GIFT CO.
36 William Street
Balaclava 3183, Vic., Australia

Distributed in South Africa by
KOLLEL BOOKSHOP
22 Muller Street
Yeoville 2198, Johannesburg, South Africa

ARTSCROLL HISTORY SERIES®
AND THE ANGELS LAUGHED
© Copyright 1997, by MESORAH PUBLICATIONS, Ltd.
4401 Second Avenue / Brooklyn, N.Y. 11232 / (718) 921-9000

ALL RIGHTS RESERVED.

This text, prefatory and associated textual contents and introductions,
including the typographic layout, cover artwork, charts and maps
have been designed, edited and revised as to content, form and style.

No part of this book may be reproduced
in any form without **written** permission from the copyright holder,
except by a reviewer who wishes to quote brief passages in connection with a review
written for inclusion in magazines or newspapers.

THE RIGHTS OF THE COPYRIGHT HOLDER WILL BE STRICTLY ENFORCED.

ISBN
1-57819-164-5 (hard cover)
1-57819-165-3 (paperback)

Typography by Compuscribe at ArtScroll Studios, Ltd.

Printed in the United States of America by Noble Book Press Corp.
Bound by Sefercraft, Quality Bookbinders, Ltd. Brooklyn, N.Y.

אריה דבי עילאה

Dedicated to the Memory of
Reb Arieh Leib Shalom Ben Yisroel, zt"l
נפטר כ"א כסלו תשל"ג

Devoted friend and supporter of the Bostoner Rebbe, Shlita, and a caring partner in his many endeavors.

A man of unusual humility, preferring anonymity to applause, he fled honor even as honor pursued him. A model of integrity and piety for all who knew him, he regarded this world as only the entrance to Olam Habah.

Together with his loving wife, Blanche, he raised a family of committed communal leaders who continue his tradition of service.

Recalling the enduring ability of his example to inspire, this 25th anniversary of his passing brings new meaning to the phrase
(כ"ה) 25 :כה לחי to life!

אתה שלום, וביתך שלום...

Foreword

We are delighted to write a few words of welcome and encouragement at the beginning of this book of stories about my father, Rav Pinchas Dovid Horowitz, *zt"l*, myself and the Bostoner community. Many of these stories have long been circulated orally among our Bostoner *Chassidim* and have now found a fitting home in this book. Others, particularly those of our early life, may be appearing for the first time. Although such stories can be entertaining, we hope that they will serve a more serious purpose as well. We hope that they will make us all more loving and more accepting of others, within an unshakable framework of a serious commitment to Torah and *mitzvos*. Such stories remind us that we are only human, and that being human also implies both an opportunity and a duty to become true *ovdei Hashem*.

The author of this book, a long-time *Chassid* and friend, shares our love of stories and our belief in their power to subtly touch and motivate the innermost recesses of the heart, recesses where the most brilliant logic cannot enter. We hope that some of that joy, optimism and warmth will fill both the author's book and life, and those of its readers as well.

Grand Rabbi Levi Yitzchak Horowitz
The Bostoner Rebbe

There was once an ignorant villager who always found a traveling guest to stay with him and conduct his Pesach seder. One year, despite tremendous effort, he could find no one. He faced catastrophe — a seder without a guest! The Heavens were in an uproar. After such mesiras nefesh, was this fair? Messengers were sent to the Highest Heavens to summon Elijah the Prophet to descend to Earth and be this simple farmer's guest.

Before the celestial guest could arrive, however, the villager went out to the barn, put a hat and coat on his favorite pony and led him inside the house. The farmer seated his dressed-up pony at the seder table and told his wife, "See, now we have a Pesach guest!"

And the angels in Heaven laughed.

They laughed, says the Baal Shem Tov, because the villager worked so hard, but look what he gave up at the last minute. They laughed, says the Bostoner Rebbe, because we all too often give up the heavenly in ourselves in exchange for the brute beast. Indeed, is there anything more ridiculous?

Table of Contents

Introduction

BEREISHIS: THE BOOK OF GENESIS
In the Beginning — 21
Bereishis
Rabbeinu Tam at Harvard • The Tree-Blessing Miracle — 24
Noach
On Fish, Challos, Noodles and the "Ice-cheh" — 32
Lech Lecha
The First Trip (1924) • The Second Trip (1929) — 38
Vayeira
The Millionaire Shochet • The Quincy Shochet — 44
Chayei Sarah
Pesach Provisions — 50
Toldos
The Third Trip (1934) • The Emir's Sister — 57
Vayeitzei
Torah V'yirah — 64
Vayishlach
Shuafat Shelanu • The Raffle — 71
Vayeishev
M.P. Smithwick, M.D. • Ship Shape — 77
Mikeitz
Boston Special Police Officer Singer
The Berditchever Rav — 82
Vayigash
Half a Shabbos • If Shuls Had Steeples — 88
Vayechi
Srulik — 94

SHEMOS: THE BOOK OF EXODUS

On Growing Up 99

Shemos
Yeshivah Torah Vodaath • Who's to Be a Rebbe? 101

Va'eira
The War Years • The Sosnovitzer Rav 108

Bo
The Mezuzah • Blind Sight 114

Beshalach
Shiras HaEast River • True Delight 120

Yisro
Zydatchov Scenes • A Wedding to Remember 126

Mishpatim
The Seaver Street Irregulars • The Home Front 133

Terumah
Eliyahu HaNavi in America • The Holy Goat 138

Tetzaveh
The Third Teletzke 144

Ki Sisa
The Snow Mikveh • The Torker Mikveh 149

Vayakhel
A Tzaddik After His Passing • Nylon! 154

Pekudei
The Curfew and the Belzer Rebbe 161

VAYIKRA: THE BOOK OF LEVITICUS

Getting Down to Work 168

Vayikra
Jewish Boston - 1944 170

Tzav
The French Bakery • Vegetable Soup 177

Shemini
Cholov Yisrael • Rav Isaac Herzog • Just Take a Look ... 182

Tazria
Made in Heaven 188

Metzora
Ornstein's Refuah • Even More 195

Acharei Mos
Amar Rabbi Akiva   203
Kedoshim
A Hospital Bris • Shabbos Shivah   208
Emor
Undone in Dorchester   213
Behar
Rav Kalmanowitz • At Home, Away From Home
The Home Run   218
Bechukosai
The Bechor   225

BAMIDBAR: THE BOOK OF NUMBERS
In Full Production   230
Bamidbar
Boston Comes to Brookline • Anything but ...   232
Naso
Hari Krishna Versus Shabbos • A Catholic Chaburah   238
Baha'aloscha
The Returned Tefillin • On the Brink
Delayed Reaction   245
Shelach Lecha
T.V. Dinners   251
Korach
Parent Problems • The Adoption   257
Chukas
The Wandering Casket   263
Balak
An Unfinished Journey • The Attorney General   268
Pinchas
To Be or Not To Be   276
Mattos
Ruth in New England • The Road Back   281
Masei
Medical Ethics • The Fountains of Rome   288

DEVARIM: THE BOOK OF DEUTERONOMY

Casting Accounts   297

Devarim
The Ponevezer Rav • The Granddaughter
Not Quite Kidnapped   299

Va'eschanan
A College of Cardinals   306

Eikev
Eliyahu in Nikolsburg   309

Re'eh
Commencements and the Jewish Question
A Cynical Sukkos   314

Shoftim
Driven • On Politics   320

Ki Seitzei
Slow to Go • The Wayward Glass
Shiluach HaKan   327

Ki Savo
The Aliyah • Double Trouble
The Lottery Ticket • The Conductor   333

Nitzavim
Boston Comes to Har Nof   339

Vayeilech
The Road Back • Three Parables • All for a Song   347

Ha'azinu
Chassidus on the Freedom Trail • Sculpt Yourself!
The Interview • A Mikveh in Nepal   353

VeZos HaBerachah
Clean Hands • On Devotion • The Kaddish   359

Genealogy   366
Glossary   370
Chronology   374

Introduction

ॐ *The Rebbe*

What you notice first and remember longest is the smile: a perpetual, accepting smile that never ceases to be amazed by the infinite variety and vagaries of life. A smile of bemusement? I think not. It is far too cheerful and conspiratorial, without a hint of aloofness or detachment. Perhaps it is the smile of a fond father watching his young children learning to walk, with a few small stumbles along the way — a pleasant mixture of humor and concern, sympathy and love.

Chassidic Rebbes generally emphasize one of two main approaches in their relationships with their *Chassidim*: greatness or simplicity. The Bostoner Rebbe, Rav Levi Yitzchak HaLevi Horowitz, *Shlita*, resembles his namesake and relative, Rav Levi Yitzchak of Berditchev, in following the latter. He seems to have three main precepts: Love G-d, love man and don't make too much of yourself in the process. Here are no retinues and pomp, although these have their legitimate place. Instead there is an unflagging interest in the common man, in every man.

The pious, the simple, even the outright antagonistic — all are welcome, greeted with the same calm, steady smile. Enter a Bostoner *shul* in Boston or Jerusalem and you will find scholars in black *kapotes* mingling freely with college students in jeans and lawyers in business suits. All are striving together; no one should remain outside.

When Rav Pinchas Dovid Horowitz, *zt"l*, the Rebbe's father, escaped from World War I in Europe to America (see next chapter), he took the highly unusual step of naming his *Chassidus* after an American city, rather than a European one. Why? "What could people expect of a *Bostoner* Rebbe?" he used to say. This gentle self-deprecation, combined with common sense and a dash of humor, remains a hallmark of "Boston" to this day.

The current Bostoner Rebbe continues this tradition of unassuming modesty. In Boston, the Rebbe and Rebbetzin used to live in a few rooms over the *shul*; the rest were filled with a diverse assortment of rotating guests. They now live across the street, to leave more room for the guests of ROFEH, the Rebbe's medical support organization. In Jerusalem, the Rebbe lives in a nice but simple apartment near the Bostoner Shul in Har Nof. The door, which is almost always open, has a small unpretentious cardboard sign that says "The Horowitzes." Only the constant stream of prominent rabbis, politicians and people needing help give away his secret.

Indeed, few important issues in the religious and political life of Israel's *chareidi* (strictly religious) community are decided without his advice. He is a member of the Council of Torah Sages, the highest Rabbinic Council of the Agudas Yisrael in Israel, and yet he walks to *shul* each night accompanied only by a neighbor or two. Asking someone else might be an "inconvenience."

Similarly, during Boston's formative years (which constitute the bulk of this book), the Rebbe would often take the initiative and personally call one of his startled *Chassidim*, when he felt that the occasion warranted it. Although Boston is now much larger, the emphasis on the personal touch remains. The Rebbe is always relaxed and somehow accessible, as if expecting someone, although his constantly ringing telephones are now first answered by volunteers.

Despite his gentleness, the Rebbe takes leadership seriously, answers questions confidently and walks with a deliberate, almost stately, step. By refusing to compromise his principles, while strenuously avoiding unnecessary conflict, he has won the respect of the community at large. The Rebbe is interested in, and takes full advantage of, modern technology. His ROFEH organization includes Boston's top physicians and he keeps in touch with many of his *Chassidim* by fax. However, he is not in awe of man or the shallow trappings of human power and technology. His gaze is fixed somewhere beyond.

What does a Chassidic Rebbe do all day? Far from being preoccupied solely with his spiritual strivings, a Chassidic Rebbe mostly spends his days in *chessed*, helping other people realize their own inner strengths and potentials. Oddly enough, although the Bostoner Rebbe's many medical activities, political connections, etc. have all been well documented in numerous articles and publications, these efforts have largely missed the mark. By emphasizing how the Bostoner Rebbe differs from other Rebbes, they have often neglected how the Rebbe resembles them, what makes him a Rebbe in the first place: his emphasis on *chessed*, humility, religious sincerity and helping the *poshuteh Yid*, the ordinary Jew.

The Rebbe is a great lover and teller of stories, and has a natural eye for detail. I have gathered from the Rebbe over 100 such short stories and vignettes: people and their problems, childhood memories, travels, *Chassidus*, stories of the Rebbe's father, and more. Through these tales a whole world comes alive — full of saints, savants, simpletons and not a few sinners — intensely personal, but at the same time universal, a testimony to "He Who varies the form of His creatures." I have selected some of those stories for this first collection, edited them only as necessary, changing some names, places and other details to preserve anonymity. I have keyed them to the weekly *parshah*, added some explanatory material on Boston *Chassidus*, and this book is the result. Although not a biography per se, I have tried to preserve the rough chronological order of the stories to provide a coherent sense of time.

❧ The Stories

Chassidic stories have their own special characteristics. Above all they are oral, not literary, creations. They are told by *Chassidim* at relaxed gatherings, such as a Saturday night *Melaveh Malkah*, or after a late night study session in the *bais midrash*. One *Chassid* tells a story, which invariably reminds another *Chassid* of two more, and soon everyone can't wait to relate his favorite tale.

Given the nature of *Chassidim* and their setting, such Chassidic stories tend to be brief, direct, simple narratives, with a minimum of stage-setting and analysis. They have also a clear ending and moral, often the greatness of a particular Rebbe or the miraculous power of faith. Their form follows their function: Sentences tend to be short, mostly nouns and verbs, not adjectives. People dominate center stage and character is revealed mostly through actions and quotes. Since much of the drama is conveyed by tone, phrasing and gestures, rather than by words, such stories are also almost impossible to capture in writing.

The stories in this book are at once part of, and quite different from, such tales. Told by a Chassidic Rebbe, they share many of the hallmarks of a Chassidic story: brevity, simplicity, empathy, an emphasis on people, limited description, and so on. But they differ in many important ways as well. First, they are not "public" stories, meant to be told to a crowd. Rather they are private stories originally told in the quiet, reflective atmosphere of the Rebbe's study (although many have somehow become known among the *Chassidim*). Second, the protagonists are mostly ordinary people living in a familiar world, a world of elevators and trolleys, not the half-remembered, usually idealized, *shtetl*-world of a Europe that is no more.

In these stories, as in his life, the Rebbe insists on demythologizing himself, on being seen as a real man in a real world. He insists on having a real past, with a real childhood — even with occasional loneliness, boredom or pain — real challenges, and thus real accomplishments. His message is clear: Man is born *basar vadam* (flesh and blood); it is what he makes of himself that matters. There are thus comparatively few tales of the imposing miracles that give Chassidishe *"myses"* (stories) their ritualistic, larger-than-life feeling. In return, these narratives gain in modesty, intimacy and relevance to our own all-too-human lives.

These stories are also quite different from the stories and appreciations of *gedolim*, Jewish spiritual leaders, that have deservedly become so popular. The latter describe the exceptional piety, learning, diligence, charity and other good traits of important Torah leaders. Taken individually these stories are inspiring but, after a while, they tend to sound similar and even repetitive since, despite accidents of external circumstances and birth, all true religious leaders are indeed extraordinarily pious, learned, diligent, charitable and so on. This often forces the writers, admirers of one great leader or another, to vie with each other in ever more elaborate superlatives, in a vain attempt to distinguish the object of their admiration from others. Words and titles soon become meaningless, perhaps because the nature of a true *tzaddik* is always beyond where words and praise, no matter how eloquent, can reach.

The stories in this book are, in some sense, the opposite of such stories. They are not stories of outsiders trying to look inward to describe a great Rebbe. They are stories of a great Rebbe looking outward, a loving *tzaddik's-eye* view of the world. They are stories not only about the righteous and important, but also about the troubled and lost. They are lessons in how to value the supposedly unimportant, about how to open-heartedly accept all men, warts and all, and how to teach them their own worth.

By accepting those who stumble, by converting the anger they arouse into an understanding smile, the *tzaddik* can bring a spirit of grace into the world. He can urge the Heavenly Court, "If I, mere flesh, can accept this person, if I can love him and help him, then so should you. You must also smile at such goings on, for such is the lot of men." This is one aspect of the Kabbalistic concept of *lehamtik haDin*, sweetening the Divine Aspect of Strict Judgment with Compassion. As for us, we too must learn to step back, to recognize that man is not big enough to take himself too seriously.

Better to realize how ridiculous our errors must seem in the eyes of Heaven and to strive to do better in the future.

The stories in this book are presented in the first person, because there is no other way to capture their immediacy in writing. Still, despite all efforts to be accurate and unobtrusive, the Rebbe of the book is, in the final analysis, inevitably close to, but not quite, the Rebbe of real life. It is impossible to capture the Rebbe's Yankee twang, his twinkling eyes and the amused yet sympathetic tone of a keen observer who clearly relishes the kaleidoscopic variety of life. Nor does asking him help. He is far too full of *chessed* to say, "No, not like that; not like that at all."

As for technical matters, we have generally followed ArtScroll's standard transliterations, although Chassidic (here Galician) pronunciation may vary. To avoid confusion we consistently use the phrases "the Rebbe" and "the Bostoner Rebbe" to refer to R' Levi Yitzchak Horowitz, *Shlita*, the current Bostoner Rebbe of Boston, not his father, R' Pinchas Dovid Horowitz (the first Bostoner Rebbe), his brother, R' Moshe Horowitz (the first Bostoner Rebbe of New York), or his nephews (the Bostoner Rebbes of New York and Flatbush). To avoid tiring the reader, epithets such as *zt"l, a"h,* etc. are generally used only the first time a name is introduced, and only infrequently thereafter.

Finally, an "occupational hazard." A Rebbe relates to his *Chassid* by descending to his level, totally identifying with him and then lifting him up. This makes it difficult to separate the individual "language" and personality of the Rebbe from those he helps. Even his everyday speech is liberally sprinkled with the Yiddish of his parents, the Harvardian English of a Boston professor and the slang of his many college student "friends."

I remember how once, when I was just starting to visit the Rebbe's *shul* in Boston, I found him engrossed in a lengthy conversation with a ten-year-old boy. They were talking enthusiastically about baseball. Later I told the Rebbe: "I didn't know that the Rebbe was interested in baseball."

"I'm not."

"Then why did the Rebbe talk to that boy about it for so long?"

Silence, a smile, and then, as if it were the most obvious thing in the world:

"Because it's important to him!"

This, then, is not a book of grand miracles, booming beatitudes, or imposing magic. Instead it presents a series of much smaller, more intimate canvases. Stories that deal with the still, small voice in all of us, with love, with compassion, with decency, hope and transformation — in short, with the most miraculous and magical things of all.

❧ *Acknowledgments*

One's first thanks, as always, are to *Hakadosh Baruch Hu*, Who in His kindness, has granted me the *zechus* to help present to others a glimpse of the inspiring mixture of warmth, wit and wisdom that is Boston.

Although space does not permit individually acknowledging all the many people who helped in this project, special mention is surely due Avrohom Biderman, Shmuel Blitz and the many talented members of Mesorah/ArtScroll in U.S. and Israel, whose constant help and encouragement were essential each step of the way. Particularly worthy of mention are R' Eli Kroen and Mindy Weil. The staff's care, professionalism and devotion to their craft show in the beautiful book this has become.

Thanks are due our readers, especially Mr. and Mrs. Moshe Adam, Rabbi and Mrs. Moshe Perkal and Mr. and Mrs. David Hoffman, for their careful reviews and comments, and to ArtScroll's readers whose comments were no less inspiring and helpful for being anonymous. We also acknowledge the helpful comments and encouragement of the Bostoner Rebbetzin, Rebbetzin Raichel Horowitz. Thanks are also due Mrs. Beth Gopin and Mrs. Nechi Perry for helping turn this taste of Boston's "oral tradition" into a printed one.

Although the Rebbe withheld and carefully disguised the identity of the protagonists of his stories, we would like to thank our unknown partners in this effort to help others. We apologize for any inaccuracies which may have, despite our best efforts, crept in (although some changes in names, places, professions, etc. may be a deliberate part of the Rebbe's insistence on preserving their anonymity).

Words fail to sufficiently express my gratitude to the Bostoner Rebbe, *Shlita*, for the time he so graciously and generously spent with me on this project. He has enriched our lives not only with his stories, but with his example, inspiration and love in a way that no book can adequately express.

Y.M.
Jerusalem 5757

A NOTE TO THE READER

Despite the stylistic use of the words "I," "my," "we" and "our" in the stories that follow, these stories are reconstructions by the author, not transcripts of actual conversations.

Bereishis
The Book of Genesis

Bereishis, In the Beginning

The Beginning. A time beyond our comprehension: our world, yet another world. The beginning of the physical world was chaos; the beginning of the moral world was Torah; the beginning of the human race was Adam; the beginning of Am Yisrael was Avraham Avinu. Before that, these things did not exist.

Chassidus also had a beginning: Rabbi Yisrael ben Eliezer, the Baal Shem Tov, who was born almost 300 years ago. His main disciple, R' Dov Ber, the Maggid of Mezritch, raised a generation of Chassidic leaders: R' Levi Yitzchak of Berditchev, R' Shneur Zalman of Liadi (later of Lubavitch), R' Elimelech of Lizhensk, R' Shmuel Shmelke HaLevi Horowitz of Nikolsburg and his brother, R' Pinchas HaLevi Horowitz of Frankfurt (the Ba'al Hafla'ah), and others. The Bostoner Rebbe is the seventh-generation descendant, son after son, the "Shabbos," of R' Shmuel Shmelke, zt"l.

The Bostoner Chassidus began with the Rebbe's father, R' Pinchas Dovid Horowitz, zt"l, who was born in Jerusalem in 1876. His grandfather, also named R' Shmuel Shmelke, and his grandmother, Rebbetzin Shayna Elka, the great-granddaughter of R' Dovid of Lelov, lived in the old Jewish community of Jerusalem, part of the "Old Yishuv." His father, R' Pinchas Dovid Horowitz, married Rebbetzin Soroh Sashe, the daughter of the Torka-Strettiner Rebbe, in 1906, and soon developed a reputation as a scholar. When World War I broke out in 1914, he was in Poland, where he had gone to represent the Yishuv in an important Jewish court case. Since he was traveling on an Austrian passport, he was technically an "enemy alien." After many narrow escapes, he made his way to Greece and boarded the last neutral ship leaving Athens for...America.

R' Pinchas Dovid Horowitz, zt"l, shortly after arriving in America

Rebbetzin Shayna Elka's brother, R' Dovid'l Biederman, a well-known Jerusalem tzaddik, had often urged R' Pinchas Dovid to go to America; but R' Pinchas Dovid had always refused. America was considered a religious wasteland in those days. In fact, as a matter of principle, R' Dovid'l usually refused to say goodbye to those leaving for its shores! Once communications were reestablished after the war, R' Pinchas Dovid sent a telegram to Jerusalem telling his surprised young wife where he was. She ran to R' Dovid'l who simply told her, "I know."

After a brief stay in New York, R' Pinchas Dovid moved to a small apartment on Barton Street, and then Chambers

Street, in Boston's (then) highly Jewish West End. He moved to a large house at 87 Poplar Street when his wife and their son Reb Moshe (1909-1982), zt"l, joined him in 1920. R' Levi Yitzchak Horowitz, Shlita, was born a year later; and his sister, the present Altstedter Rebbetzin, Faigie Thumim, soon thereafter.

The Rebbe's childhood home was an unusual one. It included a small shul, a small mikveh and a large, constant stream of guests: Chassidim, meshulachim (traveling charity collectors), newly arrived European immigrants (Boston was a major port), elderly visiting rabbis and relatives. These, plus his sister, Faigie, were the "friends" of his youth. While occasionally lonely, his childhood was far from bleak. As a young child everything fascinated him: the bustle in the shul, the house, the kitchen. This era, "the old days," roughly from the Rebbe's earliest memories until his bar mitzvah in Israel in 1934, form this first set of stories, his own personal Bereishis.

The Rebbe's home environment was fervently religious, Chassidic and "European" (R' Pinchas Dovid would speak only Yiddish). Despite the prevailing American preference for ease and compromise, R' Pinchas Dovid maintained his chumros (religious stringencies), not looking for an easy way out when it came to Jewish observance. On the other hand, he never imposed his personal stringencies or Chassidus on others. He accepted his growing band of followers "where they were at" while he simultaneously encouraged them, gently but firmly, to reject compromise in favor of pride in their Yiddishkeit.

Not realistic? Not in touch with the times? Perhaps, but as you'll see, sometimes "behind" is way ahead.

Bereishis

Hashem saw that the light was good,
And Hashem distinguished between light and darkness.
Hashem called the light "day,"
And the darkness He called "night."
(Genesis 1:4-5)

Hashem, in His absolute freedom and goodness, created the world from nothingness, from an absence of even time and space. Neither physical law nor moral law had any independent existence. All depend on Him, and all reveal His will. Man was given the ability and desire to strive toward an understanding of both the spiritual and physical world orders, so it is only natural to ask how the two types of truth, Torah and science, fit together.

To the degree that we properly understand the ultimate truths of both Torah and science, there can be no conflict between them. However, we have been working on understanding the Torah for over 3000 years, and properly trained and informed scientists are a comparatively new phenomenon. A scant hundred years ago the electron, proton and other basic building blocks of matter were totally unknown. Galaxies, quasars, general relativity, background radiation, quantum theory, the structure and importance of DNA and even the amino-acid sequence of insulin were all unknown.

Whenever some budding scholar comes to the Rebbe with yet another discourse on how modern science "proves" (or "disproves") Torah, he only smiles and says, "Maybe." We have had time to think over what the Torah says. Let's give science another 1000 years or so and then let's talk. Still, there are times when scientists and Torah scholars agree far better with each other than they do with people who lie somewhere in between, as the Rebbe points out in this story.

❧ *Rabbeinu Tam at Harvard*

It was a custom of Chassidic Rebbes in Europe to visit the small towns in their district and to give the inhabitants of these "outposts" *chizuk* (encouragement) and a sense of belonging. Throughout the 1930s Father also occasionally visited various outlying communities near Boston for Shabbos and, sometimes, we were allowed to go along with him.

We were once staying with the Andler family, close friends in Roxbury, who davened in the Shepotivka Shul. Many *shuls* in those days were still named after the towns in Europe from which their members came, in this case Shepotivka in Russia. Others were named after an occupation, like the impressive Shmatarskers' Shul in Chelsea, whose members were mostly in the *shmatah* (clothes and rags) business. The Shmatarskers were actually distinguished-looking, religious old men with long white beards; but they mostly died out, without leaving religiously involved children to replace them. There was also a Carpenters' Shul in Chelsea, part of the same "guild" tradition from Europe.

The Rav of the Shepotivka Shul also had a long white beard, but he tended to be somewhat lenient in outlook. Father held his *Shalosh Seudos* (third Shabbos meal) *tish* at the *shul* and prolonged it an hour or so after sunset, into the night. He was waiting for the extra-late end to Shabbos advocated by Rabbeinu Tam, a great medieval French Torah scholar (c. 1060-1130) and one of the *Ba'alei Tosafos*. (His opinion was accepted by R' Yosef Karo, author of the *Shulchan Aruch*, and

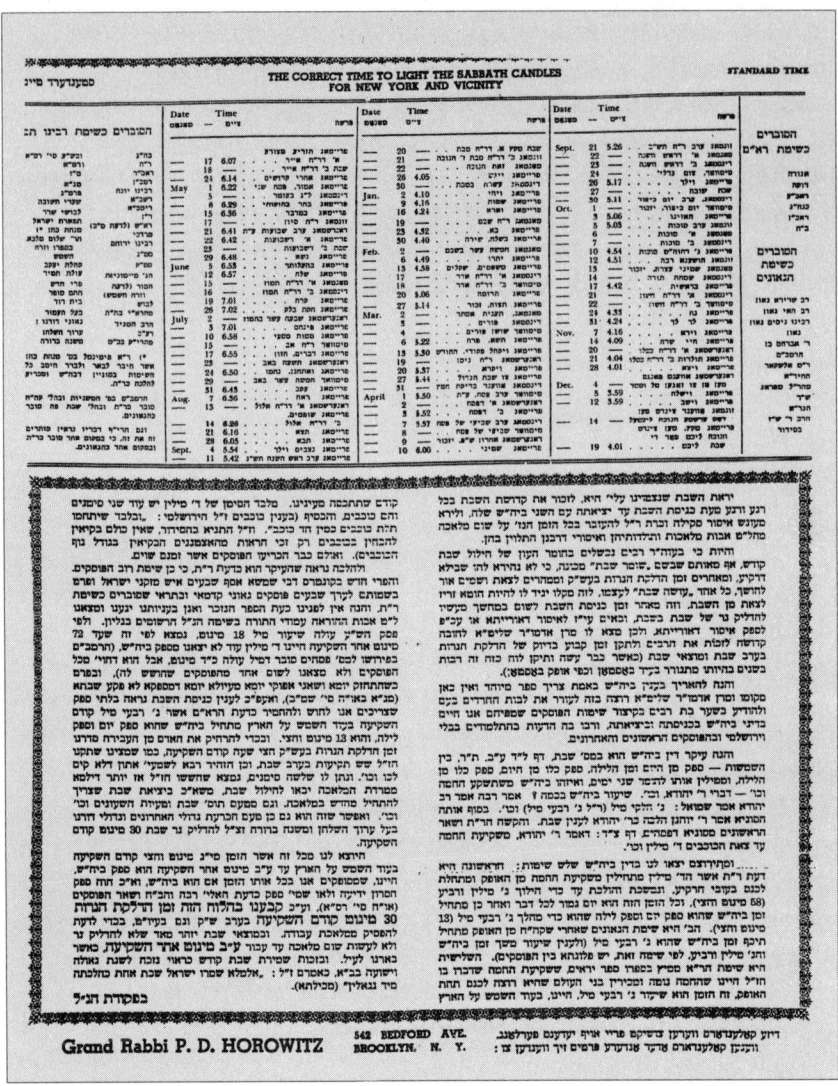

R' Pinchas Dovid's calendars consistently gave prominence to Rabbeinu Tam time. In this example, the second paragraph of the second column begins "and as for the halachah, the primary ruling is in accordance with the opinion of Rabbeinu Tam, for this is the opinion of most of the poskim (e.g., the Shulchan Aruch and Rama)."

by the *Rama*, R' Moshe Isserles, but not by the *Geonim* and the Vilna Gaon, whose opinion most communities currently follow.)

The *shul's* Rav kept looking at his watch and Father gathered from his host's uneasiness that this Rav felt under pressure for keeping his *balabatim* so late beyond their usual time of departure. When we came home, Father told us, "That Rav should know better. For *Chassidim*, night isn't night until Rabbeinu Tam time."

A few days later Father met a friend of his, Joseph S. Shubow. Although the rabbi of a non-Orthodox congregation, Shubow was very attached to Father and *Yiddishkeit*. Father had a marvelous ability to relate to all kinds of people, whatever their level of observance; and they usually reciprocated. Since Shubow was widely considered an intellectual, Father, who spoke only Yiddish, asked him to contact Professor Shipley, one of America's foremost astronomers at the Harvard Observatory, and ask him a simple question: When do astronomers declare it "nighttime"? Although only a theoretical question for Professor Shipley, this is a serious, complex issue for Jews and much depends on it. When is it Shabbos? When should a *bris* be done? Jewish halachic literature investigates the issue thoroughly, and Father was curious: What would Science say?

Shubow became quite excited by the issue and did arrange to meet Professor Shipley. The good professor said that the question was an interesting one, and agreed to write Father a brief report on it. In his long letter to Father, Professor Shipley pointed out that several different definitions of twilight are commonly used for different purposes (civil twilight, nautical twilight, etc). Astronomical twilight is when "no remnant of the sun's afterglow can be seen." Operationally, that means it is daytime until the sky no longer incrementally darkens.

For example, compare the sky 20 minutes after sunset and 5 minutes later. It darkened further in that interval, so it is still considered daytime. Try the same comparison at 40 minutes after sunset; the sky is still darkening. Once maximum darkness is reached, it is "nighttime." When does the depth of darkness stop changing? Once the sun drops 18 degrees below the horizon.

These kinds of astronomical data are all tabulated, and Professor Shipley sent Father a table showing when the sun was 18 degrees below the horizon in Boston throughout the year. Since the sun appears to make a 360-degree circuit every 24 hours, this 18 degrees correspond to 1.2 hours or 72 minutes. Although values vary somewhat with season, location, etc., they are all within reasonable agreement with the 72 minutes usually attributed to Rabbeinu Tam. Father was particularly excited by Professor Shipley's overall rationale for his calculations, that "light and day are synonymous." This was also precisely the basis of Rabbeinu Tam's definition which was, in turn, based on the verse in the first chapter of *Bereishis*: "And Hashem called the light 'day.'"

So a hard-pressed American Rabbi might accept night earlier — there are indeed other legitimate opinions — but Father always reminded his listeners that the Harvard Observatory agreed with Rabbeinu Tam.

※

> *Hashem planted a garden eastward, in Eden...*
> *And Hashem caused to grow from the ground*
> *Every tree that is pleasant to look at*
> *And good to eat.*
> *(Genesis 2:8-9)*

Judaism is not an ascetic religion. Hashem created all kinds of wonderful things for man to enjoy, and He delights in man's happiness. Still, one must not lose one's heart to the world. One must surround physical pleasures with constant reminders of Hashem's dominion and man's need to control his physical appetites. This is in part accomplished by reciting brachos and observing Torah restrictions. Within these permissible boundaries, however, physical pleasure is legitimate and often even commendable.

Fruits, which are enjoyed fresh, just as Hashem made them, occupy a special place in the Jewish hierarchy of physical pleasures, and we say a special brachah (Shehecheyanu) the first time we taste new fruits, each in its season. Similarly, the first fruits brought to the Bais HaMikdash (Holy Temple) were special and a cause for public rejoicing. As the Rebbe is fond of saying, there is a *special importance to beginnings. By saying a brachah before we eat a fruit, we are led to reflect on its source and significance at the very beginning, to appreciate its coming taste before we even taste it. Thus a brachah is largely thanks and praise for the marvelous potential of created things. Perhaps that is why our sages instituted a special brachah to be said over fruit trees in bloom, rather than when laden with ripe fruit.*

In Jewish mystical texts, the apple tree often represents Israel and the Shechinah, the Presence of Hashem in the world; and indeed a brachah can rest on an apple tree, as it can on all Hashem's physical creations.

❧ The Tree-Blessing Miracle

The Talmud prescribes a special blessing to be recited when savoring the first beautiful blossoms of fruit trees in the month of Nissan, the month of Spring. *Blessed are You ... Whose world lacks nothing, and Who created in it good creatures and trees, to benefit with them mankind.* As idyllic as that may sound, the West End of Boston, where our family lived in the 1920s and '30s, didn't grow much besides concrete. It was hardly an ideal place to locate fruit trees in full bloom. A book entitled *A Tree Grows in the West End* could never be written; there wasn't one!

Still, *Chassidim* are not deterred by such minor details, and every year Father sent out his *Chassidim* to search for the ideal place to make our annual *brachah* on the trees. In fact, the search for that *mitzvah* has been rather constant for the last 60 years. After moving back to Boston in the 1940s we began going to Arnold's Arboretum, a famous local collection of thousands of plants from all over the world. Something was always in bloom. There we gathered with our *Chassidim*, recited the *brachah* and danced in a large circle among beautiful, exotic plants.

Although we now spend the month of Nissan in Jerusalem,

which is blessed with lovely trees, we still have to send out search parties to find fruit trees that are blooming just when we need them to make the *brachah*. We often go to the Sataf, a spring in the Jerusalem Hills, where we also collect water for baking *matzos*.

The Rebbe leading his community to their annual tree-blessing ceremony at the Sataf Spring, near Jerusalem

There is a large terrace with a dramatic view across the valley, looking back towards Jerusalem. It is lovely, but one can't always rely on the timing, so we also use the garden of a local landscape artist who has a nice selection of fruit trees in his small Har Nof garden.

Back in the '30s, however, Father and his *Chassidim* would crowd into two or three cars and head for Boston's outlying suburbs, where greenery could still be found. Although only about nine or ten years old, I would also tag along.

One year we went out to Allston, which was then quite new and green (it is now considered an "Inner City" neighborhood). We drew up in front of a house that had a large plot of land, with what seemed to be fruit trees inside a tall surrounding fence. One of the drivers, Mr. Israel Sachs, *z"l*, went in to ask permission for us to enter and say our blessing over the trees. The man of the house wasn't in, but his wife, a good Italian Catholic, was quite gracious. "Of course. By all means!" Father got out of the car, and followed by a procession of his *Chassidim*, entered the gate.

We said our *brachah*, and prepared to leave, happy to have done our *mitzvah*. When Mr. Sachs went over to thank our hostess, she asked him: "Could you ask the Grand Rabbi for a special favor?"

"What is it?"

"Well, do you see that tree in the corner of the yard over there? It used to have very good apples, but for the last year or so, it hasn't produced any at all. Since the Rabbi gave a blessing to all the other trees, perhaps he could give that tree a blessing too."

Mr. Sachs translated her request to Father in Yiddish, and Father agreed. He turned around and said in Hebrew, "May this tree bring forth good fruits." We were touched that this good Catholic, who saw religious Jews saying prayers, was sufficiently impressed to ask them to pray for her too. It was a great *Kiddush Hashem*. Then we got back in the car, went back home and soon forgot about the whole thing.

That fall, Father's new *gabbai* came upstairs to tell him that a woman had come by and left him a large basket full of bright red apples. With the apples she left this message: "Please tell the Grand Rabbi that all these apples are from that barren apple tree he blessed!"

Such is the power of *mesiras nefesh* for a *mitzvah*.

Noach

[Now] every moving thing that lives
Shall be food for you, as vegetables were.
I have given you everything.
(Genesis 9:3)

Before the Flood, man was only allowed to eat plants and plant products. What we eat becomes part of us and finds fulfillment through us. The level of man before the Flood was such that he could not yet utilize and uplift the life force of animals, only plants. Adam was told, "Behold I have given you every vegetable ... and every tree ... for food." (Genesis 1:29). To control this permission, he was given one restriction: not to eat from the Tree of Knowledge. Noach was given permission to eat meat, but his greater opportunities came with greater responsibilities and restrictions: not to eat blood and not to eat flesh from a living animal.

At Sinai, the Jewish people were given the power to raise the food they ate to even greater spiritual heights, but that required even greater restrictions: proper slaughter, removing the blood, eating only kosher animals, not mixing milk and meat and the many other details of kashrus, details which make every proper act of eating ultimately an avodah, an act of Divine service.

In the Boston of the 1920s and '30s, keeping kashrus with all possible care, as the Rebbe's parents firmly insisted, was anything but easy. *Virtually nothing pre-made could be bought, and chassidim intent on maintaining their special chumros (religious stringencies) had to do virtually everything themselves. You want challos for Shabbos? Bake 'em. You want lokshen (noodles) for a kugel or soup? You couldn't just go out and buy kosher lokshen; you had to make your own. And you had to arrange for someone "special" to shecht (slaughter) your chickens and you cleaned your own fish. Compared to the ease with which kashrus can be observed today, religiously observant people were, in those days, virtually on a desert island.*

Still, the Rebbe's parents persisted, and taught by example the importance of purity, sacrifice for mitzvos and the heightened spiritual sensitivity that comes from completely avoiding the slightest exposure to non-kosher foods. The Rebbe remembers those days vividly, with all the freshness and fascination of childhood intact.

❧ *On Fish, Challos, Noodles and the "Ice-Cheh"*

To a small, young boy everything is wonderful, exciting, a real adventure. I can still remember things as simple, and yet as wondrous, as how we obtained our fish; no small deal in a house with as many guests as ours. Kosher chicken was hard to get, and usually reserved for Shabbos. Beef we had only at Pesach and Succos. Thus fish was an important staple in our busy kitchen all week long.

One of Father's *Chassidim*, Mr. Gordon, owned a fish market in Providence, Rhode Island. Although Providence is also near the sea, the main fish depot in those days was in Boston. Every week Mr. Gordon sent a big truck to Boston to pick up his fish; and every week it stopped at 87 Poplar Street to make a very special delivery before heading for home. This was a big event for us children. We woke up every Thursday morning to find a tremendous wooden crate in our hall, full of ice and whole fish, still smelling of the deep, salty sea. Looking back, it must have been a tremendous job for the women, cutting up and filleting a hundred pounds or so of fish every week. Somehow, my mother, Rebbetzin Soroh Sashe, and her trusty, efficient kitchen staff made it seem easy.

Rebbetzin Soroh Sashe was married when she was 12. Here she poses with the Rebbe's older brother, R' Moshe Horowitz – later the first Bostoner Rebbe of New York – just after they joined R' Pinchas Dovid in America (c. 1920).

On special occasions we received live carp as a "treat." To keep the carp alive, we had to put them in our large white four-legged bathtub. This was wonderful. My sister Faigie and I loved watching the large fish swim silently round and round the tub. We didn't have to go to an aquarium; we had one right in our own home. Then we had really fresh fish for Shabbos. It made a lasting impression. To this day I still prefer carp to even salmon and trout.

Fish aside, my mother's kitchen on Poplar Street was in full operation six days a week. She had to prepare not only for our family, but also for the many *meshulachim* (traveling charity collectors) who would come to spend time with us. We had 20 to 30 *meshulachim* as our guests at any one time! Boston had a large Jewish community, and the *meshulachim* came to collect donations and to service the *pushkas* (charity boxes) they left in every home. There was a lot of traffic and we had to feed and house them all for free, since there were few other places where they could get 100 percent reliable kosher food.

Mother had an assistant, Mrs. Kauffman, who helped her in the kitchen. She was a great cook, and she was there day and night, working almost continuously with Mother. Her *challos* were magnificent: large, beautifully formed and braided. Twelve of them were placed in front of Father for each Shabbos meal (*tish*), symbols of the twelve new loaves of *Lechem HaPanim* (Showbread) placed inside the Holy Temple each Shabbos. Other, smaller *challos* were distributed among the *Chassidim*.

Much of the kitchen was occupied by a big wooden table. On Fridays the whole top of the table was covered with rising *challos* — big *challos*, small *challos*, medium ones. Underneath the table there was a big wooden shelf, loaded with pots and pans. Given our large number of guests, many of the pots and pans were oversized, truly tremendous. We had enough to fill two or three walls of kitchen cabinets; only we didn't have *any* kitchen cabinets. Everything was crowded into the huge heap under the table. Finding and taking out just the right pot was no mean feat.

Even more vivid are my memories of the dining room, which had a tremendously large table, which seated 20 or so people.

The Rebbe and his sister Faigie were born in Boston. Here they pose with their mother, circa 1924.

The huge legs were each about a foot by a foot across. That was because our oversized table started out its life as a concert piano! The top had been removed and replaced. On Wednesday afternoon, this huge table would be completely covered with long flat strips of raw dough, Mrs. Kauffman's *lokshen* (noodles) in the making. After drying, the strips were rolled up like a jelly roll, cut into thin wheels, and unwound into the homemade noodles that graced our Shabbos soup. A parlor table full of drying noodles was a common sight in Europe, in the *shtetl*, but uncommon in the United States, except among those of us who wouldn't trust the *kashrus* of the store-bought variety.

Bereishis ❦ 35

Mrs. Kauffman's exquisite handmade *lokshen* were a real treat. Every Shabbos we had pan after pan of peppery noodle *kugel*, bowls full of *farfel* (small cut-up pieces of noodles) and tasty tangles of long, thin noodles floating in the chicken soup. Mrs. Kauffman had a knack for knowing just how long to let the *lokshen* dry before cooking them. We've tasted lots of store-bought noodles since; but they just don't make them that way any more.

❦

Difficult or not, *challos*, *farfel* and noodles could all be made in the kitchen; but what could a strictly kosher family do about meat in the Boston of the 1930s? Fortunately, we happened to have a professional chicken *shochet* (slaughterer) living with us, who also served as my *Gemara rebbi* by day. Every Wednesday morning, my mother would buy a few live chickens from the local market and take them, squawking noisily, home.

Every Wednesday night, we prepared for "The Big Production." First, Father would come down and inspect the knife. Then we lit two candles — a tradition rather than a necessity since there was a 60-watt light bulb overhead — and the *shochet* recited the required *brachah*. After the *shechitah*, Father would check the knife again. Then the *shochet* would give him the honor of covering the blood with earth, yet another *mitzvah* and another *brachah*. Since our little icebox hardly held anything, the chickens were *shechted* fresh each week, and soon found themselves on our Shabbos table.

We all used to call our icebox the "ice-cheh." I thought that was the Yiddish word for it, until I grew up and found out that it was just our family's pronunciation of "ice chest"! Getting the ice into the ice chest was another "Big Production." First a horse-drawn wagon with huge blocks of ice would come by on its weekly rounds and stop at our house. The iceman would cut off a block of ice, grab it with his huge ice tongs, throw it on his back and *shlep* it up the stairs to our kitchen.

We children were fascinated by how he cut the ice in his cart. First he used an ice pick to chisel a deep, perforated groove at the top of the block. Then he would neatly cleave the block all the way down to the bottom. He put the ice in the ice compartment of our ice chest and that was our total cooling supply for the week.

As the days passed, the ice block slowly melted, and the water dripped down into a large pan under the ice chest. This pan had to be emptied every so often. If we forgot to empty it in time, a not uncommon occurrence in our ultrabusy household, we soon had a flood all over the kitchen floor. This was usually followed by everyone asking everyone else, "Why didn't *you* empty the ice-cheh?"

Yes, it was a lot of work in those days; but the food had that special taste that comes from making every act an *avodah*.

Lech Lecha

*Go from your land and birthplace
And father's house,
To the land which I will show you
...and they came to the Land of Canaan.
(Genesis 12:1,5)*

The yearning for Eretz Yisrael and the ability to leave wherever we are and, like Avraham Avinu, settle in Eretz Yisrael, have been part of the Jewish people from their very beginning. They are part of the heritage of our forefathers, an indelible part of what it means to be a Torah Jew.

There is a well-known dispute among the Rishonim — the great Torah scholars who lived during the 11th-16th centuries C.E., — about the status of aliyah, "going up" to Eretz Yisrael, in our time. Ramban (Nachmanides) mainains that it is still a full-fledged Torah command: "Take hold of the land and settle it..." (Numbers 33:53). The Shelah HaKadosh, the Sefer Chareidim and Chasam Sofer concur with this view. Rambam (Maimonides) contends that living in Eretz Yisrael was never a Torah command, but rather a Rabbinic command. Rashi, Rosh and Ohr HaChaim HaKadosh agree with this view.

In either case, the Rebbe's father's top priority was always to live in Eretz Yisrael. Driven by circumstances to America, he always longed to leave his comfortable home in Boston and to follow the

"Lech Lecha" back to his roots in Eretz Yisrael. He tried three times to return and settle there — he even bought land there — but all three trips ended in failure. It was the one great disappointment of his life. His efforts bore fruit only in the next generation, when the Rebbe was able to fulfill his father's lifelong dream of returning Bostoner Chassidus to its Jerusalem home.

❧ The First Trip (1924)

Father was a *Yerushalmi Yid* and, although World War I forced him to America [see p. 2], he never ceased trying to return home. His first trip back to *Eretz Yisrael*, in 1925, was largely an attempt to reconnoiter and lay plans for a future permanent *aliyah*. He also had two other important purposes in mind: to fulfill the commandment of *kibud eim*, honoring his mother, Rebbetzin Shayna Elka, whom he hadn't seen for 11 years, and to make the special *brachah* said once every 28 years over the sun. Given Boston's inclement weather, Father felt that it was bound to be cloudy or rainy that day. He didn't want to have waited for 28 years in vain. As for the future, he said, "Who knows if I will even be here another 28 years from now?" As it turned out, unfortunately, he was not.

Father made the long sea voyage, arriving just in time for a violent Arab

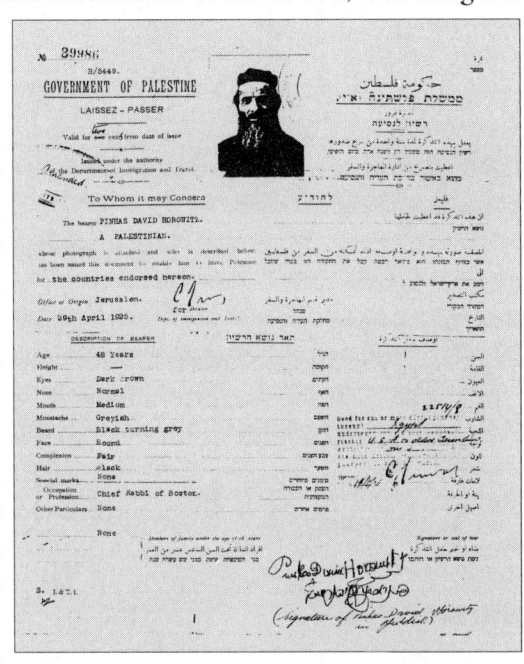

R' Pinchas Dovid was designated as "A PALESTINIAN," on this passport for his first trip back to Eretz Yisrael (1925).

pogrom. He saw his mother and made his *brachah* over the sun, but planning for the future was impossible under the circumstances. On the way home, he stopped in Vienna to consult its famous doctors regarding his eyesight, which was rapidly failing. While in Vienna, he bought the two large silver candelabra Mother used every Friday night. He also acquired the *sefer Torah* of R' Shmuel Shmelke of Nikolsburg, our well-known ancestor.

While in Vienna, Father visited R' Yisrael Tchortkover, zt"l, an important *Chassidishe* Rebbe and a grandson of R' Yisrael of Ruzhin. Unlike the more modest dynasties of Galicia, the Ruzhiner's Court was resplendent, an earthly representation of nobility and *malchus* (royalty). Although Father and the Tchortkover came from different traditions, Father and his ancestors always respected the purpose behind the splendor of other courts: to demonstrate the glory of Hashem's representatives in this world. He was also impressed by some of the very special heirlooms that dated back to the Ruzhiner himself, and beyond (the Ruzhiner was the great-grandson of the Maggid of Mezritch).

The difficulties Father faced in *Eretz Yisrael* did not dampen his enthusiasm and persistence one bit. He continued to plan, and to dream, and four years later he was ready for another try.

❧ *The Second Trip (1929)*

In 1929 American prosperity was at its peak. Everyone was a *gevir*, a rich man, or was sure that he was about to become one. Father was not feeling well — he already had serious hypertension and heart problems — but this only increased his determination to move back to *Eretz Yisrael*. How was he going to do this, support himself and maintain contact with his Bostoner *Chassidim*? He decided to reestablish the European custom of *ma'amados*, a group of people who agreed to take turns helping support the Rebbe and his household. Numerous *Chassidim* signed up, some for more, some for less, in a special *Sefer HaZahav*, "Golden Book," a *kvitel* book to be taken with Father to *Eretz Yisrael*.

We soon found ourselves packing up 87 Poplar Street for a move an ocean away, no small task. We couldn't very well take the Pesach flour mill from the basement, or the *mikveh*, or the heavy furniture, but virtually everything else was packed, boxed, baled or crated. That included Father's large library (Father was a tremendous lover of *sefarim* and an avid collector) and all our dishes, pots, pans, clothes, etc. I remember being surrounded by all the crates and containers that were to be shipped ahead as freight to "The Port of Jaffa, British Mandatory Palestine." I was only eight years old and it was all very exciting.

The Rebbe's father, R' Pinchas Dovid (left), with his gabbai and eldest son, R' Moshe, aboard the St. Louis at the start of his second trip back to Eretz Yisrael (1929).

Father announced his impending departure to his *Chassidim*, and the time and date were set for the grand farewell — the *Tzaischem L'shalom*. Although many religious Jews had already moved from Boston's West End to Dorchester and other suburbs, they came by the hundreds from all parts of Boston to see Father off, to hand him *kvitlach* and to wish us well on our new life in *Eretz Yisrael*.

There were two boats leaving from Boston that day: The Cunard Line's ocean liner left at 3 p.m., and the Hamburg-American Line's "St. Louis" was scheduled to leave at 12 noon. Agents for both lines vied for Father's patronage, since he was a local "celebrity." The St. Louis was newer and more amenable to Father's needs; but it was set to leave at noon and Father needed more time to say good-bye to all his *Chassidim* and friends. The matter was not decided until the day before we left. Then the Hamburg-American Line called to say that they would delay their sailing until 3 p.m., just "in order to have the Bostoner Rebbe on board." Needless to say, we traveled with them.

On departure day, our whole house was literally packed with people anxious to see us off. No one could move. Still, as a curious young boy, I just had to see what was going on in Father's study. After considerable struggling and pushing, I somehow managed to squeeze through the tight press of tall grownups. Father's table was covered with two large piles: a pile of *kvitlach*, and a pile of money, a pile that was a full 8 to 10 inches high. Outside the entire street was packed as tightly as our house, just a sea of bobbing heads and hats.

The mother of the manager of Boston's Checker Cab Company was a *Chassidiste* (follower) of my father, and the company reportedly donated 100 taxicabs to take everyone to the dock to see us off. Soon we were all headed to the pier which, like our house, was completely covered with *Chassidim*. At 3 p.m., departure time, the gangplank and boat were still full of well-wishers. The ship simply couldn't leave. It took the Boston police over an hour to finally clear the area. The gangplanks were raised at 4 p.m., and at 5 p.m. we set sail.

A non-Jewish photographer on board the boat saw all the goings-on and took a now-famous photograph of Father, my brother and Rabbi Baumel, Father's *gabbai* (attendant), standing on the deck of the boat. He later came down and offered to sell us the picture for a fee, which we gladly paid. Father always refused to allow himself to be photographed, but since the photograph had already been taken, there was no harm in keeping it. It is one of the very few pictures we have of him.

We first headed to Europe, to the famous spa at Karlsbad, Czechoslovakia. The hot mineral baths there were supposed to cure a variety of ills, while the spa's elaborate hotel and grounds were a popular tourist resort. The hope was that "taking the cure" at Karlsbad would help improve Father's deteriorating health.

While in Karlsbad, around *Tishah b'Av* time, we first heard the terrible reports of the 1929 Hebron Massacre. Exploiting British indifference, Arab mobs brutally slaughtered the Jewish community of Hebron, including the holy sages and students of the Hebron Yeshivah, while the British police looked "bravely" on. The mood in *Eretz Yisrael* was very tense. No one knew where the Arab murderers would strike next, and Rebbetzin Shayna Elka cabled us from

Jerusalem: "Don't come! Wait for things to calm down!" That message left us in Europe for some time. We spent the High Holy days and Succos in Torka, Poland, where my mother's father, R' Mechele Brandwein, zt"l, had been Rebbe. By then, however, he had already moved to New York, where he was known as the Torka-Strettiner Rebbe.

Unfortunately, not only did things not calm down in Israel, but the American stock market crashed, ushering in the Great Depression. Many people — those who didn't jump off the roof — became paupers overnight. All the notes and promises of support Father had received were now worthless. His second attempt at *aliyah* had now also failed; but he pressed on. Father told Mother to take my sister Faigie and me back to Boston; he didn't want to endanger our lives. As for himself, he felt that, "Once one starts to go up, one shouldn't go down." He and my older brother, Reb Moshe, went on to Israel.

Once in Israel, my brother went to learn in a *yeshivah* in Tiberias, on the shores of the Sea of Galilee. He spent Pesach with Father in Jerusalem. At the end of the year, Father returned to Boston, saddened by his second failure to strike roots in *Eretz Yisrael*. Characteristically, he quietly began planning his third try.

Vayeira

*Avraham ran to the cattle
And chose a tender choice calf.
He gave it to the young man,
Who rushed to prepare it.
(Genesis 18:7)*

Avraham, as we all know, was the archetype of chessed, which is usually translated "lovingkindness." The Talmud, however, often speaks of midas chassidus, the trait of chessed, as an undertaking to go beyond the letter of the law, to do more than required or expected, to be an "extra" Yid. This week's parshah begins with Avraham demonstrating both meanings of the term. Still in pain from his bris milah (circumcision) three days earlier, and surely not expected to entertain guests, Avraham sat at the opening of his tent, straining himself to find some opportunity to practice hospitality. Seeing some travelers, he ran to meet them, urged them to stay and personally arranged a lavish feast.

Even the slaughtering of the calf (according to the Midrash, three calves), a process called shechitah, points to the chessed that permeates all the actions of a Torah Jew, even those that, in some societies, would be mundane or brutalizing. Before slaughtering an animal for food, a shochet must first recite a brachah, thus reminding himself of the Ultimate Source of all life; and he must ensure that the animal is caused minimal pain or distress. After the shechitah of a bird, he must respectfully cover the blood, while reciting another brachah. Compare that with the history of a non-kosher hamburger!

Back in Europe, the shochtim were carefully chosen, G-d-fearing men, who were often known for their kindly personalities. Many were scholars, and almost all were knowledgeable in the complex religious laws involved in their trade. In the America of the 1920s, much of this changed. When a Yiddish-speaking Torah scholar got off the boat, he would find that there was already a surplus of rabbis. He obviously couldn't become an architect or chemical engineer. What could he do to make a living? The answer was often to become a shochet. That didn't always work out too well; but with faith, integrity and midas chassidus — going beyond the expected — one shochet the Rebbe knew made it to the top in more ways than one.

❧ The Millionaire Shochet

Back in the 1920s and '30s, *shochtim* were the very lowest rung on the American Jewish social ladder. Their work was exhausting and messy, their salary was minimal and their hours were impossible. Since there was no refrigeration, the trucks with the chickens often pulled into the *shlachthaus* (slaughterhouse) parking lot around midnight, and the poor *shochet* had to slaughter them all in time for delivery the next morning.

I remember R' Zundel Miller, who lived with us in Boston in the '30s. A Vizhnitzer *Chassid* from Tiberias, he came to America and found a job as a *shochet*. For part of the day, he also served as my private tutor. Around 11 o'clock every Wednesday night, a fellow from the *shlachthaus* would come by in his car and yell up the stairs, at the top of his lungs: "Shoche-e-e-et..!" You would think that it would have been the end of the world if Reb Zundel didn't jump out of bed and run down the stairs that split second. This was the unfortunate lot of many *shochtim* in those days.

This story, however, involves R' Mendel, a Lelover *Chassid* from Yerushalayim, who came to America and worked as a *shochet* in New York. His job was particularly hard during the freezing winters, since the *shlachthaus* where he worked was open and unheated. It did, however, have a small cubicle where one or two people could sit and warm themselves by a small stove. When the *shochtim* had to go out to work, they did so; but they hurried back as soon as they could to avoid frostbite.

One cold winter evening Reb Mendel dozed off while he was waiting in the cubicle for the truck to come in. When it finally arrived, the air was filled with his wake-up call: *"Shoche-e-e-et...!"* Up he jumped, and ran to his place. The boss and six or seven workers were already there and ready to start. Reb Mendel quickly said the *brachah* and immediately started to *shecht* the chickens, one...two...three. Then he checked the *chalaf* (knife) to make sure that it was still perfectly sharp and free from nicks (this was standard procedure). As he was getting ready for the next batch of chickens, he happened to run his hand across his head and was stunned to discover that he was not wearing a *yarmulke*!

Apparently, while he was dozing in the cubicle, his *yarmulke* had fallen off his head. *Gevalt!* he thought to himself. "What did I do? I made a *brachah* without a *yarmulke*. I *shechted* without a *yarmulke*, and I didn't even know it!"

Now the hallmark of a professional *shochet* is that he has *hargashah*, the exquisite sensitivity and focused attention that can detect the slightest jerk in the chicken's neck during *shechitah*. While not wearing a *yarmulke* might not invalidate the *shechitah*, the lack of proper *hargashah* and an unnoticed jerk does — the chicken is not kosher!

"If I couldn't feel whether I was wearing a *yarmulke* on or not, how could I tell if the chickens were doing anything or not?"

A lesser man might have hesitated, but Reb Mendel was a *chassid* through and through. He walked straight back to the cubicle, laid down his knife, and told his startled boss:

"I'm not *shechting* anymore."

"What! Why not?"

"If I can *shecht* without a *yarmulke*, I'm not a *shochet* anymore."
"Are you crazy?"
"No. I'm quitting."
"What will you do for *parnasah* (a living)?"
"I don't know, but I'm not going to be a *shochet*."

It was very hard to find work in those days, but eventually Reb Mendel found a low-paying job *shlepping* boxes in a dress shop. He worked very hard, his boss liked him and he was eventually promoted to salesman and then to manager. This went on until finally he became the boss of the dress shop. He bought a few more stores and continued to succeed until...he finally became a millionaire!

It's quite true. R' Mendel, *Yerushalmi Chassid* and ex-*shochet*, became a multimillionaire, all because he stuck to his guns religiously. Had he been willing to compromise just a little, he might still be dozing somewhere with one ear open for the inevitable battle cry: "Shoche-e-e-et...!"

※

Reb Mendel lived to a ripe old age but, at one point, he became very ill and lapsed into a coma. His family came and asked Father to pray for him. Father prayed for Reb Mendel's recovery and then gave his family a strange set of instructions. They were to go into his hospital room, lean over his unconscious form...and then shout his Hebrew name into his ear! The family was dubious that such unconventional treatment would work (What would the tiptoeing hospital staff say?); but Father insisted. They did as instructed and, after a few attempts, Reb Mendel indeed awoke and proceeded to recover.

In the Jewish mystical tradition, a person's name is his *shoresh neshamah*, the closest link of the soul to this physical world. Mentioning a person's name can help connect the two worlds and awaken the life force within. That is why our family's tradition is not to change the name of those who are ill (a common *segulah* in most communities). We don't want to tamper with that original connection.

The laws and requirements of *shechitah* are quite complex and becoming a certified *shochet* is quite difficult. First an applicant must study the staggering number of *halachos* (laws) involved. Then he must practice under the guidance of experienced *shochtim*. Getting certification from a rav can take years. The slightest nick in the knife or tremor in the *shochet's* hands can render the animal unkosher, or result in exceedingly complicated legal issues. As in most areas of Jewish practice, *shechitah* is one area where good intentions, while laudable, just aren't enough. In fact, they can often do more harm than good. Doctors, lawyers and airplane pilots often say that the same applies to their expert professions, but the Rebbe's favorite case involves....

The Quincy Shochet

There was a nice fellow from Quincy, Massachusetts, who used to come by from time to time. Everyone called him the "Quincy *Shochet*." Why? It went back to the Florida real estate boom of 1928.

In the late '20s people started moving in large numbers to Florida for the warm climate. They were the forerunners of today's Florida condominium success story. Our friend from Quincy joined this mass migration and arrived in a small sunny town in Florida, along with a lot of other newcomers from the North. He asked the locals, "Where can I get kosher chickens around here?" And they told him: "Nowhere. There's no *shochet* anywhere in this part of Florida."

He started thinking about it: all these people and no kosher meat. He said to himself: I'm no *talmid chacham* (scholar) and no *shochet*, and maybe I'm not all that observant, but I do keep kosher. That's a must! How can I watch this whole community just eating *treif* and losing their *Yiddishkeit*?

"Finally," he told us years later, "I decided to get a real *chalaf* (slaughtering knife) in New York, and go into business."

What did our friend know about being a *shochet*? In Europe his family had lived across the street from the local slaughterhouse. As a little boy, he enjoyed watching the *shochtim* rush about *shechting* cows and chickens there. It seemed easy enough, so he went to New York, got himself a *chalaf* and put up a sign:

> ATTENTION
> ALL THOSE WHO ARE
> CONCERNED ABOUT KASHRUS
> AND WHO WANT THEIR
> CHICKENS SHECHTED
> SHOULD COME TO ME
> AND I WILL SHECHT THEM!

This sign made quite a stir, and many of the people there were very happy that they now had a "*shochet*" in their midst.

Of course, there was still one small problem. Our friend really didn't know much about *shechitah*; but he was a resourceful fellow and soon found a "solution" for that too. He put a *pushkah* (charity box) outside his door and, after he finished killing someone's chickens, he would ask that person to throw a few coins in the box for *tzedakah* (charity), just in case the *shechitah* wasn't all right. The idea was that this act of charity would somehow cover whatever went wrong with the chickens! Everyone was satisfied with this arrangement, except perhaps the chickens, until one fine day our friend closed down his operation and moved back up north to Quincy.

Once we all heard that story, he was ever after known in our community as "the Quincy *Shochet*." One can't help admiring his intense desire to do good, but hopefully, no child who once lived across the street from a brain surgeon will buy a scalpel in New York and decide to strike out on his own.

Chayei Sarah

> And Yitzchak brought her [Rivkah]
> To the tent of Sarah his mother.
> (Genesis 24:67)
>
> She resembled Sarah his mother...
> A lamp burned from Erev Shabbos to Erev Shabbos,
> And there was a blessing in the dough.
> (Rashi, quoting Midrash Rabbah)

Throughout the generations, Jewish women — each one a woman of valor, an Aishes Chayil — have successfully held the Jewish people together. Hashem told Avraham to listen to Sarah, his wife, and she alone fully understood the danger of Yishmael and the greatness of Yitzchak. Similarly, Rivkah alone fully understood the danger of Esav and the greatness of Yaakov. The Jewish woman has always been the guardian of the continuity of the Jewish people and, indeed, being born a Jew depends only on the Jewishness of the mother.

When the angels looked for Sarah, she was listening from within her tent. Rivkah carried on this tradition of modesty, stability and accomplishment within that very same tent. Kol kevudah bas melech penimah, say our Sages, "all the glory of the king's daughter [remains hidden] within." The man goes about his business and studies in the Bais Midrash, while the woman forms the bedrock of the home. She is the light that burns in the home *from one generation before the Messiah (Erev Shabbos) to the next; and she gives the blessing to the dough that nourishes her family, both spiritually and physically, until then.*

The Rebbe's mother's tent — her combined palace, social hall and operations center — was her kitchen. There the lights and oven also burned all week long, preparing for an endless stream of guests, almost without stop. She and her trusty kitchen staff dished out massive amounts of food and chessed along with unforgettable lessons in dedication, commitment and the importance of hard work to her young children who were allowed to watch, "if you don't get in the way." The entire year was a major effort, but Pesach (Passover), when even the smallest crumb of leavened ingredients (chametz) was strictly forbidden, was something else again. The Rebbe still remembers every detail, every beloved precaution and exertion to make sure that everything was just right.

❦ *Pesach Provisions*

When I was a child, many commercially available Kosher-for-Pesach products were questionable and, instead, we had to do everything ourselves. We even ground our own salt from solid blocks of clear rock salt. This was first baked — almost burned — in our *matzah* oven to remove all possible impurities. It was as black as pepper, although it still tasted like salt. Our pepper, on the other hand, was dark red. It was hand ground, using a mortar and pestle, from dried cayenne peppers. Mr. Singer, the lucky "volunteer," would wear a special coat and gloves for the occasion. He covered his whole head with a big scarf, with only his eyes peering out through narrow slits, but they watered for hours afterward all the same.

Tea was no problem: We just didn't drink it at all, because there was concern that tea had some doubtful additives. Raisins and dried fruits were another casualty, since they were occasionally dried and stored in a dusting of flour.

As for *matzos*, we baked our own to make sure that everything was done just right. This was a major saga, beginning several months before the holiday. Father always distrusted American *matzah* flour, so much so that, during his first few years in America, he even planted his own wheat! He also bought a large electrically operated flour mill, with six-foot-tall grinding stones, which he kept in our basement. Although the mill eventually fell into disuse, I remember, as a child, playing with the large throw-switch on the wall. It didn't do anything by then, but we children loved swinging it back and forth anyway.

The Rebbe and his father, R' Pinchas Dovid, circa 1929. The Rebbe is eight years old.

After World War I was over, Father began importing *matzah* flour from Israel. He felt that the weather in America was too wet and rainy, whereas the weather in Israel was hot and dry. Every year our relatives would send three cloth bags of *matzah* flour, which they had hermetically sealed in large tin cans for the sea voyage. Of course, the U.S. Customs Bureau couldn't just let the cans through without inspection. They might have contained contraband diamonds or gold (nowadays, seeing all that white powder, they might suspect heroin!). Conversely, Father couldn't just let them open up his precious *matzah* flour cans without proper supervision. So every year we would alert the U.S. Customs Bureau in advance, and they would call us when our tins arrived. Then we would go down to the Post Office building and the customs agents would carefully open the tins in front of us.

Baking the Matzos for Jewish Passover Holiday

Seder Feast!

Boston's newspapers regularly carried articles on the Rebbe's father, "R' Pinchas Dovid Horowitz, Embodiment of Wisdom of Centuries to his 5000 Jewish Followers." Here the Boston Daily Advertiser (c. 1928) reports on matzah baking at the original New England Chassidic Center. The Rebbe's sister, Faigie, is the young girl on the left.

We continued getting annual flour tins all the way up to the early '40s and World War II. By then, however, *kashrus* in America had improved and properly supervised Pesach flour was available, with difficulty, in New York. We drew our own special water (*mayim shelanu*) for kneading the *matzah* dough from springs in the Blue Hills, not far from Boston. Then we were in business ... once we had an oven.

A *matzah* oven cannot just be built out of concrete blocks and cement. For the oven to withstand the necessary high temperatures without cracking, special oven tiles and oven bricks must be used. Our Poplar Street oven was big enough to bake all our *matzos*, and it lasted over 20 years without cracking.

When our family eventually returned to New York (1939), we didn't have room for a large brick oven, so we had to make do with a small portable metal one, just large enough to bake a few special *matzos* for the *seder*. When we returned to Boston in 1944, one of the first things we did was to start building a large brick *matzah* oven in our Dorchester basement. Thanks to the local experts on oven tiles and baker's ovens — almost all Italian — Boston soon had a reasonable replica of the original Poplar Street *matzah* oven. Eighteen years later, after moving to Beacon Street in Brookline, we had to do it all over again. Building three ovens should give us a *chazakah*!

Bereishis ❦ 53

Our *matzah* bakers were never professionals and our *matzos* didn't look much like the store-bought variety. They were often somewhat thick, lopsided and hard. Once Father's *matzah* oven caught fire and almost burned down our whole house; but our *matzos*, in those days, looked char-broiled every year!

Only a few women, who were accustomed to rolling thick dough to make their own noodles, succeeded in making beautiful round *matzos*. Once someone held up a fine-looking *matzah* and called out, "This is the most beautiful *matzah* baked today. What will you bid, as *tzedakah* for the *shul*, for this beautiful *matzah*?" A few bids, and then someone piped up, "I'll give five dollars for that *matzah*!" We were amazed. Five dollars in those days, the 1920s, was a small fortune. Five dollars for a *matzah*! Being a young, awestruck child, I didn't realize that our Rothschild of a *matzah*-bidder was the *husband* of Mrs. Annie Siagel from Newton, the proud woman who had rolled it!

Pesach preparations, circa 1960, in Dorchester. The Rebbe (center) prepares for bedikas chametz with (L to R) his daughter Tobeh Leah, Dovid Thumin (a nephew), R' Ya'akov Thumin (the Altstedter Rav) and the Rebbe's sons Reb Mayer and Reb Naftali.

Although Pesach is biblically only a seven-day holiday, it is observed for eight days outside *Eretz Yisrael*. This eighth day, the *Acharon shel Pesach*, was ordained by the sages of the Talmud to accommodate doubts in the Diaspora concerning the proper dates of the festivals. Although we were ultrastrict about the first seven (Biblical) days of the festival, for that last day, some of our extra stringencies — such as not drinking tea — were lifted.

For example, during the first seven days of Pesach, *Chassidim* don't eat *gebrochts* (literally, "broken pieces"), *matzah* crumbled in water and used for cakes, dumplings or soups, because of the very remote possibility that unbaked flour in the *matzah* could become *chametz*. That ruled out *kneidlach* (*matzah* balls) until the evening of the eighth day of Pesach. Then the women came downstairs to cook this long-awaited treat.

While we waited, one of the *meshulachim*, our ever-present guests, would make *Kiddush*, everyone would say "Amen," and then we would all drink wonderful glasses of steaming hot tea, the first tea we had had for a week. Later everyone went to the *Yom Tov tish*, made *Kiddush* themselves, and had wonderful *matzah* balls and soup.

In Israel, the Rebbe's Pesach preparations include collecting special cold water (mayim shelanu) from the Sataf Spring for baking his own seder matzos.

We sweetened our tea with *hittel-sukar* ("hat sugar"). This came all the way from Poland where it was made under the supervision of the Pshevorska Rav. His special sugar was known all throughout Poland for its highly reliable *kashrus*. It came in large bricks shaped like a hat, hence its peculiar name. It was beautiful to look at, and we broke off small pieces whenever we needed sugar. We used to keep a steady supply of small chunks in our sugar bowl throughout Pesach, ready for use.

Mitzvos were harder to keep in those days, but they had more *ta'am* (flavor), and so did the food.

༄

By the early '50s, "*hittel-sukar*" had long been a thing of the past, and there were few American alternatives which maintained such a stringent level of *kashrus*, especially in Boston. Undeterred, we decided to try to organize things our own way (we seemed to specialize in trying the impossible as if that were completely normal). In this case, representing Boston's barely visible Chassidic community, we simply called up the manager of the giant Revere Sugar Company, one of America's largest sugar refineries, and asked to inspect their facilities! Much to our surprise, he not only didn't hang up, he said "sure" and offered to personally show us around.

The refinery was huge, and the tour began on the top of the eight-story main building, which was located near a dock on the Somerville waterfront. A large boat had pulled up outside and was unloading a steady stream of brown, unrefined sugar crystals onto an open conveyor belt. The belt disappeared into an entrance on the roof, through which the sugar was sent to the refinery through sieves, which removed gross impurities. On and on the process continued, floor after floor. Finally, on the lower floors, the gleaming white sugar was packaged and sealed for shipment.

The process was encouraging. It was almost completely sealed, highly automated and, in any case, a halachic principle called *bitul* would nullify small amounts of unintentional "contamination" before Pesach. There was only one potential problem, an open trough around the bottom of the big processing vat. The area was used for taking samples and testing the fluid as it passed by on its way to the next floor. We asked the manager if food could accidentally fall into the trough.

"No."

"How can you be so sure? What about a worker eating a sandwich while he worked?"

"Well, Rabbi," he said, "I guess there would be nothing to stop it, but frankly, most of our workers don't work even when they have to. I wouldn't worry about them working during their lunch hour!"

We were pretty satisfied with the whole thing but, in the end, we didn't use their sugar. In addition to dealing with the trough, we would have had to send someone to Cuba to check out the unrefined sugar at its source. Much later, the Satmar Chassidic community in New York apparently did just that.

Toldos

[Yitzchak] dug another well, and they
[The Philistines] didn't quarrel over it.
And he called its name Rehovot [Spacious], saying,
"Now Hashem has made room for us
And we will be fruitful in this land."
(Genesis 26:22)

The Pelishtim, or Philistines, were a group of seafaring peoples who eventually settled in five major cities — Gaza, Ekron, Gath, Ashkelon and Ashdod — along the southern coast of Canaan. In the time of the Judges they often ruled over Israel with an iron fist. They captured the Holy Ark, blinded Samson, and killed King Saul and his son Jonathan, before finally being subdued by King David. This week's parshah as well as *Vayeira* seem to refer to an earlier, smaller, more benign phase of Philistine settlement. Still, their level of moral development, even then, left a lot to be desired. Avimelech's "criticism" of Yitzchak (Genesis 26:10) was essentially: Why didn't you tell us that Rivkah was your wife? Didn't you realize that, otherwise, we would feel free to seize her?

Time passed and the Romans conquered Israel, renaming it Palestina (Philestina, Palestine). And now after centuries of Arab pogroms, the Hebron Massacre of 1929, and constant calls to "Kill the Jews," here we are again. The Palestinians and Gaza are back in the news. True, these Palestinians are different, Arab descendants of Yishmael, not strangers from (possibly) Crete — but not all that different. Yitzchak did indeed make a treaty with Avimelech and the Palestinians of his day, but it was based on strength and first-hand experience, not on weakness or naivete. More important, the Philistines were not motivated by ulterior motives or material gain. They were attracted by Yitzchak's moral superiority, as they stated: "We clearly saw that Hashem is with you, and [therefore] we said, 'Please let there be an oath between us'" (Genesis 26:28). Negotiations must be made from a position of spiritual strength.

Although the Rebbe's father's second trip to Israel was thwarted by the bloody Arab attacks of 1929, his third trip, in 1934, illustrated quite different options for Jewish-Arab relations.

~ The Third Trip (1934)

In 1934, when I was almost 13, Father told Mother that he didn't want me to become *bar mitzvah* in Boston, but in *Eretz Yisrael*. This was still during the Depression years, and we couldn't realistically expect much help from the *Chassidim*; but he convinced Mother that, by practicing various economies, we could save enough money to get started. Mother would first take us, the children, to *Eretz Yisrael*, and Father would follow once enough "savings" had accumulated.

We traveled to *Eretz Yisrael* on the S.S. Aquitania. There were no crowds or fanfare as there had been five years earlier, and the crossing itself was uneventful. First landfall was in the Madeira Islands which, although owned by Portugal, are located 360 miles off the coast of Morocco. The scenery was spectacular: snow-capped mountains inland (the tallest, Pico Ruivo, is 6100 feet high) towering above the lush greenery on the warm tropical coast. We passengers disembarked for a day excursion which featured a tour of the wine cellars where the world-famous Madeira dessert wines are made. Unfortunately the free samples at the tour's end proved too much of a *nisayon* (trial) for some Jewish passengers. They decided that just tasting non-kosher wine was not the same as drinking (it is) or that Madeira was not a wine but a special local beverage (it isn't). We abstained, while taking in all the new sights and sounds around us.

The British Colony of Gibraltar, our next stop, guards the Spanish side of the entrance to the Mediterranean. The Sephardic Jewish community there welcomed us and showed us local sights of Jewish interest, including, unfortunately, the torture chambers used by the Spanish Inquisition. Since it had been some time since we had tasted fresh kosher meat, they also brought us several chickens we could *shecht*. "Is there a *shochet* among you?" they asked. "Yes, yes," an 80-year-old fellow passenger piped up, "I used to be a *shochet*, and I am sure that I still know how." That may have been true, but our memories of his trembling hands during the voyage sufficed to convince us to do some more sightseeing instead!

After a week on the open sea it was a wonderful feeling to cruise the Western Mediterranean where one can, with effort, see land on both the European and African sides. At night, the faint lights on both sides gave one a sense of being surrounded by life, a particularly comforting feeling after a week of seeing only emptiness.

The next stop was

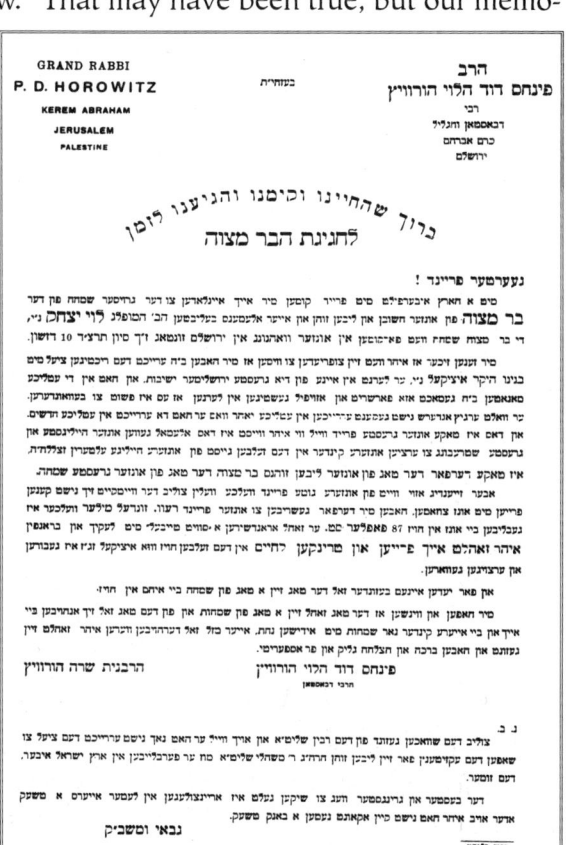

The Rebbe's bar mitzvah invitation (Jerusalem, 1934)

Bereishis ❦ 59

Algiers, where we were, at last, enveloped in the exotic world of the Arab Middle East. Dress, drinks, customs, language — all were a world apart. Could *Eretz Yisrael* be far away? We visited the teeming world of the Casbah, an endless tangle of narrow streets full of Arab traders and shopkeepers, trying to unload their wares. Then as now, tourists were prime targets, although their "great bargains" didn't always stand close scrutiny.

The most exciting moments, however, were on that dark dawn when, at 5 o'clock in the morning, the foredeck of the ship was packed with people waiting for their first glimpse of *Eretz Yisrael*. Finally it became light enough to see that long-awaited speck on the horizon. That was it! That was our beloved *Eretz Yisrael*! Some people burst into tears, others said prayers or some kind of personal *Shehecheyanu*. The closer we approached, the more excited we became. Finally, the Aquitania anchored off the port of Haifa and smaller boats ferried us ashore.

The Old City of Jerusalem (there was very little new city), nestled in its beautiful hills, was another unforgettable sight. To conserve our limited resources, Mother rented us an apartment in the very last house in Kerem Avraham, then a new Jerusalem neighborhood near Geulah. It was like living at the end of the world. Looking out of our windows, we could see the vast empty spaces and hills that led from this last outpost of Jerusalem, which is now near the city's center! We really suffered at first. Although it was already the Jewish month of Shevat, roughly February, it was still very wintery and cold, and we had almost no heat.

One day we received an unexpected cable from Father: "Have left for Israel! Mr. Singer is with me." All the calculations were apparently designed to convince Mother to leave for *Eretz Yisrael*. As soon as we left, Father secretly began making his own travel arrangements for the Aquitania's next sailing, a month later. Then, on Purim, he went down to his Purim *seudah* and announced to a room full of startled *Chassidim*: "Good-bye, I'm leaving soon for *Eretz Yisrael*."

Father's boat also stopped in Gibraltar, where the head of the community greeted him warmly, and presented him with a beautiful old *sefer*, authored by a *chacham* with ties to their community. Father's boat arrived in Haifa on Saturday, and he refused to disembark until Shabbos was over. The steward told him that they couldn't very well hold up the entire ocean liner just for him, and that he simply had to get off, otherwise he'd find himself en route to Beirut. This made no impression at all on Father. It was Shabbos and he wasn't getting off, period! The captain himself came down to persuade Father to leave. He wouldn't have to write, he wouldn't have to do anything, except get off the boat. Father refused to budge.

Finally, they asked him just when he could leave. Sundown? No. When three stars could be seen? No. When then? Only when it was completely dark, the latest opinion on when Shabbos ends (held by Rabbeinu Tam). Finally, they decided to wait for him, even if it threw the whole ship off schedule.

At Rabbeinu Tam's time for the end of Shabbos, a small boat came out with British customs inspectors and immigration officials. All the passport formalities were handled for Father on deck, and then he disembarked. The next day Jerusalem's newspapers all carried the unprecedented news that a gigantic ocean liner and His Majesty's immigration officials had both waited for the Bostoner Rebbe's Shabbos.

❧ The Emir's Sister

Once Father arrived, our tiny Kerem Avraham apartment was too small, and we moved to the second floor of a fancy new building near the Mandelbaum Gate. This was still during the British Mandate, 13 years before the partition of 1947, and the area — later a no-man's-land — had no special connotations. In fact, the British governor lived on the first floor of the building.

This governor was no lover of Jews, and he was always complaining about the daily *minyan* Father held upstairs in our apartment. To him we were all just "natives," and His Honor would personally run upstairs and start yelling at us for every slightest noise. In short, he caused all of us much unpleasantness.

Meanwhile, difficulties developed in financing the land Father had purchased in Shuafat, outside Jerusalem. Father, much to his regret, eventually had to return to America to find more investors and to handle other matters. He tried his best and his letters reassured my mother that things were going well, but he eventually had to admit that the situation was almost hopeless. The rest of us tried to stay in Jerusalem as long as we could (another year, as it turned out). To save money we made arrangements to move to a smaller apartment a few blocks away.

In those days, almost all moving in Jerusalem occurred on one special weekend each year, so we prepared to move out on that Sunday, as specified in our lease. A few days before moving day, we had a visit from a tall, impressive-looking Arab. He solemnly announced that our apartment had been rented by the sister of the Emir Abdullah, who was later to become the king of Jordan, and comparatively friendly to Jews. Her family had a problem. They had to vacate their present apartment on Friday, and our apartment would not become available until Sunday. They wanted to know if they could move into just part of our apartment for those few days, as they had nowhere else to stay. Mother, who was in charge now that Father had left, agreed to let them have half of the apartment. So we shared it for the weekend, with *cholent* and Shabbos *zemiros* on our side of the apartment, and prayer rugs and chanting on theirs. It went along well enough; and M...other had several nice conversations with the Emir's sister.

During one of their talks, Mother mentioned all the trouble we had had with the governor downstairs, and warned her to be careful.

The Rebbe's family shared this "deluxe" apartment building with a none-too-friendly British governor in 1934. The next tenants, headed by King Hussein's aunt, promised to put him in his place.

"What were you doing that was so terrible?" she asked.

"Nothing — just a little noise."

"Don't worry," she said. "We despise him, and we will teach him what it means to have troubles. In Arabic cooking, we constantly do our own grinding, chopping and pounding right here in the house. Wait until he hears all the racket. He will soon pine for the days when you were his neighbors, and after a week [she snapped her fingers] it will all be academic. He won't last that long!"

The weekend itself passed uneventfully, and was a good example of how "the cousins," the descendants of Yitzchak and Yishmael, could get along — at least for a while. We can only hope that her grandnephew, King Hussein of Jordan, will do as well.

Vayeitzei

*And Yaakov went out from Beersheva
And went toward Haran.
(Genesis 28:10)*

*[From these calculations] you learn that
After [Yaakov] received the blessings,
He secluded himself in the House of Study of Eiver
For fourteen years.
(Rashi on Genesis 28:9)*

Hashem's commandments to Noach formed the basis of a tradition carefully guarded and transmitted by his son, Shem, and Shem's son, Eiver. The Midrash, noting an unfilled gap of 14 years in the life of Yaakov, asserts that they were spent learning in the Yeshivah of Shem and Eiver. This total immersion in Torah study was essential preparation for his withstanding the challenges of Lavan, which lay ahead. Much later, Yaakov sent Yehudah ahead to Egypt *lehoros lefanav*, "to teach before him." The Midrash interprets this as "to establish [before he arrived] a House of Study, from which the teachings should come forth" (Rashi on Genesis 46:28). From the Jewish nation's very earliest days, Jews were expected to assure their spiritual growth by periods of intense Torah study with their peers within the all-encompassing atmosphere of a yeshivah.

Isn't it possible to learn Torah alone? Yes, but it's not the same. The give-and-take between two *chavrusos*, study partners, and their "battle in Torah," deflates self-importance, prevents self-delusion and sharpens the mind. Their joining with other *chavrusos* in informal group discussions, meals, prayers and shared experiences develops a sense of purpose and community. Their relationship with, and awe of, the Rosh Yeshivah, an experienced senior scholar, develops a sense of what man can achieve and the tremendous effort required to achieve it. It is not only the learning that counts, but what it leads to: a love of Hashem and His Torah, a thirst for purity and a sense of how holiness can, and must, fill every moment, every action. As the enigmatic *tzaddik* Reb Leib Sarahs once said: "I came to the Maggid [of Mezritch] not to learn Torah from him, but to see how he tied his shoes."

The Rebbe likes to tell about his yeshivah years, and the powerful influence they had on his life.

✺ Torah V'yirah

There were no religious *chadarim* or *yeshivos* in Boston when we were growing up, so there were no *frum* children our age to play with, much less to learn Torah with. Father was very strict about avoiding improper influences which, while understandable, often left us lonely. I grew quite close to my sister Faigie, who faced similar difficulties. She, our older brother (13 years my senior), some elderly *meshulachim* and occasional visiting relatives were my main childhood companions.

Father did hire private tutors for me, all older men from Europe. They may have been, perhaps, great *talmidei chachamim* (scholars), but pedagogues they were not. In fact, they usually ended up taking a nap while still seated next to me! Of course, their nap did not disturb me all that much. Sometimes, when things became too boring, I was just waiting for it to happen! Obviously these study sessions didn't compare with the eight to ten hours a day of intense learning boys my age received in a European *yeshivah*. It was enough to whet my appetite for real Torah study, but it was no way to become a *lamdan* (scholar).

This situation changed dramatically in 1934, when my family moved back to *Eretz Yisrael*. There we lived in a Yerushalayim chock full of *Chassidishe* boys my own age and wonderful *yeshivos*. It was the opportunity of a lifetime. The Yerushalayim of those days, while poverty stricken, was filled with great spiritual riches, just waiting to be claimed.

Thus excited, if unprepared, I went off to learn Torah at Yeshivah Torah V'Yirah in Jerusalem's old Meah Shearim neighborhood. It was, at the time, a particularly good *yeshivah*, and politically neutral. My *chavrusah*, R' Levi Rabinowitz, later became known for his *sefarim* on *Yorah Deah*. He was part of a group of boys from the Diskin Orphan Home which was located "way out of town" in Givat Shaul, in those days a remote, desolate hill. Now it is a densely populated suburb of Jerusalem, near our Bostoner neighborhood in Har Nof.

After his family moved to Jerusalem, the Rebbe attended Yeshivah Torah V'Yirah. Here, a decade later, the historic building is being gutted for extensive renovation.

In the 1930s, Givat Shaul was served by the number 11 bus line, just as it is today, although during that British Mandate era there was no Egged Bus Company. Instead it was *Hamekasher*, a privately owned bus company, that ventured so far from "civilization." I remember once meeting the *Ma'aseh Ilfas*, an old Lithuanian scholar, who lived out in Givat Shaul. He came into Meah Shearim one night to speak at our *yeshivah*. He was very good at *meshalim* (parables), the Dubno Maggid of our generation. The last *Hamekasher* bus left at 10 p.m., and it was 10:30 by the time he finished speaking. We were all quite concerned. Nowadays, many Bostoner *Chassidim* walk from Har Nof to the *Kosel* at 3 a.m. every Shavuos morning but, in those days, the trip was regarded as long and dangerous.

"What will you do now? How will you get home?"

"With the 'elover' (number 11)."

"How? The number 11 stops at 10 o'clock!"

"Oh, I have my own 11," he said, pointing to his two legs, which did rather resemble that number.

⚜

The *bachurim* (students) at Torah V'Yirah were all very special, truly devoted to Torah and *yiras shamayim*. The *menahel*, R' Aharon Katzenellenbogen, was a great *talmid chacham*, although, of course, I was in a much lower *shiur* (class). My own Rebbe, R' Ze'ev Cheshin, later became an important person in the Bratzlaver Chassidic movement.

We had a *mussar shmuess* every Shabbos afternoon after *Shalosh Seudos*, given by R' Yankev Rottman, who was very adept at "delivering the goods." I will never forget the incredible fervor of the *Maariv* we davened every *Motza'ei Shabbos* after his *shmuess*. The *hislahavus* (burning enthusiasm) that filled the *bais medrash* was incredible.

R' Aharon Katzenellenbogen, z"l, the saintly Rosh Yeshivah of Torah V'Yirah during the Rebbe's stay.

Although many of us had electricity in our homes, the *bais medrash* was lit by a *blitz lomp*, a powerful kerosene light which seemed very bright when you looked at it. One day we got the great news that electricity would be installed in the *bais medrash*. We could hardly wait and, when the big day came, and the lights went on, it was literally "*Vayehi Ohr*, Let there be light!" All the dim shadows and nooks of the *bais medrash* were illuminated, and the pages of our *Gemaras* sparkled with an unaccustomed bright glare. Things had a special feeling of permanence. It was wonderful.

We boys had also always hoped that similar changes would take place in our so-called bathroom. It was a rather basic Arab-style affair, just a series of open round holes in the cement floor. It was unpleasant to pass by that area, even on the outside. Alas, such further physical improvements were not to be, at least not while I was there.

෴

The poverty in Jerusalem in those days is hard to describe. There were no government social programs or other centralized support. People of all ages faced a daily struggle, especially when the breadwinner of the family passed away. There was a young man in our *yeshivah*, just a few years my senior, whose father had passed away. His family was immediately thrown into turmoil, then crisis ... and then the horrible news: *Binyamin iz arois gegangen in gass!* Binyamin is leaving the *yeshivah* for "the street!"

In other words, Binyamin was leaving full-time Torah study to work at some menial trade. Now he would never claim his full share of Torah, never be a true scholar. All gates, all his spiritual opportunities, were closing before our very eyes. Everyone felt very bad, although we all understood. His father had died and there was no one else to support his family. *Yeshivah* study led to neither a *parnasah* nor ease in *shidduchim* in those days. What would he end up being when he got out — a *bank-kvetcher* (bench-sitter), who only knew how to sit all day?

R' Yankev Rottman, z"l, was remembered by bachurim at Jerusalem's Yeshivah Torah V'Yirah for his fiery mussar shmuessin. The Rebbe was an inspired 13-year-old listener, circa 1946.

Still, the *yeshivah* could not just pass over the fact that a young man was leaving the *yeshivah* for the outside, working world. The allure of the street was very powerful in those days and it was essential to try to stem the tide. So our *rabbanim* called a special assembly.

All the classes met together in the *bais medrash*, and R' Yankev delivered a searing fire-and-brimstone *mussar shmuess*. He described the seriousness of the situation in awe-inspiring detail: what it means when a pure *yeshivah bachur* leaves the world of the *yeshivah* for the crass, material world of the street, the loss to himself, the loss to the whole *Olam HaRuchni* (the Spiritual World), the irreparable damage caused when one pure spirit leaves the *yeshivah* world ...

Another favorite speaker was R' Ben-Zion Yadler, the Yerushalayim Maggid.

After his *shmuess*, R' Yankev called on us to say *Tehillim* (Psalms), the traditional Jewish response to an impending calamity. Our sole intent was to be that this Jewish soul, the soul of Reb Binyamin ben Ploni, should come back to the Torah world. I still remember the fervor of our prayers, the whole *yeshivah* praying in unison with all our might, "May he return! May he return!"

In fact, Binyamin did not, could not, return. We teenagers all knew that he was a "goner." Imagine, then, my surprise when, just a few weeks later, I was walking down Rechov Meah Shearim and saw Binyamin walking on the other side of the street. It was him, really him! What a shock. Our view in the *yeshivah* was that he was "gone," not with us, out of our world, out of this world ... and yet there he was, looking completely normal, just walking down the street. He had somehow reappeared. Had he just come from Mars, I couldn't have been more surprised.

Bereishis ∞ 69

Later, as an adult, I tried to understand. Why had the *yeshivah* done all this: the assembly, the *shmuess*, the *Tehillim*, the prayers? After all, Binyamin really had no other choice. He was already out, and it was virtually certain that he could not return (in fact, he remained a devout Jew and went on to raise a religious family).

Perhaps it was partly to tell any other *bachur* who might be thinking of leaving the *yeshivah* for some less noble reason, "Do you remember the 'hesped' we said over Binyamin? Well, we are all going to get together and pray with all that fervor that you come back to Torah learning too!" If so, it was very strong medicine, and very effective as well.

Vayishlach

And Yaakov came complete to the city of Shechem
Which is in the land of Canaan...
And he bought the plot of land
Where he pitched his tent...
For a hundred kesitah [coins of silver].
(Genesis 33:18-19)

Every Jew wants, somewhere deep inside, to buy a plot of land in Eretz Yisrael and to sink his roots deep into the Land of his Fathers. When one moves to Eretz Yisrael and buys a plot of land there, he is a citizen, "at home," at once.

Avraham bought Me'aras HaMachpelah near Hebron; Yaakov bought a field and pasture near Shechem; King David bought the threshing-floor that became the Har HaBayis in Jerusalem. Not only were these purchases involved and difficult at the time (not to mention overpriced!), but today it is precisely these three places — Hebron, Shechem and the Old City of Jerusalem — that the non-Jews contest most hotly and try most strenuously to take away from us.

The Rebbe's father also yearned, with all his might, to buy his own plot of land in Eretz Yisrael. Unfortunately, his experience was much the same.

⌘ *Shuafat Shelanu*

One major purpose of Father's trip to *Eretz Yisrael* in 1934 was to buy a piece of land. He wanted to establish a new community that would be attractive to religious Americans and would help convince them to move to Israel, much like our community in Har Nof today. In those days, however, convincing Americans to make *aliyah*, or even to visit *Eretz Yisrael*, was a big challenge. The trip was two weeks or more each way by boat, and Arab marauders, pogroms, discrimination and hostility were poorly policed, if not abetted, by the British.

Father had his eye on a large plot of Arab-owned land in Shuafat, near Beit Hanninah. Buying it was not easy to arrange, since Jerusalem was in the middle of a local real estate boom. Even at the last moment, after months of difficult negotiations, a competitor might jump in, offer a bit more money and grab the land away. All the Jewish infighting only made the Arabs richer and more difficult to deal with.

Finally, Father got a deal brokered by R' Amram Blau, *zt"l*, famous in the Western press as the leader of the Neturei Karta movement. He also worked as a real estate broker, and every day he would drive up to our house in his "Cadillac," a little donkey, which he tied up outside. He spoke Arabic well, and would report on the success of his protracted negotiations with the Arab landlords. Given the Arab birthrate and the Arab system of inheritance, this was anything but simple.

The original large plot had been broken into many smaller pieces, each now owned by one of the numerous heirs of the heirs of the original owner. One had to get all the dozens of people who had any claim to the land to agree before it could be sold. All this had to be done very quietly, so potential competitors wouldn't know that someone had already pieced together a useful-sized plot of land. Otherwise, they would jump in and try to trump the deal at the last minute. There was another reason for secrecy. An Arab owner who dared sell his land to Jews could find himself, even in those days, threatened by extremists.

One day, R' Amram showed up with 15-20 Arabs, whom he settled into our large living room. They were from all over Mandate Palestine and they were going to spend the night with us, so we could consummate the deal in the morning! Although they couldn't write well enough to sign the necessary documents themselves, they could put their fingerprints on it, a perfectly legal procedure in those days. The owners of all adjacent properties also had to "sign" with their fingerprints to guarantee the borders. The strangeness of the whole scene made quite an impression on us, especially when every so often our Arab "guests" took out their small prayer rugs and dropped to the ground, singing exotic-sounding chants on their knees.

The following morning, after the deed was signed and sealed, Father went out to Shuafat, to the land he had purchased. He then walked once completely around the border to perform the Talmudic *kinyan* (formal acquisition) of *dosh ametzra*. Doing that uncontested in the presence of others is, in Jewish law, a sign that the land is yours; and Father wanted to acquire his land in *Eretz Yisrael* by this special *kinyan* of the *Gemara*. He was very happy that he had finally acquired part of *Eretz Yisrael*; and he planned to build his Givat Pinchas community there.

Unfortunately things didn't work out that way, and Father soon had to return to America. The American real estate market had crashed, trapping many of his supporters, and money was tight. Then the Italian-Ethiopian War broke out, which discouraged many would-be settlers; and then there were more Arab attacks on the Jews in Israel. Finally, World War II began. All Father's plans fell through. There simply were no takers, beyond the first two or three contracts. No one had money to invest in a plot of land outside a Jerusalem they might never see. Father passed away in 1941, his dream unfulfilled.

After the Partition of 1947, Shuafat was on the Arab side of the border and there was no hope of reclaiming it until after the Six Day War of 1967. Then, once Shuafat was back in Jewish hands, our family tried to reclaim it from the Israeli government. The government, however, had seized all the land from Ramot to Shmuel HaNavi by "eminent domain." They told us, "If we give you your land back, we will have to give back land to thousands of Arabs, so forget it." They finally gave us meaningless "compensation." Not only was it insufficient to relocate the whole 90-*dunam* Givat Pinchas development elsewhere, it was not even enough to buy a quarter of a used apartment in any decent neighborhood! We tried to ask the Government for 90 *dunams* of land somewhere else in exchange; but they just said that they "didn't believe in exchanges." So that is how Father's land was "liberated" in 1967, and his dream destroyed once more.

That is not the end of the story, however. In 1992, when we were already living in Har Nof, R' Menachem Porush, a religious member of the Knesset and a prominent leader of the Agudas Yisrael organization of Israel, invited me to speak at the inauguration of a new religious neighborhood on the outskirts of Jerusalem. It was a particularly large plot of land that had been kept by the Government for "greenery" for many years and was now being rezoned for housing. I receive many invitations to speak, so I just entered the date on my calendar and didn't give it much thought.

On the appointed day, the Agudah sent someone to drive me to the ceremony. As the car was going along, I noticed something strange. We were going to Beit Hanninah, and then ... to Shuafat. There I was, probably standing on the

Once he had his land in Shuafat, R' Pinchas Dovid tried to convince frum American Jews to make aliyah and move in. Plots in Kiryat Boston were sold through "the Palestine Land Improvement Company of New York."

very land that Father had purchased from the Arabs for his new religious neighborhood, so many years ago.

What extraordinary *hashgachah* (Divine Providence) that I, of so many Jewish leaders, had been asked to make this particular speech in this particular place at this particular time. What had seemed just another ground-breaking ceremony had become the fulfillment of Father's dream, a dream I had witnessed on this same spot as a child. It just demonstrates once again that, when a *tzaddik* plants a seed, although it may take more than a half-century to grow, it will eventually blossom and bear fruit.

ꕤ

And Esav said "I have great [wealth]..."
And Yaakov said... "I have everything [I need]."
(Genesis 33:9-11)

Both Yaakov and Esav were blessed with great wealth, but they viewed their material possessions differently. Esav, the original "conspicuous consumer," boasted that he had far more than he needed for his daily necessities (see Rashi), while Yaakov was grateful that he had what he needed to raise his family and to serve Hashem properly. Esav constantly wanted more — "He who has 100 zuz wants 200." Yaakov was satisfied with his lot. Wealth is indeed relative, as the Rebbe found out during the year (1934/35) his family spent in Jerusalem.

ꕤ The Raffle

In Jerusalem's *Yeshivah Torah V'Yirah* I certainly stood out as "*der Amerikaner yeshivah bachur.*" This sometimes had its humorous side. For example, not long after we got there, the *yeshivah* held a raffle. The first prize was one British pound sterling, about $5 — a princely sum in those days, especially for the *yeshivah's* penniless students. I also bought a ticket but, *auftzulochus*, the night of the big drawing found me sick in bed. Around 10:30 p.m. there was a knock on the door and three boys burst in with the great news. "You won! You won the raffle!"

I was very happy, until one of them gave a blow-by-blow description of the dramatic scene. Once they had drawn my number, one of the *Roshei Yeshivah* turned to another and said, with a wouldn't-you-know-it expression, *"Gelt gait tzu gelt* (Money goes to money)!"

Our family was so poor by American standards that we soon had to leave Jerusalem for America. However, I had forgotten that, compared to the grinding poverty of the Yerushalmi students, I was a rich American "tycoon." "Who else," they said, "would have won the raffle?"

Vayeishev

*And when the Chief Baker saw
That [Yosef] had interpreted well,
He said to Yosef, "I also dreamed...
The bird ate the [bread] from my head-basket."
And Yosef answered..."[Pharaoh] will hang you
On a tree and the birds will eat your flesh."
(Genesis 40:16-19)*

This week's parshah is a parshah of dreams. Yosef, the tzaddik who must connect Heaven and Earth, dreams of both sheaves (earth) and stars (heaven). The butler dreams of his fruitful service; and the baker, through his dream, reveals his guilt. We Jews didn't need Dostoevsky's Crime and Punishment to tell us about man's need to confess and seek atonement. Nor did we need Freud to tell us that dreams open unique, if hazy, windows into our subconscious and the soul. Rather they needed us to add that, "dreams go after the interpretation"; that dreams can stir us to action and reveal positive possibilities we had never previously considered. We can then move from failure to teshuvah (repentance). We can then rise above our experience, transforming it and doing something positive to heal ourselves and the world.

Of course, to see beyond the facade, to accept and mold the good and to transform the bad, this requires a true tzaddik. Not only a Biblical tzaddik like Yosef, but his spiritual heirs, the true *tzaddikim of every generation, have this power, as the Rebbe learned from his father, while still a young child.*

✥ M.P. Smithwick, M.D.

Father's private physician was Dr. M.P. Smithwick, a general practitioner and surgeon. He was a refined, soft-spoken Yankee gentleman, a frail, dignified white-haired old man, of a type no longer seen.

Dr. Smithwick couldn't speak a word of Yiddish, and Father couldn't speak a word of English, yet they had an unusually close relationship. If there is such a thing as a non-Jewish *Chassid*, Dr. Smithwick was Father's. When Father was sick, the doctor would sit quietly next to Father and hold his hand for hours, in a way that silently showed his deep affection and admiration.

Dr. Smithwick would often tell Father a story about one of the Mayo brothers, the founders of the famous Mayo Clinic in Minnesota. While recovering from a surgical operation, one of his patients developed a high fever which, despite all the surgeon's efforts, became worse and worse. Finally, in a desperate attempt to save his patient's life, he performed a second operation. Once the patient was opened, it was discovered that the surgeon had left one of his instruments inside the original surgery, causing all the subsequent complications. The patient died soon thereafter.

This was the story as Dr. Smithwick used to tell it, and from his tone, one could gather that he didn't much approve of such a careless surgeon becoming so famous. At times, there even seemed to be a touch of envy and satisfaction. He told this story so many times that I once asked Father about it. How could one of the Mayo brothers do such a careless job?

Father shook his head quietly and said, "No. The doctor that accidentally left that instrument inside and killed his patient was not Dr. Mayo. It was Dr. M.P. Smithwick." According to Father, Dr. Smithwick had a guilty conscience. That was why he felt an uncontrollable need to tell this story over and over again to others. He couldn't very well tell it about himself, so he told it about one of the Mayo brothers whom he envied.

Father had an extraordinary ability to accept people as they were, relating to the good within them, without letting other facets of their personality interfere. And his feelings about Dr. Smithwick were no exception.

Father also told me that the holy Baal Shem Tov had already discussed such things, long before Freud. When a person does something wrong he has to speak about it — directly, indirectly, even subconsciously acting it out. But Father went further than merely understanding others. He could help others win back their sense of self-worth. He could heal his doctor, even as his doctor healed him.

> *In Egypt the Medanites sold [Yosef] to Potiphar,*
> *An officer of Pharaoh*
> *And Captain of the Guard.*
> *(Genesis 37:36)*
>
> *You did not send me here, Hashem did.*
> *He has made me a father unto Pharaoh,*
> *Director of his government, dictator of all Egypt.*
> *(Genesis 45:8)*

Hashem's ways are beyond our understanding. Nowadays, if someone wanted to become president of the United States, he would do well to be born into a rich, prominent political family, with a long history of public service, study political science in college, build a large financial nest egg, develop a local political following and parlay that into increasingly responsible and visible positions. In contrast, Yosef's recipe for success — to be sold as a penniless slave in a land he had never set eyes on before, to be arrested and have to languish for years in jail — does not seem very promising.

Yet that is how Hashem shows Who rules this world, declaring by His will alone who will be a slave and who a king, who will be trapped and who free. This is the secret of our history: Be true to the Torah, avoid sin, believe in Hashem and trust His ability to save every Jew from the most impossible situations. Indeed by obeying His will, we have every right to hope that things will be ...

ೞ **Ship Shape**

My nephew, R' Avraham Horowitz, *Shlita*, the current Bostoner Rebbe of New York, tells a story about my father, R' Pinchas Dovid, which occurred a few years before I was born.

World War I was raging in Europe, when a worried couple came to see Father in Boston's North End. They told him that their son had received a draft notice and, since many Americans were being shipped to the war in Europe, they feared for his life. Father listened attentively and then asked them only one question: "Do you keep Shabbos?" "No," they said, "we simply can't ... the business ... this is America ... it's just impossible."

"I'll make a deal with you," Father said. "You keep Shabbos 100 percent, and I'll promise you that your son will never go off to the war." They hemmed and hawed, talked it over, and finally took the plunge. They gave Father their solemn promise and left. They kept Shabbos conscientiously after that; but the U.S. Army kept "doing its thing." Their son soon received a notice to appear at the designated time and place for his physical examination. His parents panicked and ran back to Father. He calmed them by saying simply: "I promised he will not go to Europe, and he won't."

However, their son passed his physical in fine form and soon had another letter: "Greetings..." He was to appear at a specified time and place to be inducted into the Army and pick up his uniform. The parents ran back to Father — "Look, we're keeping Shabbos ..." — but all Father would say was: "I promised you, and a promise is a promise."

Another letter, another visit to Father ("A promise is a promise"), and off their son went for basic training. And so it went. Finally, one last letter: Their son was to appear in two weeks' time to board a ship with his company, destination Europe! Again the parents ran to Father and again they received his promise. But the days ticked slowly by with no deliverance in sight. No last-minute messenger came.

The parents paid Father several more visits, the last one on the very day their son was to set sail; but Father refused to become excited. He merely asked, "Are you still keeping Shabbos?" and, when they said yes, he calmly reiterated, "I promised…"

On the last day, the hours ticked by. But nothing happened.

They left the house for the dock. Still nothing happened.

They said their tearful farewells. Nothing.

Then their son, with all his shipmates, ascended the gangplank to the top of the ship. As he reached the top, he turned to wave one last, sad farewell and then it was all over…

Well, not quite. The next soldier in line, not expecting the sudden turn, accidentally pushed the man who was waving. While falling, he caught his foot in a hole in the deck. There was a small commotion at the top of the gangplank, and our friend was soon slowly carried back down. He had twisted his ankle, and it was quite a bad sprain, one that could take weeks to heal. The young man quite literally missed the boat!

A few weeks in an Army hospital did wonders and the young man was soon up and about. He was eventually assigned to a new unit; but he never did see service in Europe. To Father, it was an example of the power of keeping Shabbos; but his *Chassidim* saw it as a clear example of *Tzaddik gozer v'HaKadosh Baruch Hu mekayem*, a tzaddik decrees and Hashem fulfills — After all, "A promise is a promise."

Mikeitz

> And Pharaoh took his ring off his hand,
> And put it on the hand of Yosef;
> And he dressed him in clothes of fine linen
> ...and they called out before him: "Avrech!"
> (Genesis 41:42-43)

There is no question that clothes make the man. They strongly influence his self-image, which affects the way others view and interact with him. This, in turn, reinforces his self-image. Traditional Jewish dress has long been an important part of Jewish identity, and we are told that the Jewish people emerged from the exile in Egypt only because they preserved their distinctive language, names and dress. Jewish dress is a symbol of both Israel's modesty and its majesty. In fact, when a Jew walks into shul in the morning, wearing his tallis and tefillin, he is wearing his uniform, what the Zohar calls, "the robe and crown of the King," simultaneously a symbol of his allegiance and his closeness to the Divine.

Chassidim have developed their own special dress, based partly on the somber dress of 18th-century Polish nobility. A long black coat (bekeshe) is surrounded by a black sash (gartel), which divides the upper (more spiritual) and lower (less spiritual) halves of the body for prayer. On Shabbos, the plain wide-brimmed black hat gives way to a costly fur hat of sable, either a tall cylindrical spodek or a flat, disk-like shtreimel. On Shabbos, Yerushalmi Jews often wear a gold-colored robe with thin brown and blue pin-stripes. Wearing such special clothes, one cannot help but act, think and daven differently. For a Chassid, they are not only a sign of "having arrived" religiously; they are, even more, a way of getting there.

Of course, serious or shallow, every time and society has its symbols of authority and greatness in dress. For Mr. Singer, the Rebbe's trusty handyman, shamash and orderly, for example, it was the shiny dark-blue uniform of the Boston Special Police.

❧ Boston Special Police Officer Singer

Mr. Singer was a colorful figure, who came to live with Father as a young man. I remember him proudly taking us children out for walks wearing his beloved blue Boston Special Police (B.S.P.) uniform. Every hotel and official residence in Boston had special private guards, and Mr. Singer felt that the New England Chassidic Center deserved one too. He applied for a license, passed some written tests, and then went out to get his uniform. Although he was timid and frail by nature, the uniform made Mr. Singer feel important. He even got himself a pair of blue pants with a shiny dark-blue stripe down the sides, normally only the prerogative of a sergeant or captain! Mr. Singer wanted to apply for a gun too, but Father wouldn't let him. He was afraid he would shoot the *meshulachim*, against whom Mr. Singer waged a lonely, fruitless battle.

After that, Mr. Singer would never be seen in the street without his uniform; and soon everybody knew about the Yiddish-speaking "Special Police Officer" who walked the Bostoner Rebbe's children to the park. In the summer he used to take us to the outdoor concerts on the Boston Esplanade. The Boston Pops Orchestra, which used to perform there, was conducted by Arthur Fiedler. In fact, Mr. Singer knew their family quite well, since Emmanuel Fiedler, Arthur's father, had been Mr. Singer's violin teacher.

Although an excellent babysitter, Mr. Singer was somewhat less successful as a policeman. After 1930, the Jews started their migration from our West End neighborhood to Roxbury and Dorchester in the (then) suburbs, and Poles and Italians began moving in. Most were nice, but some of the younger ones could be pretty tough. Our windows would be broken every so often but, whenever we would call the police, they would say, "You have your own police officer. Why doesn't *he* take care of it?" Unfortunately, Mr. Singer, our one-man Special Police Force, was too meek to be of much help. Whenever a brick sailed through a window, he would run up to his bedroom, rather than venture out in hot pursuit.

In 1934, Father and Mr. Singer came to join us in Israel. Mr. Singer had never ventured outside of Boston before, except for his biweekly trip to a farm in Chelsea to pick up *chalav-Yisrael* milk for the family. The sea voyage was quite an experience for him. Of course, he continued wearing his Boston Special Police uniform, but on the boat no one seemed to notice. They were accustomed to people wearing all kinds of uniforms. When Mr. Singer arrived in Jerusalem, however, Her Majesty's British Mandatory authorities, who were ruling Israel at the time, did not find his dress amusing.

Boston Special Police Officer Mr. Singer cut a dashing figure in his uniform.

Our family soon received a call from the Mandatory Police informing us that they had detained a certain Mr. Singer, who was being held in custody for "impersonating a police officer." Was it true that he lived with us? We explained that he was harmless, and that he served as a private police officer at the New England Chassidic Center in Boston. "Maybe," they said, "but he can't be a private policeman here in Jerusalem. He has to promise to never wear that uniform again, as long as he resides in Palestine."

The authorities finally released Mr. Singer; but he was quite disheartened. Now, after 15 years of wearing his policeman's uniform, he would have to go around in a plain jacket like any ordinary citizen. It was a bitter blow, and even we children felt his disappointment. A while later, Mr. Singer said he missed the States and headed home to familiar territory.

He stayed all alone in our house in Boston, grappling with the *meshulachim*, who still came as guests. Of course, the moment he planted his feet on American soil, Mr. Singer put his uniform back on. We returned a few months later, and Boston Special Police Officer Singer once again patrolled the streets from our house to the park.

The real police officers in Boston's West End got to know Mr. Singer pretty well, and used to play along. Whenever they saw him taking us for a walk, wearing his pants with the captain's stripe, they used to salute! This simple gesture used to make his whole day.

Once there was a new policeman on the beat, who neither knew nor cared for Mr. Singer. One day an elderly lady wanted to cross Charles Street, a busy intersection near the *shul*. Mr. Singer just walked into the middle of the street, raised his hand and stopped traffic! This policeman was outraged, and he pulled Mr. Singer into Station 3 for a reprimand. B.S.P. or not, he certainly had no right to go around stopping Boston traffic.

The officer at the precinct told Mr. Singer that, since he had broken the law, he would have to reapply for his B.S.P. license. By that time, however, Mr. Singer was already an elderly man. To retake all the exams and reregister was simply too much for him. He regretfully put his memory-filled uniform away, this time for good, marking the end of an era of devoted, if erratic, public service.

※

> *Yosef sent them portions from his table,*
> *Giving Binyamin five times as much as the rest.*
> *(Genesis 43:34)*

As you can see from this week's parshah, it was an ancient custom for a king or other important person, even the master of the house, to personally give portions to his guests. This both expressed and reinforced the relationship between the giver and receiver, both their differences and their underlying unity.

In Chassidus, this has evolved into the custom of sherayim. The Rebbe makes a berachah and tastes part of a dish first. The remainder (lit. sherayim) is then passed out among the Chassidim, who thus all eat from the same plate. Often, in the case of easily hand-held items, such as apples, the Rebbe calls each Chassid individually, and personally puts the item into his hand. This form of a Rebbe's giving berachos to his followers has its roots in Kabbalah. Sometimes, however, a Rebbe must remember to give a berachah to himself.

෴ *The Berditchever Rav*

The following story is told about my older brother, R' Moshe Horowitz, zt"l, the first Bostoner Rebbe of New York. In his later years he suffered from heart trouble. Once he suffered a severe stroke and went into a coma. After a miraculous recovery, he described what he had seen while "beyond":

> *I was in a big, beautiful hall. Father (R' Pinchas Dovid, zt"l) and I were sitting together at a large table, holding tish. The hall was packed with a large crowd of standing Chassidim. We began to prepare to give out fruits to the Chassidim as sherayim. However, there was something going on, at the back of the hall.*
>
> *Soon the crowd began dividing as a short, robust man, with a bushy red beard and a wide smile, began rushing up the aisle, heading for where we sat. I was annoyed and asked Father, "Who is that?" But Father turned serious and said, "We had better move over and make room for him; that is the Berditchever Rav [R' Levi Yitzchak of Berditchev, one of the most famous of all Chassidic Masters]."*
>
> *The Berditchever Rav sat down between us, and I tried again to give out sherayim. The Berditchever Rav stopped me and said, "Why are you in such a hurry to give out sherayim to others? You have to eat some yourself first!"*
>
> *I understood that he was gently criticizing me: Why do you always give others brachos to get well, and now that you are sick, forget to give yourself a brachah first?*
>
> *I followed his advice and gave myself a brachah on the spot. The scene faded and I soon opened my eyes and found myself on a hospital bed, back in this world, on the way to recovery.*

הסכמות

אשר נמצאו בכתובים על הפירוש כתר נהורא.

הנה הראה לפני ה"ה מוהר"ר **אהרן** כ"ץ מ"מ ות"נ דק' **בילגוריא** סידור על פי כוונות שויתי ה' ילדעתי הוא טוב מאוד ויכולו מחמדים וכל הכוונות בסידורים קם קודם וזאת הכוונה של שויתי ה' הוא ק"ק שכולו ירחת ה' וקיבול עול מלכות ה' ורוממות אל להמליץ חא ה' בשמים ונארץ וד' רוחות העולם והוא חרב פיפיות להכרית הקליפות ולמהר העולמות ובמה שבחין שבחין חכמי הזיה"ק להרטיח מהימנא על הק"ש ובסהמל"ו כ"ש בסידור זה שכולו נתיסד על כוונה זו ע"כ אני מסכים להדפיסו ונח"ה על כל המדפיסים לבל ישיגו גבולו להדפים סידור זה משך עשרה שנים אחר כלות דפום של מוהר"א הנ"ל:

נאום הק' **לוי יצחק**
בהנגן מוהר"מ
פק"ק ברדימשוב יצ"ו

היות כי כבר נתתי הסכמה לה"ה מוהר"ר **אהרן** כ"ץ מ"מ ורלאב"ד ומ"נ דק' **ועליחוב** יצ"ו על ספר שהדפיס ושמו **אור הגנוז לצדיקים** ועתה בא בידינו שניות שאתן לו הסכמה על סידור שויתי ה' אשר חיבר ולדעתי כי טוב הוא כוונות פשטיות לקיים שויתי ה' כו' בשעת תפלה וכולו ירחת ה' וקבלת עול מלכות ה' אשר ראוי לקיים זה כל היום כ"ש בשעת תפלה וגם הפירוש עייינתי בכולו וטוב הוא ע"כ אני נותן לו הסכמה ומלינדה פרוסה בח"מ ע"כ המדפיסים לבל ידפיסו סידור זה משך י"ב אחר כלות הדפוס של מוה' אהרן הנ"ל:

נאום הק' **ישראל**
בהר"ר שבתי
מ"מ פק"ק קאזניץ יצ"ו

הנה אני הח"מ מונע עלמי שלא ליתן הסכמה על שום ספר כי אין זה מדרכי אך לה"ה מוהר"ר אהרן כ"ץ מ"מ ורלאב"ד דק"ק **ועליחוב** יצ"ו אשר הרם' סידור בכוונות שויתי ה' שחיבר ע"פ התקוני זוהר הקדוש ור"מ ומרומז בתיקוני זוהר בכמה אתר שיהי' בעולם סידור וכוונות בעקבות משיחא ובפרט שכבר הסכים הרב הקדוש מ"מ דק' קאזניץ ומי כמוהו מורה ע"כ באתי עה"ח:

נאום הק' **יעקב יצחק**
במהו' **אברהם אליעזר**
הלוי הורוויץ מלאנגש הדר
בק"ק **לובלין** יצ"ו

ואשר טוב עשה בתוך עמיו ה"ה מו"ה **אהרן** מ"ן ורלאב"ד ומ"מ דק' **זעליחוב** יצ"ו אשר הראה לי סידור בכוונות שויתי ה' והם כוונות ע"פ פשוט כי הגם כי כל הסידורים עם כוונותיהם טובים לככוש המחשבה הטרודה לשיעבוד הכוונה אך הם כוונות עמוקות עפ"י סוד הקבלה ולא כל מוחל סביל דא אך הכוונות האלה של שויתי ה' ויראת ה' ואהבת ה' החיוב לכל אדם לקיים כל היום אפי' שלא בשעת תפלה כ"ה בשעת תפלה וזה עפ"י התקוני זוהר ור"מ ובם ירחלים ואין זה בכלל מ"ש המנ"א סי' נ"א ס"ק א' בשם הזוה"ק כל ב"נ דאתי ליחדא כו' לכן נ"ל שמי שאינו יודע בעלמו שיוכל לכוין לקיים זה תל יכוין כלל בשמות ויחודים כו' היינו לבתפלל ויחודים כמו בסידור הכוונות אבל לקיים שויתי ה' לנגדי תמיד חיוב על כל אדם כל היום כמ"ש גרים ש"ע או"ה וכן להיות מחשבת אדם כירחת ה' ואהבת ה' כתב כסי' החינוך להרמ"ה שחיוב תמידי לא יפסקו מן הלאדם אפילו רגע א' מכל ימי חיו. ותהלות נחמר כל הנשמה. תהלל יה ואר"ל תן הילול על כל נשמה וכן קבלת עול מלכות ה' כמ"ש מרנצ"ן תיני שומע לכם לכפול מתנו עול מלכות שמים אפילו שעה אחת ואין זה בכלל כוונת שחות ויחודים שבת המנ"א. ע"כ אני אומר יישר כחו וחילו להדפיס וראוי לכל בר ישראל להיות לו לעזר ולפותר להיות מוכה את הרבים ונח"ה על כל המדפיסים שלא להשיג גבולו להדפים בלי רשותו משך עשרה שנים מיום כלות הדפוס של הסידור הנ"ל:

נאום הק' **עזריאל** הלוי אים הורוויץ חופ"ק **לובלין** יצ"ו

R' Levi Yitzchak of Berditchev wrote on of the three original approbations to the prayer commentary, Keser Nehora, which was first printed in a siddur in the 1890 edition of Siddur Tefillah Yesharah. The other two approbations are from the Koznitzer Maggid and the Chozeh of Lublin. The siddur and commentary are still used by the Bostoner Chassidic community, which has republished it several times.

Vayigash

> *And Yaakov said to Pharaoh...*
> *"Few and troubled were the years of my life*
> *And they didn't approach the days*
> *Of the years of my fathers' lives..."*
> *(Genesis 47:9)*

Yeridas hadoros, the declining of the generations, is a sad fact of our history, and an inescapable part of the American Jewish scene. Despite heartwarming counter-examples, especially in the larger Orthodox urban communities — baalei teshuvah, day schools, yeshivos, religious publishing houses, kollelim — the vast majority of American Jewry has been following a tragic downward spiral.

First, there were the firmly religious great-grandparents in the shtetl — they attended cheder and maybe even yeshivah, and breathed Yiddishkeit in the streets. Then came the poor but ambitious immigrant grandparents, determined to become "American." Anything smacking of the Old World and its old religion was an embarrassment. Chaim became Charles; Baruch, Bradley. Their children "made it," at least materially. They fought their way into the colleges and the professions, and they sent their children to once-a-week Sunday Schools, under protest.

Then their beloved Jason and Jennifer found themselves out on the troubled streets of the '60s with no Jewish education and no Jewish roots to speak of. No beauty of Shabbos, no home full of kashrus and mitzvos, just some unshakable baggage ("Don't forget you're Jewish"), some Jewish jokes and perhaps some weak secular identification with Israel. Is it any wonder what happened to them? Their only hope is for us to open our homes to them, to open our hearts to them, to treat them like our own lost children. Ready or not, worthy or not, we must give them something they can hold on to, someplace they can belong.

Yosef's greatness was his ability to withstand all the materialistic and sensual seductions of his success and position in Egypt. He acknowledged his Jewish brothers, honored his "old-fashioned" father and all that he stood for, and proudly presented them to Pharaoh himself, without embarrassment or apology. Yosef's refusal to compromise or hide his Jewishness eventually won the non-Jewish world's respect, a point well worth remembering.

Today's problems did not develop overnight. They are the result of the self-indulgence and compromise that were already apparent a half-century or more ago. Just contrast this week's Yosef with the many weaker souls the Rebbe has met from his childhood on.

∽ *Half a Shabbos*

During the 1950s there was a fellow who came to our shul in Dorchester to say *Kaddish* for his father. He was a fine but simple fellow, from a religious family, whom circumstances had led into various religious compromises. He was far from being a scholar — he could just barely read Hebrew — but one thing he did know: He had to say *Kaddish* for his father. One thing led to another and he was soon *davening* with us every morning, even after his year of *aveilus* (mourning) was over. Gradually he became more and more involved in our community and the *shul*.

He soon realized the importance of keeping Shabbos, but he had a problem. For 30 years he had been a deliveryman, dropping off big stacks of newspapers from the back of a truck at newsstands all around town. Of course, it was a six-day-a-week job, Shabbos or no

Shabbos. He now knew that it was wrong to work on Shabbos, but how could he give up his seniority and his pension benefits? He was not yet on a *madreigah* (spiritual level) where he could relinquish all that.

So what did he do? Every Shabbos, as soon as he got off the delivery truck, he ran into his house, changed into his Shabbos clothes and came to *shul*. He never missed a Shabbos *Minchah* (afternoon prayer service) and this became his special way of observing the Sabbath, at least half a day. Eventually, he convinced his employers to let him off on Saturdays, and he became fully *Shomer Shabbos* (Sabbath observant), and a generous supporter of our *shul* and many other charitable causes.

R' Pinchas Dovid tried to stem the tide of Shabbos violation by publishing Der Shabbos Buch, a tract that emphasized the need of proper observance. It was an early harbinger of Boston's outreach to the wavering and non-observant.

This gentleman's half-day schizophrenia was far from unique. The 1920s and '30s were full of such tragic cases, full of people who couldn't resist the test, but who didn't want to give up the *ta'am* (flavor) of their *Yiddishkeit* altogether. They made up their own rules and compromises as they went along, each in his own peculiar way.

One such gentleman in Father's *shul* in the West End was a European Jew with bright red cheeks. He prayed fervently, but he wouldn't *daven* with us on Shabbos mornings because he had to go to the "early *minyan*" in the Chamber Street Shul. Now some of you may be familiar with the early-morning Shabbos *minyanim* that sprang up in the 1960s. Their purpose was to allow husbands to *daven* early on Shabbos and return home in time to babysit the children, while their wives attended the "regular" *minyan*. These bear no relation to the early *minyanim* of our story. In the 1930s, virtually every early Shabbos *minyan* in the United States had only one purpose: to let the *Kaddish*-sayers finish *davening* in time to go to work on Shabbos! That was par for the course. On the one hand, people still knew that they had to say *Kaddish* for their father or mother — today, *Kaddish*, in many communities, is literally a dying institution. On the other hand, mother or no mother, they wouldn't dream of being late for work on Shabbos.

Our red-cheeked friend used to lead his early *minyan*, and then go to work. What was interesting about him, other than the fact that he *davened* even without having to say *Kaddish*, was that, once he finished, he didn't rush off to work with the others. He remained standing at the *amud*, the prayer stand near the *aron*, and first recited his "*Yom Tehillim*," the set of psalms for that day, recited by the particularly devout. So there he was, getting up early to *daven*, leading the entire congregation in *tefillah* (prayer), saying his *Tehillim* with fervor and then, *nebach*, rushing off to violate the Shabbos at work! Only Hashem could really judge such a person — saint, sinner, neither, or both — man sees only the deeds, not what lies in the heart.

I remember hearing about another case from those years, where the father, while not knowledgeable, was still quite religiously observant. His son, as so often happened, was not. So there they were every Shabbos morning, an odd couple indeed. The father would get up early and start quietly reciting *Tehillim*. Then, around 7 o'clock, he would start saying his *Tehillim* out loud, louder and louder. Why? He had to wake his son up so he wouldn't be late for work!

That is how our Sages describe the world at its chaotic beginning: "*Ohr v'choshech mishtamshin ba'arbuvya*," light and darkness all mixed up together and serving at the same time. Here the holy *Tehillim* were being used to simultaneously bring a man closer to Hashem and to make sure that his son wasn't up too late to sin!

Bereishis ❧ 91

*When Pharaoh calls you and asks
What you do, tell him,
"Your servants have always been cattlemen."*
(Genesis 46:33-34)

*So he will send you far away
From him and settle you there [in Goshen].*
(Rashi)

Yosef sought to insulate his family from the assimilation and the worst excesses of the larger, secular culture. But that is a negative definition of Jewish identity: We are not gentiles. What are the uniquely Jewish values that must take their place?

Volumes could be written on the differences between Jewish and gentile perspectives on life; but most boil down to the Jewish insistence on living a Torah life, a life that remains forever within the confines of halachah. Every thought, every action must be seen in a Divine context. Not just in shul, or at the times set aside for prayer, but in every place, at every time. Our lives must be lived so that even the non-Jews recognize that "Hashem is [always] with you (Genesis 25:28)." That is the true secret of our success. The Torah covers every act of life, no matter how minute, and raises it to an act of Divine service — another lesson the Rebbe learned at an early age.

❧ *If Shuls Had Steeples*

When I was a young boy in Boston's West End, I once had a conversation with an elderly gentleman who *davened* in Father's *shul*. At one point he asked, "Did you ever notice how churches all have a tall steeple with a bell inside?" Actually, I had noticed nothing of the kind. What did I have to do with churches or steeples? They simply weren't part of my world. But he went on anyway, without waiting for my answer, to make a very interesting point.

"In Russia," he said, "all the churches have steeples and the *goyim* ring bells to call the worshipers to prayer. Any kind of steeple, any kind of bell. How different are we! If *shuls* had steeples and bells, we would have a whole fifth *chelek* (section) of the *Shulchan Aruch* filled with *halachos* (laws) that would tell us exactly how to make and use them. What is the proper height and width of the steeple? Of what material should it be made? Of what should the bell be made? How large should it be? And the same for the clapper. And exactly where should the clapper strike the bell?"

The old man was right. That is indeed the difference between the Jewish approach and the non-Jewish, or barely Jewish, approach to life. Our steeples are ultimately built, not out of wood, but out of *halachos*.

Vayechi

[Yehudah] will bind his donkey to the vine,
And to the vine-branch his donkey's foal,
He will wash his garments in wine,
And his clothes in the blood of grapes,
His eyes are red from wine.
And his teeth are white from milk.
(Genesis 49:11-12)

As Yaakov's blessing to Yehudah indicates, the power of wine to "make glad the heart of man" was never underestimated by our tradition, and the Sages of the Talmud call wine "the best of medicines." Indeed, rejoicing in Hashem and the wondrous world He gave us freely from His overflowing kindness is a key tenet of Chassidus. On the other hand, the effect of wine on Noach was also not forgotten, emphasizing the need for self-control and moderation. In this sense, wine represents Din, the aspect of strict Divine Judgment, and Chassidim pour in a little water, the symbol of Torah and Divine Mercy, before drinking.

Returning to the beginning of Bereishis, the Chumash we are now completing, our Sages tell us that there are 13 words between the first mention of Hashem's Name (Elokim, the Name associated with strict Judgment) and the second. There are five words between the second mention and the third, which, we are told, represent the five fingers that surround the Cup of Blessings. Perhaps the meaning is that Hashem created the world through His Thirteen Middos (Aspects) of Mercy, and man must complete it by using his five fingers (and the Five Books of the Torah) to raise up the good things of this world, the wine-filled Cup of Blessings, to the level of mitzvos and avodah (Divine service).

Of course, there were always some who took the enjoyments of life more literally, and whose irrepressible joi de vivre couldn't help but win one's heart. Such a religious bon vivant was Reb Srulik, Chassid and Cognac-maker Extraordinaire, Vintner by Appointment to the Court of the Grand Rabbi of Boston and the New England Chassidic Center of the West End.

❧ Srulik

Reb Srulik was a distant cousin of ours from *Eretz Yisrael*. He was a descendant of the sages of Tzfas (Safed), where he established a reputation as a kindhearted and learned man. He was entrusted with the important task of being a *sheluchah de-Rabbanan*, which involved raising funds for the Kollel Rabbi Meir Baal HaNes of Jerusalem, and representing the Jerusalem community on his many trips to America. Later, in the late 1920s, he moved to America permanently and lived near us in Boston's West End. He was a jovial, congenial man, heavy set and rather round, almost barrel shaped. This was quite appropriate, for Srulik had a special talent; he was one of the finest wine-makers in Prohibition Boston.

Chassidim could not, of course, get by without wine for *Kiddush*, *Havdalah*, Pesach *sedarim*, *Sheva Berachos* and all the other special occasions that crown the Jewish year. Nor did they have to; since the law specifically *allowed* the use of wine for "sacramental" purposes. But that was scant comfort in those days. You couldn't just go to the corner grocery store and buy a bottle of strictly kosher French Bordeaux or Spanish sherry. Enter Srulik, our local connoisseur and wine *maven*, who graciously accepted the honorable task of keeping the New England Chassidic Center stocked with a year's supply of homemade, strictly kosher Zinfandel (red), Muscatel (white) and

Wine plays an important role in many Jewish religious observances. Here the Rebbe recites Grace After Meals over the Kos shel Brachah (Cup of blessings), in a state of dveikus (clinging to the Divine).

Malaga (traditional) wines. Srulik's Malaga, by the way, wasn't cloyingly sweet like the commercial brands. Instead of adding processed sugar, he simply stopped the fermentation early — leaving natural grape sugars — and fortified the wine with alcohol. Father completely trusted Srulik's meticulous attention to both *kashrus* and his craft.

In the fall, shortly after Succos, our basement at 87 Poplar Street was turned into Srulik's wine factory and we all readied ourselves for another "Big Production." Of course, one doesn't just go into a fruit store and ask for 40 crates of grapes. The expense alone would have been prohibitive. Instead, Srulik would head for the railroad shed in Charleston, where the huge freight cars of grapes were unloaded. Sometimes we children were able to go along with him, and what a special occasion that was: the dim golden light of the late autumn afternoon, the trains in their large shed, the stall-keepers and the vendors all greeting Srulik, tasting grapes, exchanging news about the harvest and tips about wine. By the time the various brightly colored grapes had all been selected and paid for, and the wooden crates loaded onto a rented delivery truck, it was already night.

The grapes were first pulped in a large hand-cranked grinder, about a yard across. Then they fermented in barrels. Finally we set up the large 6-foot-tall wine press. Since our basement was too small to leave the press intact all year long, the 4-foot-wide wooden barrel

Chassidus teaches raising up the pleasures of this world, such as wine, to a level of kedushah (holiness). From R to L: The Bostoner Rebbe; Av Beis Din of the Eidah Charedis (and former Chief of Strassbourg); and the Biala-Pzsyscher Rebbe at a Bostoner simchah tish

that held the fermented pulp came in two sections, which fit together inside a wider but much lower tub. The cover was put on top, the handle was inserted and turned, the cover squeezed down on the pulp, and the wine-to-be poured out between the wooden slats of the central barrel to be collected in the surrounding tub. After the first pressing, 2-inch-thick spacer boards were added and the grape mash was squeezed further. Then more boards and so on. It was very exciting, even for those of us too young to really appreciate wine. Finally the juice was drained through a spigot into barrels to age.

The wooden grape crates were apparently of value and, once empty, were sold to someone. We remember this detail because stacking the crates, four at a time, was a job for us children. The first crate was laid open-side-up on the floor. Then two more crates were set up vertically, back-to-back, inside. Then another crate was set face-down on top to hold them in place.

The compressed fermented pulp was also not wasted. Srulik mixed it with water and transformed it into that more exciting (although less legal) cousin of "sacramental wine" ... "sacramental brandy"! In fact, the local connoisseurs assured us that Srulik's was the very best, the very finest of brandies. It always amazed me how Srulik would pour dark red wine or pulp juice into the metal still, and how the crystal clear droplets of brandy would emerge from the condensation coils at the other end. This was yet another "Big Production." Srulik would fuss around the still with his thermometer, while we waited for the very first, finest drops, the "96," to emerge. These were caught in a small silver cup and given to Father, who made the first *brachah* on the new year's crop. *Baruch Hashem*! Another year of plentiful wine for Shabbos and a *l'chaim* for the *Chassidim*, who could drink brandy but not grain-derived spirits, on Pesach.

Srulik made some wine for himself on the side, but there was really no market for fine kosher wines in those days. Cognac and brandy, however, were more in demand. Years passed and Srulik, who had moved with Father to New York, moved back to Boston and settled near us in Dorchester. One day I heard fire engines racing past our house, stopping a few blocks away, just outside Srulik's door. His basement distillery had exploded and then caught fire! My immediate thought was that, once the firemen saw his still, Srulik would be arrested. Prohibition was over, but homemade "sacramental" spirits were still less than fully legal.

Srulik apparently foresaw the same scenario — himself in handcuffs — and quickly rushed back and forth to hide what he could; but the whole idea was ludicrous. His brandy-flooded basement literally reeked of alcohol. The firemen burst in, in full regalia, and put out what was left of the blaze. They looked at poor Srulik, his life's work in shambles, they looked at each other and then left quietly, without saying a word. They just didn't have the heart to cause him further pain.

Srulik contemplated the wreckage for a while, cleaned up, thought a bit more and then, as irrepressible and jovial as ever, passed the word to his latest customers and friends ... "Srulik rides again!"

Shemos
The Book of Exodus

On Growing Up

The child grows up and ventures forth into the world. So too our people "went down to Egypt ... and became a nation there" (Deuteronomy 26:5); as the Pesach Haggadah explains: Israel developed its distinct character there. This pattern repeats itself in our individual lives as well. The child leaves the familiar, comfortable environment of his home and goes off to live among strangers, whether in yeshivah, university or workplace, while he creates a new, increasingly adult personality. Developing new powers, he readies himself to make his own unique contribution to Hashem's plan.

Apparently, experiencing the unsettled, undefined world of the unfamiliar is an important transitional state. It helps loosen and rearrange outgrown childhood patterns, prompting growth. One of the Rebbe's close chassidim, R' David Gottlieb, often gives newcomers to Israel an excellent piece of advice: "Don't settle where you're already comfortable. Settle someplace you want to grow into, some place where you would like to be comfortable a few years from now."

The Book of Shemos chronicles the Jewish people's maturation far away from home, first in Egypt and later in the desert. Its climax is the receiving of the Torah. The Rebbe's own transitional period, his adolescence and early adulthood, was also spent away from home (Boston), in Eretz Yisrael and then New York, acquiring his broad Torah knowledge. After his father's passing, the young R' Levi Yitzchak returned with his Rebbetzin to Boston. Their task was to reestablish Bostoner Chassidus in the spiritual desert that Boston had become in the mid-1940s.

Shemos

And when Hashem saw that [Moses] turned aside
To see, He called to him ... and said:
"Don't come closer to here...
Because where you stand is holy ground."
(Exodus 3:4,5)

Moses, impressed with the marvelous vision of the burning bush, wanted to "turn aside" and leave this mundane world to approach the Divine. Hashem stopped him and said: "No! Your job is not to make My World, the World of the Heavens, holy. Your job is to make your earthly world, where you stand, holy." To recognize the potential for holiness in even the barren ground of a desert, and to work a lifetime to realize that potential, that is the purpose of every Jew. It is not easy. The ground is cold, rocky and often unreceptive; but it is our task nonetheless.

Yet before he can receive this message and undertake the burden of leadership, Moses must first see the bush aflame. He must experience a light-filled world beyond the mundane to truly lead either flocks or men. The yeshivah is one such protected world beyond the day-to-day clamor of life, a place to learn to see the light of Torah and to prepare for the challenges ahead. So it was for the Rebbe as well.

⚜ Yeshivah Torah Vodaath

My first exposure to *yeshivah* life at *Yeshivah* Torah V'Yirah in the Old *Yishuv* of Yerushalayim (1934-36) was a wonderful experience but, when our family returned to Boston, Father was hard pressed to find an American *yeshivah* that met with his approval. Instead, I learned privately with my brother, Reb Moshe, for another two years. I was 14, and he was 27.

In 1938 Father befriended Mr. Edward Gerber, a religious up-and-coming Boston lawyer, who later became the brother-in-law of R' Yosef Ber Soloveitchik, *zt"l*. He taught me English, and I taught him Talmud. He saw how lonely I was, and after one of his trips to New York, he told Father: "What are you keeping your son here for? There's a very good *yeshivah* in New York. A real *yeshivah*, where they learn well and the *Chassidishe bachurim* have beards and *peyos*."

The *yeshivah*, of course, was Mesivta Torah Vodaath, one of the very few *yeshivos* in America at that time. The Mesivta had about 200 students under the general guidance of R' Shraga Feivel Mendlowitz, *zt"l*. At first Father wouldn't hear of it. He couldn't believe that there could be anything suitable in America. Finally, however, he decided to go to New York to speak with R' Mendlowitz. R' Mendlowitz came to see him, and soon convinced Father of the advantages of the *yeshivah*; and Rosh Chodesh Iyar 1938 was set as my enrollment date.

First, however, I needed a place to stay. Father was one of the few Chassidic Rebbes in America before World War II; and it wasn't easy to make appropriate arrangements. *Kashrus* was a major issue. Father did not permit eating beef or veal outside our home, only chicken, and even then we had to be very careful about the *shechitah*. Someone suggested a respectable family whose *kashrus* was 100 percent reliable, and who were willing to rent out a room to a *yeshivah bachur*. Neither was very common, since there were few out-of-town *yeshivah bachurim* in those days.

My brother, Reb Moshe, went with me to New York to help make arrangements for the room. First we *davened Minchah* and *Maariv* at Torah Vodaath in the big *yeshivah* building, a block or so away from the Mesivta. There we met my prospective host and walked home with him. As we walked up the stairs, he made a loud, peculiar announcement: "*Menschen gain! Menschen gain*" (People are coming!). At first we couldn't figure out what was going on. Then we surmised that his wife was angry with him, and he wanted to alert her not to greet him with a hot "*Mi Sheberach*" at the door! Needless to say, Reb Moshe quickly decided that this was no place for his shy younger brother to spend his *yeshivah* years. If even the husband was afraid to come home, I certainly didn't stand much of a chance!

The Rebbe, Mr. Edward Gerber, z"l, and Rav Yosef Ber Soloveitchik, zt"l, in Boston in later years (when the Rebbe was about 30).

Eventually we found a wonderful family, the Eisdorfers, with whom I stayed for several years. The father, Mr. Moshe Eisdorfer, was a refined, reserved European gentleman from Hungary. Mrs. Eisdorfer was Litvish but, despite their different backgrounds, they were a lovely, harmonious couple. The *kashrus* and food were both excellent, although I was never a big eater, either then or now. Mrs. Eisdorfer used to joke that she never had to cook for her husband. She would just cook for me, and the *sherayim* (leftovers) were more than enough for another meal.

My roommates varied over the years. One was the son of a distinguished New York Rav. Whenever he would act up — he was only 13 — Mr. Eisdorfer would say to his wife, "*Loz im loifen*," literally "let him run." Every time he heard this, our young friend, as if to illustrate his host's words, would jump up and run around the table!

My first day in the Mesivta's *Bais Medrash* was full of surprises. Where were all the Chassidic *bachurim* with beards, frock coats and *peyos*? After my experiences in Yerushalayim, I was not expecting *yeshivah bachurim* dressed in short, light-colored American suits. They reminded me of the Irish Barber Shop Quartet that used to sing outside our window on Poplar Street in Boston. They were all clean shaven, except for one fellow in the corner who had also just arrived that day; and they wore no hats, only *yarmulkes*. Were these *yeshivah bachurim*?

The *Gemara shiur* was something else. The *Maggid Shiur*, R' Shlomo Heiman, *zt"l*, was very special and his *shiur* was a popular one. Listening to a formal *shiur* and publicly asking questions was a new experience for me; but I was, once again, disappointed with some of the other students. One *bachur* even asked a question, using blatantly incorrect Yiddish grammar, about *"der"* (masculine) *"frau"* (feminine). What was going on here? They couldn't even speak Yiddish straight!

The *shiur* lasted two hours, from 11 a.m. to 1 p.m. It was followed by a lunch break, the afternoon *seder* (learning session) and then *Minchah*. At *Minchah* I looked up and saw a completely different group of people. The Poplar Street Barber Shop Quartet had suddenly been replaced by a serious group of Torah Jews, in light-grey hats, *davening Shemoneh Esrei* with tremendous *kavanah*. That made me feel a lot better. If they could *daven* like that, things were going to be all right. Later someone pointed out the best boy in our class: the boy who couldn't speak Yiddish! It was a powerful, instant lesson in how not to judge people by their externals.

In fact, not only was that boy something special, the whole *Bais Medrash* was. That one *Bais Medrash* produced many of the prominent American-born *rabbanim* and educators of that generation: R' Eliyahu Moshe Shisgal (R' Moshe Feinstein's son-in-law), R' Moshe Leiberman (my *chavrusah*, later a *Maggid Shiur* at Torah Vodaath), *zt"l*, and *yb"l*, R' Elya Svei (Philadelphia *Rosh Yeshivah*), R' Ya'acov Weinberg (*Rosh Yeshivah* of Ner Yisrael), R' Binyamin Goldenberg (long-time head of Torah U'Mesorah), R' Manes Mandel (*Yeshivah* of Brooklyn), R' Simchah Schustal (Stamford *Rosh Yeshivah*), R' Don

Ungarischer (Bais Medrash Elyon, Monsey) and many others. In fact, when the Lubavitcher Rebbe, R' Yosef Yitzchak Schneersohn, *zt"l*, emigrated to America in 1940 and needed ten outstanding young men to start his own *yeshivah*, he took six or seven from our class. The Chassidic student who entered on my first day, R' Shmuel Teitelbaum, became the Chinchkiventzer Rav, later a cousin of mine by marriage.

Torah Vodaath taught me some other important extracurricular lessons as well. Although only 16, I felt that a Rebbe's son belonged in the *Bais Medrash*, engaged in independent study with the advanced students, not in the formal classroom setting reserved for students one *shiur* below. I insisted, won my case...and always regretted it. Without that extra preparation I had to work overtime just to keep up. Although, *baruch Hashem*, successful, I always wondered what I had missed. Sometimes it pays to listen.

Torah Vodaath was a truly great pedagogical institution. As the forerunner of most American *yeshivos*, it influenced the entire religious American Jewish community of its time.

❧ Who's to Be a Rebbe?

Despite its many great teachers, lecturers and scholars, the guiding light of the *yeshivah* was R' Shraga Feivel Mendlowitz. He was exceedingly modest — hence his insistence on being called "Mr." rather than "Rav" — a great *tzaddik*, an inspiring leader and a friend to all. On the other hand, he didn't brook too much nonsense from us boys. We were there to learn Torah and every minute was precious.

R' Mendlowitz used to come early to the Mesivta on Bedford Avenue. After the bell rang, he would often go and stand outside to "greet" the latecomers as they walked up the 12 steps from the street to the Mesivta building. A boy really knew he was in trouble when he ran up to the building and saw R' Mendlowitz standing at the top of those 12 steps with his pocketwatch in hand.

Walking up those 12 steps under his watchful eye seemed to

take an eternity. He never actually said anything; but the experience was a full course in *mussar* all by itself. Once a latecomer reached the top step, he would be shown the pocketwatch: It said 9:10, not 9:00, and you made a mental note to never, ever be late again. We were in such awe of him that R' Mendlowitz's silent feedback was more dramatic and effective than any reprimand a principal could give.

There were only three or four other Chassidic students in the whole school, so we really stood out. One day, during study session, three of us were "congregating," having a brief chat, when R' Mendlowitz walked in. We were deeply chagrined, but instead of scolding us, he put his fatherly hands on two of our shoulders and said, "I'll tell you now what you are going to be after you leave the *yeshivah*." Then he turned straight to me and said, "You are going to be a Rebbe."

I was in a state of shock. I had no intention of becoming a Rebbe. Two other Chassidic boys in the *Bais Medrash* did indeed have such aspirations — one even invited people to his *Melaveh Malkah tish* — but not me. R' Mendlowitz was a *tzaddik*, but his

The Rebbe, then an 18-year-old yeshivah bachur with a beard (R), was on hand to greet R' Yosef Yitzchak Schneersohn, the Lubavitcher Rebbe, zt"l, upon his arrival in New York City in 1940.

prediction was hard to believe. I was so shy and low key. Furthermore, Father was sick and I didn't want to even think about anything happening to him (a son doesn't usually become a Rebbe while his father is still alive). And here was R' Mendlowitz, a very special person, whose words carried weight, and who had just walked up to me and said, "You are going to be a Rebbe." It shook me up so much that I never did hear what he told the others.

R' Shraga Feivel Medlowitz, zt"l, the saintly, energetic menahel of Yeshivah Torah Vodaath, was a pioneer in building Torah education in America.

To this day we have never figured out how R' Mendlowitz knew that the quiet young man on the sidelines was the one who actually would become a Rebbe. He was an amazing man, a legend in his own time.

Va'eira

And I have heard the groaning
Of the Children of Israel
Whom the Egyptians have enslaved.
(Exodus 6:5)

The suffering of the Jewish people throughout the centuries defies description. The forces of darkness have mercilessly, relentlessly attacked the forces of light again and again, all but extinguishing them in blood and pain. Yet the light burns on, fed by martyrdom, determination and faith in the ultimate victory of all that is good and right.

To speak of this suffering is not easy. We cannot fully understand Hashem's plan, and to try to "explain" such suffering, reducing it to our own comprehensible size, is to profane it. But we do understand what is demanded of us: to stand firm, to resist, to rebuild. We instinctively recognize the truth of R' Nachman of Bratslav's cry, "Gevalt, brothers! Just don't despair!"

Rebuilding does not mean providing a decent burial for our past, our Torah and our way of life; it means living it. It is the "civilizations" of our Egyptian taskmasters, Roman persecutors and Nazi murderers that belong in museums. We belong in the land of the living, in our rebuilt yeshivos, synagogues, day schools and kollelim. Air-conditioned Holocaust museums are *no substitute for warm Jewish hearts and living Jewish communities. The best way to remember the fallen is to take their place on the front lines of Yiddishkeit, and to live their lives that were so tragically cut short.*

❦ *The War Years*

In America, the years of World War II were incredibly frustrating. There was not much a young man in *yeshivah* could do to help, although we did give the *maaser* money from our *nadan* (dowry) to help get Jews out of Europe, during the brief period when that was possible.

We knew, of course, of the ceaseless efforts of R' Avraham Kalmanowitz, the Mirrer *Rosh Yeshivah*, to try to get the American authorities to stop the slaughter of the Jews of Europe. Even on Shabbos, he, R' Aharon Kotler and the Kapitchenitzer Rebbe all went to see someone who might be able to help them see Cordell Hull, the apathetic U.S. Secretary of State. R Kalmanowitz would literally faint when speaking in synagogues, describing what he imagined to be the desperate plight of European Jewry. Later, when he found out the full truth, he said that all that he had thought, all that he had said, all the nightmares that he had had, were only a *tipah sheb'yam*, a drop in the sea, compared to what had actually occurred.

We also knew of a group of activists, loosely affiliated with the Revisionists who were trying to get the U.S. Administration's attention. Their plan? To organize a "Rabbis' March on Washington." Peter Bergson, a prominent Jewish activist (and a nephew of R' Avraham Y. Kook,) organized the trip; and the well-known American philanthropist and playwright, Ben Hecht, helped pay the train fares.

There were no *kollelim* in America in those days; but the older students in our *yeshivah*, those already learning independently, were asked to join the *rabbanim*. There were 200 of us in all. The trip itself was highly depressing. The situation in Europe was terrifying, and we doubted that the U.S. Administration would pay the slightest attention. It seemed a hopeless, "stonewall" situation. We felt that President Roosevelt would never receive us or accept our petition (he didn't); but the organizers were trying their best, and we felt that we should try our best too.

Once in Washington, we all waited outside the White House... and waited ...and waited. R' Eliezer Silver, President of the Union of Orthodox Rabbis of the United States and Canada, had gone inside with a few prominent *rabbanim* to try to see President Roosevelt. Six million Jewish lives hung in the balance; but President Roosevelt was far too busy to see Rav Silver, even for just a few minutes!

We were all, of course, very upset. It was yet another sign of the disregard for Jewish issues and lives that characterized our government at that sad time. Later we found out that one of Roosevelt's "Jewish" advisers had told him, "Don't even bother listening to them. What do a few Orthodox Rabbis matter?"

From the White House we went to the Capitol where we were met by Vice President Wallace. He gave us some fine-sounding words of comfort, which was about all he could do. Finally we went

R' Eliezer Silver (center) and R' Avraham Kalmanowitz (to his right, with long beard) led the Rabbis' March on Washington, a tragically fruitless attempt to petition the U.S. Government to stop the Holocaust.

The Melitzer Rebbe leads the Rabbis' March on Washington in reciting Tehillim for the Jews of the ongoing Holocaust (1943). The Rebbe is the young man with the black hat and black beard, five rows from the speaker (right of center).

en masse to the Lincoln Memorial, where the Melitzer Rebbe, led us in reciting *Tehillim*. There is a well-known photograph of that scene: the Melitzer Rebbe at the top of the Memorial, with all the *rabbanim* crowding around. And somewhere in that mighty crowd you will find a young man with a small, black beard, learning more about the importance of having democratic leaders willing to listen to Jewish concerns.

That was the tragic end of the Rabbis' attempted meeting with President Roosevelt. We went back to New York on our special train, and the Jews of Europe continued to go to their deaths in the cattle cars of their Nazi murderers, and the President of the United States of America continued to be "too busy."

※

On the train, I was seated next to Dr. Yehudah Leib Gordon, a psychiatrist who used to write for the *Morning Journal*. We got to talking about the general situation — the psychiatrist and the *yeshivah bachur* — and he explained an interesting statement from the *Gemara* from both a psychological and religious point of view.

The *Gemara* says: "Whoever becomes angry is as if he served idols." What's the connection? Imagine someone who walks into a dark room and bumps into a chair. It hurts, but after all, it is dark, so what can he do? He walks out on the other side and finishes his business. Then, on the way back, he bumps into the same chair again, quite hard. It really hurts. What does he do now? He grabs the chair and, livid with rage, shoves it aside.

What did the chair do? Why should he get angry with an inanimate object? It must be that, in his moment of anger, he did regard the chair as having somehow hurt him. That is, in his anger, he attributed life and power to a piece of wood. That is the essence of all *avodah zarah* (idol worship)

ೞ *The Sosnovitzer Rav*

I had the privilege of witnessing the life of the East European *shtetl* when, as an 11-year-old, I traveled with my family to my brother's wedding in Poland (1932). There we met our great-uncle, the Rebbe of Sosnovitz, R' Alter Biederman.. His daughter was married to a great *talmid chacham*, known simply as "Reb Motteleh," and they had one son, Reb Mosheleh. Two years later Reb Alter passed on and Reb Motteleh became the Sosnovitzer Rav.

By 1939, Poland was already enacting anti-Semitic laws as the clouds of war began to gather over Europe. Poland had ordered all alien Jews, such as "Palestinians," to leave; and this included my great uncle's family, which had originally come from Yerushalayim. However, Palestine, then under the British Mandate, wouldn't let them back in! They were trapped, and Reb Motteleh sent us an urgent letter asking for help in entering the United States.

This was no simple matter, as the gates of U.S. immigration were also closed. He would be admitted if — and it was a big if — an American *shul* would formally hire him as their rabbi and guarantee him a credible salary, at least on paper. Many *shul* leaders of that time were secular "big shots" — some were arrogant and overbearing boors — who treated their Rabbis as "employees" and were averse to doing *chessed* in any form. They were more interested in taking than giving. In fact, Father couldn't convince a single *shul* board in Boston to sign the papers necessary to save Reb Motteleh and his son.

Instead it was the rabbi of a non-Orthodox temple, R' Joseph S. Shubow, a very special person and a great admirer of my father, who promised to get the necessary papers. He went to his temple's board meeting and made the outrageous proposal that they offer the Sosnovitzer Rav a position with an annual salary of $5000, a huge sum in those days. "What on earth are you talking about?" they said. "You want us to give some Orthodox rabbi in Poland, whom we don't even know, a contract? What if he comes here with his contract and demands his money? Then we'll all be stuck!"

R' Shubow was unperturbed. He told them, "First of all, if this *rav* does ask for your $5000, you can deduct it from my salary. Second, this *rav* not only won't come to ask you for $5000 for being your rabbi, he won't even step foot in your building, because he would regard it as *treif*!" Father never forgot R' Shubow's incredible selflessness and sacrifice for a fellow Jew.

Next Father went to a small *shul* in West Warwick, Rhode Island, which agreed to formally offer a position to Rav Motteleh's son. Now both families were covered, and all the necessary papers were sent off. Unfortunately, the Polish Consulate staff in Warsaw were real *reshaim* (villains), and put every possible difficulty in the path of Jews trying to leave.

They sent Reb Motteleh a letter saying that there was a U.S. visa waiting for *him* in Warsaw, but said nothing about his son. He sent us an urgent telegram saying that he couldn't possibly leave his only son behind. What should he do? Father immediately got in touch with a senator in Washington, and the Senator got in touch with the U.S. State Department, and the U.S. State Department got in touch with the Polish Consulate in Warsaw. There they said, "Oh, we're quite sorry," the letter had been intended for both of them. They gave Reb Motteleh and his son a new date, around September 3, for receiving their visas in Warsaw, but by then it was too late.

World War II began with the Nazi invasion of Poland on September 1, 1939, and Sosnovitz was near the German border. Reb Motteleh and his family were among the first inhabitants of Sosnovitz to be shot by the Nazi invaders. They were among the first victims of the Holocaust.

Bo

And they shall take some of the blood [of the pascal lamb],
And put it on the two mezuzos (doorposts)
And on the lintel of [their] houses.
(Exodus 12:7)

Contrary to the opinion of some, the proud public performance of mitzvos does not increase the hostility of the non-Jewish world, but its respect. This was made clear at our nation's very beginning. The Jews in Egypt marked their doorposts with the blood of a sheep (an Egyptian god) and, rather than attacking them, the Egyptians lent them their most precious vessels of silver and gold. Far from increasing Jewish vulnerability, such mesiras nefesh (self-sacrifice) for mitzvos was powerful protection against the deadly plague that followed (the death of the firstborn).

The mezuzah scroll prominently displayed on the doorposts of every Jewish home (Deuteronomy 6:9) proclaims the same message. Its outside contains the Holy Name "Almighty" in Hebrew, whose three letters are an acronym for Shomer Dalosos Yisrael, Guardian of the Doors of Israel. In fact, on that first Pesach night, the Leil Shimurim (the Night of Guarding), Hashem Himself guarded the mitzvah-marked homes from all ill, and no Jew was afraid to say, "A Jew lives here!" The same principle holds true today.

A young friend of ours, a leader in a national Orthodox student organization, once had a yechidus (private meeting) with the late Lubavitcher Rebbe, R' Menachem Mendel Schneersohn, zt"l. The Rebbe surprised him by asking, "Do you put on tefillin each morning?" "Of course," he said. "And do you walk across the campus to get to your minyan?" Again, "Of course." "So tell me, do you carry your tallis bag with the Hebrew letters facing outside or in?" An embarrassed silence followed. "In," he mumbled. "So do this one thing for me. From now on carry it with the Hebrew letters facing out. A Jew should be proud of his tefillin."

The Bostoner Rebbe's father exemplified this "mezuzah attitude" in his dress, his speech and his attitude towards mitzvos. Every mitzvah, every second he could be doing a mitzvah, was precious to him, as the following incident shows.

❧ The Mezuzah

By the time Father moved to Brooklyn in 1939, things were very rough for him, both financially and physically. After serving in Boston for 25 years, he left as a very sick man, suffering from the effects of high blood pressure. For some reason, our family traveled all night from Boston to New York by train. It was a terrible ordeal. Father was so weak and frail by then that we were worried that he might not make it to New York alive. Some loyal friends met us at Grand Central Station at 5 or 6 a.m., and we went on together to Williamsburg, which was, even in those days, a religious neighborhood.

By the time we arrived at the building where we were to live, several other friends from the neighborhood had gathered. Father's *shul* was on the ground floor and our living quarters were on the next floor, at the top of a steep set of stairs. We all escorted Father as he entered the building and, ever so slowly, began his climb to the top of the stairs. With each step we became more and more grateful and relieved. He was already halfway up the stairs, another step, another step, soon he would enter the apartment and lie down at last.

We ran ahead and opened the door but, when Father reached the doorway, he stopped and wouldn't move. No matter what we did, he just stood there, carefully rummaging through his pockets. He wouldn't budge. Finally, he reached into his coat pocket and pulled out a little hammer, a *mezuzah* and some nails. "I'm not going in," he said, "until I put up a *mezuzah*."

He said the *brachah* and carefully hammered his *mezuzah* into place. Then he entered our new home and half-collapsed on his bed. The story of his *mesiras nefesh* for the *mitzvah* of *mezuzah* soon spread throughout Williamsburg and was the talk of the whole community for days.

> ## Hassidic Rabbi of Boston Departs After 25 Years
>
> ### Pincus D. Horowitz Embodiment of Wisdom of Centuries to His 5000 Jewish Followers
>
> By Julius Kaplan
>
> The last thing Rabbi Pincus David Horowitz did, before bidding Boston goodbye after 23 years, was to bake some matzoth for Passover, of flour imported from Palestine.
>
> He wouldn't think of doing as most Jews do nowadays—go out and buy the unleavened bread in the nearest store. For Rabbi Horowitz is a representative of more than one Hassidic dynasty, going back to the founding of the orthodox sect by Rabbi Israel Baal Shem, 230 years ago.
>
> The unpretentious house at 87 Poplar street, near the Charles River, center of Hassidism in New England for a quarter of a century, is vacant today. Senator Walsh and the late elder Senator Lodge were once visitors there.
>
> The grey-bearded Rabbi Horowitz and his black-bearded older son, Rabbi Moses Horowitz, and other members of the family took the train Monday night for Brooklyn, N. Y. There was a new congregation waiting for them there, or more accurately, a new following.
>
> When Rabbi Horowitz came to this city from Palestine, he was the only Hassidic rabbi in New England, and the second in America. To his orthodox Jewish followers, he was the embodiment of the wisdom of two and a half centuries of Hassidism, a blood descendant of such rabbis as the Rabbi of Lublin, Poland, whom his followers called The Seer, saying that he had vision over 100 miles and could work miracles.
>
> There was the time Rabbi Horowitz created a great stir in Boston, drawing a throng of some 10,000 people in Roxbury to watch a marriage ceremony. Police had to handle the crowd. Hassidic custom required that a wedding take place under the open sky, and Rabbi Horowitz performed this particular ceremony outdoors in the midst of a raging February blizzard.
>
> Hassidism came into being in 18th century Russia as a movement to meet the religious needs of the laboring Jews, who had become estranged from the rather erudite and inaccessible rabbis of the congregation. Hassid, freely translated, means "good Samaritan." The Hassidic rabbis are the last word in orthodoxy. They always have beards, and on the Sabbath and holidays wear long silk robes and fur hats. In New England, Rabbi Horowitz had some 5000 followers.
>
> His great-grandfather left Austria 90 years ago to settle in Palestine, and there Rabbi Horowitz and his children were born. His younger son, Levi, who has a sprouting beard, is studying for the rabbinate in Brooklyn. His grandson, son of Rabbi Moses, a little boy named Abraham, has blond ringlets curling about his ears.
>
> There have been several instances, Rabbi Moses said, where Christians have come to his father. They had heard stories of Hassidic miracles from their immigrant parents. The Hassidic rabbis disavow miraculous powers, but their followers often make claims for them.

R' Pinchas Dovid's departure for New York in 1939 was the occasion of this Boston newspaper article, which provides interesting glimpses into American impressions of Chassidus and the Rebbe's family at mid-century.

※

116 ❦ AND THE ANGELS LAUGHED

They could not see each other...for three days
But all the Children of Israel
Had light in their dwellings.
(Exodus 10:23)

Seeing is a matter of spiritual level as well as physics and physiology. Thus the Jews saw the light, while the Egyptians could not. The first primal light, which Hashem Himself pronounced "Good," was enjoyed by Adam HaRishon for only 36 hours: the 12 hours before he sinned, and the 24 hours of the Holy Sabbath that followed. According to the Midrash, this was a special light with which Adam could see from one end of the universe to the other. It was then hidden until the End of Days, when the tzaddikim (righteous), because of their own high spiritual level, will be able to enjoy its brilliance.

Where was this all-encompassing light hidden? In the Torah and its mitzvos, says Chassidus, and thus a glimmer of it exists in every generation. That is one mystical aspect of the 36 Chanukah lights, which correspond to the 36 hours during which Adam enjoyed the pure, primal light. Indeed, the tzaddikim of every generation still see with their righteousness, as well as with their retinas.

❧ Blind Sight

Father moved to Williamsburg in 1939 and began to strengthen the Chassidic community there. Before World War II, almost all the great rebbes were still in Europe; and American *Chassidim* needed someone nearby to help them with their day-to-day problems and needs. Many became Father's "adopted" *Chassidim*; and soon hundreds of people began attending his Friday night *tish*. Among them were three prominent "Moshelach," one of whom was R' Moshe Smith, the president of a prestigious *shul* in Williamsburg.

Nowadays, it is common for Jews to leave their old neighborhoods for the suburbs and, tragically, their *shuls* become churches. In the case of Williamsburg in the early 1940s, the opposite was true. Jews poured into Williamsburg, and often bought old churches to become their new *shuls*. Such was the case, among others, with R' Moshe Smith's *shul*, which was looking for a new *rav*. He suggested that my older brother would be an ideal candidate; but Father flatly refused to consider it. He opposed *davening* in any *shul* building that had previously served as a church. The halachic conditions under which such trans-

R' Pinchas Dovid's new apartment and shul, at the corner of Bedford and Wilson Avenues, housed the first community-wide Chassidic tish in Williamsburg, New York.

The Rebbe's brother, R' Moshe Horowitz, never accepted the position in the "converted" shul. He became the Bostoner Rebbe of New York (in 1941) and a member of the Moetzes Gedolei HaTorah of the Agudath Israel of America. This Moetzes meeting shows him (second from L) engaged in discussion with the Novominsker Rebbe (L), R' Moshe Feinstein, and R' Yitzchok Hutner, and R' Yitzchok Ruderman (R).

formations are permissible are so stringent and demanding that Father felt they could never be fully met in practice; and he battled incessantly against such "conversions."

R' Moshe Smith refused to take "no" for an answer. He pointed out that the *shul* had been meticulous refurbished according to *halachah*. The roof had been changed somewhat, all non-Jewish symbols had been removed, and so on. Father still didn't like the idea but, given his *Chassid's* unremitting arguments, he agreed to inspect the building himself. At this point in his life, Father was practically blind and walked slowly with a cane. This didn't exactly make him an ideal building inspector, but he went anyway.

At the *shul* Father was met by an appropriate delegation of dignitaries who proudly showed him the sanctuary on the main floor. He listened silently as they pointed out the many improvements they had made and then, without comment, said "Now I would like to see the upstairs." They escorted him to the hall and began walking up the staircase to the women's gallery.

Halfway up the stairs, Father stopped and stuck his cane between the staircase the *shul* had added and the original church wall. At that point the wall had been breached for a long stained-glass window, whose Christian scenes had long since been replaced with plain glass. Father, with his half-blind eyes, turned to R' Moshe and said, "What's this?" R' Moshe looked down to where the cane touched the window and there, half-covered by the staircase, was an unreplaced stained-glass panel with a big cross!

Pandemonium broke out; R' Moshe almost fainted. They had *davened* in that *shul* for 30-odd years, walked up and down that staircase hundreds of times, and had never once seen what my "blind" father saw.

My brother didn't take the position after all; the *shul* was converted back to a church in the '90s; and people learned that a *tzaddik* sees more, and differently, than other men.

Beshalach

*Then Moses and the Children of Israel sang
This song to Hashem saying:
I will sing to Hashem for He is very great,
The horse and his rider He tossed in the sea.
(Exodus 15:1)*

How does a Jew relate to the miracles of this world — those that occur every day (waking, living, learning), those that occur but once a lifetime and those that occur but once in history, such as the giving of the Torah and the splitting of the Reed Sea? A Jew says shirah (sings). Although a Jew knows all too well the pain of this world, he also knows the joy of being a Jew. He knows that the true essence of the Creator and His Creation are joy, that the Presence of Hashem rests only where there is joy.

When victorious over the Canaanites, Devorah says shirah. When she bears her long-awaited son Shmuel, Channah says shirah. Throughout the many trials and triumphs of his life, King David says shirah. The response may be natural, but for the song to be holy, the singer must be holy and the joy must be holy.

The root of all these songs is the Shiras HaYam, the Song of Moses at the Sea (Exodus 15:1-18). After the Jews had been saved from Mitzrayim (Egypt) and their own meitzarim (spiritual limitations), their response was spontaneous song. How could 600,000 ex-slaves spontaneously and simultaneously sing such a complicated song? The Sfas Emes, the second Gerer Rebbe, answers that this song, like every truly holy song, sings itself at all times. It is like the radio waves that fill the air, waiting for a tuned receiver. All man has to do is to reach the spiritual level that the song represents, merge with it, and the song will sing itself through him.

This applies to all men at all times, and not to man alone. When the Philistines placed the Holy Ark on the backs of the oxen taking it back to *Eretz Yisrael*, the oxen bellowed all the way. According to the Sages of the Talmud (Avodah Zarah 24b), this was their way of saying *shirah*. In fact, according to R' Yochanan, they sang the *Shiras HaYam* itself. So too, the spiritual presence of the Ark, and the Torah inside it, can make even the animal in us sing.

So *Chassidim* sing. They negate the negative, fill with joy the positive, celebrate miracles through song, and create them the same way.

✼ Shiras HaEast River

In Williamsburg people still remember Father's *tish* on the seventh night of Pesach, the night of the splitting of the Reed Sea. The *Chassidim* came back to *shul* at midnight, the very time that the Sea split for our ancestors as they left Egypt. They poured water on the floor to represent the Sea, and marched through it singing the *Shiras HaYam*.

This symbolic reliving of the Exodus was a very moving experience, one which our family never failed to celebrate. The *tish* itself was a big communal occasion, and its climax was Father's recitation of the *Shiras HaYam* at the *amud*, verse by verse.

Usually the *tish* was very joyous. *Chassidim* from all over Williamsburg, especially the *Eretz Yisrael* ones, would come and dance on top of the tables. But in 1941, during the Holocaust, a Galician (Polish) Jew stood up, banged his hand on the table and complained: "In Europe, Jewish blood is flowing, and here you are dancing?" That brought everyone down at once. The Nazis were murdering the Jews of Europe, destroying whole communities. There was numbing, chilling pain. No one could move.

After a short pause, Father asked the *Chassidim* to sit back down at the table. He had something he wanted to say. Then he tried to explain the relationship between a Jew's obligations and his mood through an interesting Torah thought. *Rambam* says that one of the *avodos kashos shebamikdash*, one of the most difficult tasks in the *Bais HaMikdash*, was *simchah* (rejoicing). Why was *simchah* such a difficult *avodah*? After all, when things are going well, and one has everything he wants, it is easy to rejoice. Shabbos comes and one celebrates; *Yom Tov* comes and one celebrates. So why is *simchah* an *avodah kashah*? Because when, G-d forbid, things are difficult and frightening, and one has to be *same'ach* anyway, because the Torah calls *Yom Tov* a *"z'man simchaseinu"* (a time for rejoicing), then one truly performs the *mitzvah* of *simchah*, and it is hard indeed. But since Hashem wills it so, we rejoice nonetheless.

Every year after the *tish*, around 1 a.m., we would walk as a group to the East River (later, in Boston, it was the Charles River) and sing the *Shiras HaYam*. We couldn't sing out loud while we were walking, because we didn't want to wake up all the neighbors, but we hummed softly until we arrived at the grounds of the large Shaeffer's beer factory that faced the river. Then we could sing out loud again. We continued this tradition even during the war, when the brewery became a navy yard, although then we had to get special permission to be allowed onto government property. Throughout the Williamsburg of that generation people knew, "The seventh night of Pesach? We're going with the Bostoner Rebbe to the East River to say *Shiras HaYam*."

Father, R' Pinchas Dovid HaLevi Horowitz, passed away a few weeks before Chanukah 1941. In 1942 I received my *semichah* (rabbinic ordination), *"Yoreh Yoreh, Yadin Yadin,"* from R' Shlomo Heiman, *Rosh Yeshivah* of Torah Vodaath. (While Torah Vodaath does not usually offer this special form of *semichah*, we had requested it because it was our family tradition.) My Rebbetzin, Raichel Horowitz, and I were married in 1942; and in 1943 we had our first child. In 1944 our young family returned to the Boston area — Dorchester, to be exact — to undertake the improbable task of reestablishing Bostoner Chassidus virtually from scratch. Few members of the old Bostoner community remained, and those who did were aged and frail. It would have taken a series of miracles to have succeeded but, fortunately, the miracles came.

One case in point was our first Boston *Shiras HaYam* in 1945. Of course, Dorchester, Massachusetts, wasn't Williamsburg, New York, and most of our 80-year-old congregants were not good candidates for coming back to *shul* at midnight; but we persevered. We rounded up the few people we could count on, and after *Maariv* on the seventh night of Pesach, told them, "We have to make a *minyan* at midnight tonight. Make sure that you all come back for *Shiras HaYam*." It seemed like a good idea at the time, but midnight was soon fast approaching, and we had only nine people, one short of the ten people required for public prayer.

One fellow who was supposed to come, the caretaker at the *mikveh*, lived just around the corner; so we sent someone to fetch him. We waited and waited, with no results. At first, we weren't worried; we assumed that our two congregants were just talking to someone outside, and that they would all come back together. Not so. Our messenger came back empty-handed: "No luck! I knocked on the door as loud as I could but there was no answer." Well, there we were with only nine people — not a *minyan*. More agonizing moments passed.

What could we do? At midnight there are no religious Jews wandering around the streets of Dorchester; and we couldn't just knock on random doors at that hour and say, "Hi! Why don't you come make a *minyan*?" As we were agonizing over all this, the outside door opened and a little fellow walked in. He was sort of barrel shaped; in fact, downright stout. He sat down at the *tish* and we took a second look at him. It was none other than Heller, the attorney who used to *daven* in Father's *shul* in the West End of Boston in the 1930s, 15 years earlier.

Heller had been one of Father's most enthusiastic *baalei teshuvah*. During the '30s, it was almost unheard of for a Boston lawyer to be *shomer Shabbos*. Heller was not only a *shomer Shabbos* lawyer, he was a real *kana'i* (zealot). He always took the most extreme position possible. Heller had never shown up at 61 Columbia Road before, and never came again. He came just that one time, without fuss or explanation, at midnight on the seventh night of Pesach, to make our *minyan* and to say *Shiras HaYam*. After that, until his death 10 or so years later, we did not see Heller again.

We couldn't help but feel that, if it was not *Eliyahu HaNavi* in the body of Heller, it was, at least, some other special spiritual force that woke Heller up just before midnight and told him, "Listen here, there are nine other *Yidden* at the Bostoner Rebbe's new *shtibel* waiting for a tenth man to say *Shiras HaYam,* and you had better get up and go there!"

❦ True Delight

One of the very special people who used to dance on the tables at Father's *Shiras HaYam tish* was R' Pinchas Lazar Paksher. He was an impressive, aristocratic-looking *Yerushalmi*, a *Chassid* of Father's uncle, R' Dovid'l Biederman. He visited America often, collecting money for various worthy causes, and then he would visit my father. In Jerusalem, he *davened* every day with Reb Dovid'l.

Reb Lazar enjoyed telling and retelling the story of how, one day after *davening,* they realized that it was the *yahrzeit* of a famous *tzaddik*. In Chassidic circles, such an occasion calls for a celebration, but the members of Reb Dovid'l's *minyan* were too poor to afford a *seudah* (festive meal). They decided to go home and bring their breakfasts back to *shul* to make an improptu *seudah*.

They did, and, poverty coming in only one flavor, each of them returned with exactly the same meal: a *pita* (flat bread), a piece of herring and a bit of *shiris* (a low-grade edible oil). They were too poor to have any special food on hand.

Then they ate their "royal" breakfast with gusto, singing beautiful *niggunim*, exchanging *divrei Torah* and Chassidic stories. For a brief hour they were in seventh heaven, far above the daily world and its problems.

Reb Pinchas Lazar would always conclude his story by saying, "I was young then, and many, many years have passed. On my travels I have been to great weddings and elaborate banquets, filled with the fanciest delicacies. But never did I experience *simchah* and loftiness to compare with that very special *yahrzeit seudah* of *pita*, herring and *shiris*. That was true delight."

Yisro

And Moses led the people out
To meet Hashem.
(Exodus 19:17)

This teaches that the Divine Presence
Went out to meet them
Like a bridegroom welcoming his bride.
(Rashi)

The special relationship between Hashem and the Jewish people is so close, so intense, that the Giving of the Torah that inaugurated it can only be described as...a wedding! As described in our mystical tradition, Hashem was the groom, Klal Yisrael (the Jewish People) was the bride, Moses and Aaron were the groomsmen and the Torah was the kesubah (marriage contract). The engagement was on Pesach, the marriage on Shavuos and the bride's arrival at the groom's home was on Succos. The ultimate effect of marriage is that two become one. So our Sages tell us that "Hashem, Klal Yisrael, and Torah are one," unique, interconnected and inseparable.

This accounts for the incredible sanctity attributed to a Jewish marriage throughout the ages. It is a reflection of the deepest relationship underlying and sustaining all existence. The husband and wife undertake to create their own universe of Torah and service to Hashem, and to fill it with new souls, the children they are granted. This, and so much more, was built into the rich, elaborate symbolism of the traditional wedding in the shtetlach (villages) of pre-war Europe. Europe, however, was not so much a place as a state of mind; in fact, one could, like the Rebbe, get married "in Europe," in Brooklyn.

✥ *Zydatchov scenes*

*I*n 1932 my older brother, Reb Moshe, was married in Zydatchov, Poland. His *kallah*, Rebbetzin Lea Fraidl, was the daughter of R' Chaim Avraham Eichenstein, the Zydatchover Rebbe. They had met during Reb Moshe's first visit to Poland in 1929; but the match was delayed for three years, partly because her family wasn't sure that she should leave Poland for America. We all went over by boat: Father, Mother, my brother, my sister and a certain thrilled 11-year-old boy.

We traveled by train much of the way; and then by car. When we reached the small river just outside Zydatchov it was almost sunset.

The Rebbe, age 11, is sitting next to his sister and mother (with white kerchief) en route to his brother's wedding in Zydatchov, Poland. The woman with a full-length shawl is the mechutaniste of R' Areleh Rokeach, zt"l, the Belzer Rebbe at the time (1932).

The whole city turned out and lined up on their side of the river, forming a reception party to greet the *chassan* and his parents. Their *kapelia*, a small-town band, played music and sang, while we slowly crossed the bridge. It was all very impressive and beautiful. There was certainly nothing like it in Boston.

Zydatchov itself was a small town; some streets were paved, but only a few. There were several fine old *shuls*, the oldest having served the famous Zydatchover dynasty of Chassidic Rebbes. The bride's brother, who had by then succeeded his father, lived in a very large, if plain, brick building with plenty of room for a large *tish* and other public celebrations.

There were very few cars, but there were plenty of horse-drawn carriages and *fiakkers*, hansom cabs. There, despite my young age, I quickly learned a valuable practical lesson. When riding in a *fiakker* always sit in back, not up front with the driver. In front, one is right behind the horses and the smell is quite impossible. On the other hand, seeing all the horses and carriages was very exciting.

The Sosnovitzer Rebbe, Father's oldest living relative, was *mesader kiddushin* (officiant). My brother stayed on in Zydatchov with his

The Rebbe (L) and his mother (R) try out a fiakker, Zydatchov's "taxi service." Also shown (R to L): the Rebbe's sister, brother and R' Yisroel Sharf ("Srulik").

wife's family, and learned Torah there for two years, while the rest of us went back to Boston. As for Zydatchov, the town, its good folk, jolly *kapelia* and fine old *shuls* were all tragically destroyed in the war. It was my last view of the special, intense Jewish life of the *shtetl*.

✌ *A Wedding to Remember*

Ten years later, it was my turn to wed; and my parents arranged a *shidduch* (match) for me with Raichel Horowitz, the daughter of R' Naftali Ungar, and Rochma Miril Horowitz, the daughter of R' Alter Ze'ev Horowitz, the Stryzover Rav. We had a lot in common, including our dreams for the future, and we've worked at them together for the last 55 years (*kein yirbu!*).

Our wedding was unique in its time — an American *chasunah* (wedding) with all the Chassidic trappings and traditions of Europe. It was, for all intents and purposes, as if we were also getting married in Zydatchov, with one important difference. Since the requisite facilities did not exist here, we had to do everything ourselves.

The first hurdle was finding a suitable wedding hall or, to be more precise, *two* wedding halls, one for the men and one for the women. This was unheard of in New York at that time. One hall was upstairs and one hall was downstairs, because we expected about 3,000 people for the *chuppah* and 1,000 people for the meal. Virtually everyone in Williamsburg had some connection to us, and we also had quite a crowd coming from Boston and from Cleveland, where my *kallah* had lived with her stepfather, R' Meir Leifer, the Nadvorna-Clevelander Rebbe.

Then we had to provide our own *hashgachah* (*kashrus* supervision). Of course, the hall had a sign saying that it was kosher, but that wasn't enough for us, given the questionable standards of the time and our many *chumros* (stringencies). We started by ordering 1,000 new plates and 1,000 soup bowls for our guests. Since our budget wouldn't allow the fanciest settings, we procured seconds. They were beige

Unique in its time, the Rebbe's chuppah was attended by 3,000 guests; his wedding tish, by almost 1,000. All were treated to New York's first large-scale, fully Chassidic wedding.

with a rather plain pattern, but they were unused and served the purpose admirably. Some of the plates survived to cover our *kugel* pots for 30 or 40 years after the great event, each with their little chip — they were seconds, after all — *zecher l'churban*. Several thousand pieces of flatware were *kashered* in boiling water. All the chickens were *shechted* by our own *shochet,* and so on.

We even had to tutor our band, the Warshaver Kapelier-meister. They knew only a few Chassidic *niggunim* (melodies); and we taught them many, many more — including some from Yerushalayim and one that had been played at my brother's wedding in Zydatchov. Many years later, when the need arose, we had to do the same for a band in Boston. Both were very busy after that playing at Chassidic weddings, since they were the only ones who really knew Chassidic music.

Our wedding was unlike many Chassidic weddings in that everything went by a strict schedule. Specific music had to be played at specific times: *Vayehi biYeshurun Melech* when the *chassan* went to the *chuppah,* and so on. Since ours was the first Chassidic wedding of this scale in Williamsburg, most subsequent weddings followed pretty

The chassan's tish was a relatively unknown institution when the Rebbe was married in 1942. The Chinchkevitzer Rebbe (l) is seated to his right.

much the same pattern (if not timeliness!). Since Father had passed away the year before, my brother, Reb Moshe, officiated as the *mesader kiddushin* and the Kapitchenitzer Rebbe read the *kesubah*.

The Bostoner Rebbetzin, Raichel Horowitz, has supported and encouraged the Rebbe in his many endeavors for over 50 years.

The wedding *seudah* (meal) and the *mitzvah-tantz* that followed were highly unusual in their time, the first on the New York scene. There were no official photographs — what did pictures have to do with the *halachos* and *minhagim* of a wedding? — but a fellow *bachur* from Torah Vodaath happened to bring an old box camera and took ten or so snapshots: the *chassan's tish,* the *chuppah* outside, the Kapitchenitzer Rebbe.... Later, numerous people asked him for copies, and it gave him an idea. Why not start taking pictures at weddings? He soon became one of New York's best-known photographers and the head of Trainer Studios. Not only did he start his career at our wedding, he met his own wife there!

Not all of our European and *Yerushalmi* customs caught on. For example, following an old *Yerushalmi minhag,* our family had baked a large bagel-like pastry and broke it over our heads just before we entered the *yichud* room for the required privacy after the ceremony. Still, our wedding did show that Chassidus could flourish here in all its forms; and that "Europe" was more a matter of mind than geography.

Mishpatim

If [the ox's] master did not guard it,
He shall surely pay [for any damage]...
[If he steals], he shall surely pay...
If the theft is found in his possession....
He shall pay double.
(Exodus 21:36; 22:2,3)

One way to view this chapter is as a long list of what not to do. A closer look, however, will show that it is really a long list of what to do, a guide to how to fix things up once the damage has been done. In short, it is a detailed introduction to teshuvah (repentance) and tikkun (repair), setting things right. The first, most obvious, steps are returning misappropriated items and paying for any loss.

Teshuvah means returning to one's true inner self, completely rejecting one's spiritually tainted, dysfunctional self and recasting oneself anew. A person who succeeds in this task, or who is on his way to succeeding, is called a baal teshuvah, a Master of Repentance. The reward for such an immeasurable spiritual accomplishment, one which affects all subsequent generations, is equally immeasurable. Indeed, the Talmud teaches us that, "Where [in Heaven] the baalei teshuvah stand, even the completely righteous cannot stand."

The Rebbe has helped literally thousands of baalei teshuvah during his many years in Boston. Most were college students from

Boston's large, constantly changing student population. His first experiences in this field, however, were not with college students ... quite the contrary.

✿ The Seaver Street Irregulars

In the summer of 1944, I moved from New York back to Boston, with my Rebbetzin and infant son (Reb Pinchas). Mother and my sister Faigie soon followed. The Boston of 1944 was not the Boston of 1929, or even 1939. Most of Father's *Chassidim* had long since passed away or moved to New York, which by then had become the major center for Jewish life in America.

Father's congregation, along with the whole well-organized Jewish community of my childhood, had "evaporated." They say that Boston's Wall Street *Shul* used to have 80 people learning a daily *blatt Gemara* but, with the passing of the older generation, their children began to assimilate and were lost. The same sad story repeated itself in all the old Torah-filled *shuls* of Boston. How could we ever reestablish Bostoner Chassidus in such an unpromising new environment?

After a few weeks in Boston's West End, the home of so many special memories but no longer a Jewish neighborhood, we moved to the corner of Seaver Street and Columbia Road in the then up-and-coming suburb of Dorchester. There we found few *Chassidim*, plenty of apathy and a generally low level of religious observance.

It was immediately obvious that we needed to recruit people from the general community if we were going to have a *minyan*, especially on weekdays; so we set about doing just that. There were a few retired old-timers living nearby. They were not very religious, but at least they had the time to attend *shul*. So we began to urge them: "Come on. Let's start a *minyan*!" Finally enough said, "O.K. If I am the 10th man, I'll come," and we got started. Making *baalei teshuvah* is never easy; but we were only 23 and our first *baalei teshuvah* were all over 70!

There was, for example, one fine old gentlemen, about age 83, who started coming around. One couldn't help looking at what he called his *tefillin*. They were tiny things, obviously bought for his *bar mitzvah* 70 years earlier, when he was 13. Now, as you might guess, *tefillin* smaller than ¾ inch or so aren't likely to be optimal, but there was no use in arguing with him first thing in the morning. One has to build a positive personal relationship with someone, before one's words will be heard. Still, I felt that he should at least wear his *tefillin* on the proper part of his head, above the hairline. In this man's case, the *tefillin shel rosh* drooped down until they were literally hanging between his eyes!

I went over and, as respectfully as possible, tried to coax the wayward *tefillin* back up into a higher position; but they kept falling down. His comment on all this was rather interesting. He told me: "*Oy, der kop hot oisgedart,* Oh no! My head must have shrunk!" It had been 40 years since he had last put on *tefillin*. That's when I first learned that heads can shrink without "shrinks." They can certainly shrink without *mitzvos*.

On the other hand, his putting on *tefillin* that year, the last year of his life, and his helping fellow Jews make a *minyan* to pray, surely stood him in good stead when he went to his final reward.

Several other *shul*-goers became true *baalei teshuvah* in every sense of the word. One, in particular, changed his life, his clothes, his speech, his innermost being, all in a comparatively short time. No one looking at his long beard and frock coat would ever have guessed that, just a short while before, he had not even observed Shabbos, *kashrus* or other mitzvos. Hearing him *daven* before the *amud*, pouring out his *tefillos* with all the beautiful, heartfelt *kvetchen* (tearful musical flourishes) of Ukrainian Jewry, was always a moving experience. He soon became very involved in the *shul* and the broader Jewish community.

This gentleman continued working very hard on his *teshuvah* and *tikkun*, trying to set right whatever he had done wrong. He would come into the *shul* in the wee hours of the morning and say *Tehillim* and private prayers, standing in front of the *aron kodesh* in the darkened *shul*, crying and pleading his case before Hashem. One morning, one of the *meshulachim* noticed a small puddle of tears on the floor where this *baal teshuvah* had stood in prayer.

He also asked for help in doing *teshuvah* in those cases where a simple *tikkun* (restitution) was no longer possible. For example, years before, he had owned a small grocery store. It was during the Depression and no one could pay right away, so he kept a monthly ledger and charged people at the end of the month. Unfortunately, he would pad the bills a bit, and people overpaid him without checking, since they trusted the friendly grocer. He felt awful about it now, but what could he do? It had all happened 20 to 30 years before.

I really felt for him, and told him what the *Gemara* says about money one can't return: It should be used for a *tikkun rabbim*, a project that benefits the general public, which will hopefully include some of the wronged or their heirs. At the time, Boston was building a new communal *mikveh*, and he donated his estimated overcharges to that.

That was one problem solved but, when he wasn't busy overcharging customers, our friend also used to extend loans on interest. Here, although no fraud was involved, both he and his borrowers were violating the Torah's prohibition against usury (the various methods Jews and Jewish banks use to avoid this problem were not applicable here). This also weighed heavily on his conscience, and again he sought a *tikkun*. I suggested that he establish a *gemach*, an interest-free loan fund. He did so, and for the rest of his life was known for helping all who turned to him. He was a *baal teshuvah*, a Master of Repentance, in the finest sense of the term.

The opposite of letting go of destructive behavior patterns and starting over again is remaining stuck in a rut. *Rambam* (Maimonides) compares this to *hatovel v'sheretz b'yado*, which requires an explanation. Someone who has touched a dead *sheretz*, e.g., a lizard, becomes spiritually unclean, *tamei*. He can regain his spiritual purity, *taharah*, by immersing in a special pool of water called a *mikveh*.

Imagine someone, says *Rambam*, who wants to be pure but takes the *sheretz* along with him to the *mikveh*. There he holds it in his hand, *b'yado*, while immersing! What good will his immersion do him as long as he still holds on to the *sheretz*? All his good intentions will be in vain, since the *sheretz* will recontaminate him time and time again. Similarly, one cannot do true *teshuvah* while retaining one's old destructive habits. The Rebbe has met many successful *baalei teshuvah* but, regrettably, he has also met all too many people who were unwilling or unable to change.

❧ *The Home Front*

Shalom bayis (domestic tranquillity) can be a difficult, if worthwhile, goal. Still, most couples manage to make a go of it. All rules have exceptions, however, and we remember one couple, let's call them the Brands, who fought tooth-and-nail all throughout the '30s, when Father was still living in Boston. They came to see Father time and again for advice, but their problems were chronic and apparently incurable.

The years passed. I went off to *yeshivah* and, a few years later, Father moved to New York. In due course, I received *semichah*, married and moved back to Boston.

A few months later, we were visited by none other than Mrs. Brand. She was still alive, still well and still having "domestic problems." Just like old times, she launched into a long recital of her problems with her "impossible" husband.

This was only the first of many such visits. Although most of her visits have long since blended into one long litany of complaints, I distinctly remember her visit on V-J Day 1945. The rest of the country was celebrating the Allied victory over Japan, but there was no rest for Mrs. Brand.

She recounted once again her pathetic story, her long list of grievances and then her triumphant summation, a quote I shall never forget: "Rebbe: The German war is finished. The Japanese war is finished. But *my* war goes on!"

Terumah

From every man whose heart is willing
Take My offering.
(Exodus 25:1)

Three offerings are mentioned here:
One the offering of a beka (half-shekel) to make the sockets...
[One] the beka for the communal chest, to buy communal sacrifices,
And one for [building] the Mishkan.
(Rashi)

The Jewish people form a community, all dedicated to a common goal. People contribute to a community in two distinct ways. One way is to contribute as unique individuals with differing talents. Some offer gold, some silver, some blue-dyed wool; but together they can build a Mishkan (Sanctuary), a communal receptacle for Holiness in which Hashem can dwell.

The second way goes beyond the particularities of talent or birth. On a deeper level, all Jewish souls are equal, springing from the same spiritual source. This equality is reflected in the offering of the machatzis hashekel. In that case (Exodus 30:11-16), Hashem asked for exactly the same contribution from each of the 600,000-plus Israelites in the desert. When a Jew offers not only the contents of his heart, but the heart itself, all Jews are indistinguishable sparks of the same Divine flame.

There are many such mitzvos which emphasize the importance of each and every Jew. For example, on Succos we bring together the arba'ah minim (four species): the lulav (palm), esrog (citron), hadasim (myrtle branches) and aravos (willow branches). One contributes fragrance, one gives taste, one has neither, and one has both. Together they represent the four types of Jews: those with learning, those with good deeds, those with neither, those with both. Yet the mitzvah of arba'ah minim cannot be performed if even one of these 4 species is missing. Similarly, the eleven spices in the k'tores, holy incense, include chelb'nah, whose smell is unpleasant. Although it may represent a Jew whose deeds are unworthy, the community's incense cannot be offered to Hashem without it.

Thus we find that 10 Jews, even the most distant or non-observant, form a minyan, the minimum community needed to sanctify Hashem's Name through the recitation of Kaddish or Kedushah. The moral? Everyone has their place, their contribution, their role; and the community can form a resting place for the Divine Presence only when all work together as one. This goal is so important that even Heaven itself is often willing to help achieve it.

❧ *Eliyahu HaNavi in America*

When we moved to Dorchester, Massachusetts, a suburb of Boston, in 1944, a house was already waiting for us. In 1941 Mr. Marx Spitz, a Boston real-estate agent, had bought a large rambling old house for Father, in the hope that he might return from New York. The building had been deserted for so long that the locals called it "The Haunted House." It was a bargain at $2,500, but it was in such poor repair that it had to be almost gutted before it could be made ready for use. The building wasn't habitable in time for our first High Holidays in Dorchester, but the small *shul* on the first floor was ready, so we made arrangements to stay nearby.

The Rebbe and a band of faithful followers gather in 1954 to lay the cornerstone for the first addition to the Dorchester shul. From L to R (from cornerstone): Jacob Prilluck, Israel Sacks (rear), Rubin Grossman, the Rebbe, Julius Kalman, Louie Weiner (rear), Marx Spitz, Joseph Mael, Joseph Goldstein

Since we had almost no followers left from Father's days, and since the few that were left were quite old, we were afraid that we might not have a *minyan* for the *Kol Nidrei* service on Yom Kippur Eve. After all, everyone in the neighborhood already belonged to a *shul*; and we had just arrived. Still, we didn't want to give up our "Chassidisheh davening": our traditional Bostoner *niggunim, piyutim, Shir HaYichud* and *Mishnayos shiur*.

A few days before Yom Kippur, we carefully counted our tiny flock and called some of our friends among the *meshulachim* in New York. We invited them to come to Boston to help complete the 10 Jewish men that are absolutely required for a *minyan*. We checked and rechecked to make sure that everything was all right. However, as the sun began to set on Yom Kippur Eve, one of our regulars, an elderly gentleman who lived far away, hadn't arrived. We were only nine!

The situation was desperate. At that late hour on *Kol Nidrei* Eve, any Jew with a spark of Jewish feeling was already in *shul*; and anyone not in *shul* certainly wouldn't be interested in the long service we *Chassidim* would provide. A few men went out to look anyway, but the streets were, as expected, deserted. No *minyan* for Yom Kippur. What a disaster!

At the last possible minute, the door opened, and a rather nondescript little fellow walked in and looked around. There was nothing particularly remarkable about him, certainly nothing we noticed as we rushed to start before the time of *Kol Nidrei* passed. A *"Sholom Aleichem"* and a friendly chat could wait for later. Carried away by our *tefillos* and tremendous gratitude, we plunged into the *davening*. We had just barely made it.

As soon as the official service was over, the stranger came by and shook my hand but, since I was still saying extra *tefillos*, I could only nod my greetings in return. That was all right. He would surely *daven* with us again the next morning.

But he didn't. Instead, the next morning brought Reb Baruch, our regular 10th man, who had been ill the night before. We waited a bit, and then started, keeping an eye open for our expected guest; but he never returned.

We lived in Dorchester for many years, but none of us ever saw him again. Who was this stranger, who came just once from nowhere to an almost nonexistent *shul* at that late hour on that very special night? I don't know; but he didn't *look* like *Eliyahu HaNavi*.

The Rebbe often likes to tell stories of the great Chassidic Masters of years gone by, usually to make a point. For example, he uses this story to illustrate the phrase from the first verse of this week's *parshah*, "from every man whose heart is willing to take My offering." Beyond the heart's impulse to give there is indeed a higher, more carefully weighed and considered level of giving. But, beyond that, there is at least one level more.

The Holy Goat

The Kotzker Rebbe was a burning flame — intense, sharp, demanding. He could not bear the minutiae of life, the utterly insignificant things people did with their lives instead of devoting them to Divine service. Even some of his close disciples left him, feeling that his opposition to the mediocrity of ordinary life was too strong. They began their own dynasties, attracting *Chassidim* of their own. Finally, for the last years of his life, the Kotzker closed himself off almost entirely from "the little men, the flatterers" he was unable to bear. He used to say of himself, during those years of seclusion, "*Ich bin der Heilige Tzap*, I am the Holy Goat," and tell this parable.

Once there was a man who used to give the people in *shul* a *shmeck tabak*, a pinch of strong snuff, to help rouse them to prayer. He kept it in a beautiful *tabak pushkah*, a silver snuff box. One day his beautiful silver box disappeared. He was beside himself with grief and left *shul* a broken man. Then whom should he meet outside the *shul* but the Holy Goat.

The Holy Goat had a great holy heart and he asked the man, "Why are you so upset?" The man told him his story and ended by saying, "So now how can I give *tabak* to people?" Touched, the Holy Goat said, "Take out your penknife and cut off a piece from the tip of my long horns. Make yourself a new *tabak pushkah* and continue giving out your *tabak*." So he did.

The man's new horn *pushkah* was soon the talk of the town and everyone wanted to know how they could get one. "Ask the Goat," he said. So they did, each with his sad story, his penknife and his new *pushkah*. The end result was that everyone in town soon had a beautiful goat's-horn *tabak* box and the *Heilige Tzap* soon had no horns left at all.

The Kotzker was talking about himself, of course; he had used his powers to help raise group after group of disciples, who went on to become Rebbes and start communities of their own. Now, like the Goat, he too had nothing left to give.

Sometimes people give everything they have to their children, their friends and their community and end up left out and hurt, just like the Kotzker's fabled Holy Goat. But maybe they should stop and think: Perhaps that's what made him Holy.

Tetzaveh

And this is what to do to them
To sanctify them as Kohanim to me:
Take one ox from the cattle,
And two perfect rams [without blemish] ...
And they shall eat them,
To be an atonement for them.
(Exodus 29:1,33)

One of the great goals of Yiddishkeit is temimus, perfection. Ideally, a mitzvah should be done with all one's heart — 100 percent, not 85 percent. "It's all in perfect shape, it just has this little dent here, this little bump there" may be fine for a used- car salesman, but it won't do for a mitzvah.

This is particularly true for shechitah, which involves taking an animal's life, and using its energy to power a Jew's Torah learning and avodah (service), raising the animal's essence to a higher level. The slightest knick in the slaughtering knife, for example, disqualifies it. The slightest adhesion on the smooth surface of the animal's lungs makes the whole animal questionable. Although further tests may render it kosher, it is not glatt (literally "smooth") and those who keep glatt kosher won't eat it.

This concern for physical perfection reminds us of the concern we should also have for spiritual perfection. The meat we take in and make part of ourselves must be 100 percent pure, 100 percent perfect; but so must the news we take in, the books we take in, the conversations we take in, the thoughts we take in. This is a lifelong task, but one well worth pursuing.

In the Boston of the 1930s and '40s, however, even physical kashrus, in its most basic, literal sense, was quite a challenge.

✥ The Third Teletzke

Although our family had always insisted on *glatt kosher* standards, in the Boston of the 1930s *glatt kosher* beef was not to be had. We used to *shecht* chickens in our basement; but we couldn't very well walk a full-grown cow through the streets of Boston to our basement and *shecht* it there. In Europe the local *shochtim* were generally scrupulous in their approach to *mitzvos*, careful in inspecting their *chalaf* (knife), and fully aware that they were involved in something religiously serious. This description didn't quite fit many of Boston's *shochtim* in those days. Most were suspected of being less than they should be for such a serious task, and several were even suspected of being *mechalel Shabbos*!

Still, Shabbos and *Yom Tov* are enhanced by *basar v'dagim* (meat and fish), and Father made a special effort to get properly slaughtered meat twice a year, for Pesach and for Succos. A few days before the holiday, late at night, we would "smuggle" a small calf into our basement. The *meshulachim*, who were already there for *Yom Tov* — why shouldn't they take a week or two "vacation"? — would all gather around. Usually one of them could *shecht* beef, quite different from *shechting* chickens, and would do the job under Father's watchful eye.

We always worried that the calf might start to bellow or make noise. This operation was all taking place right in the middle of Boston's crowded West End residential district. If the neighbors had suspected anything, they would have called the police, and we would have had a lot of explaining to do to them and the local Health Department.

Why didn't Father simply go to a local *shlachthaus* and bring his own *shochet?* One local owner had invited him to do just that. It was more convenient and they had all the necessary facilities; but Father wouldn't hear of it. He didn't want to "embarrass" their regular *shochet.*

After returning to Boston in the 1940s, we wanted to renew Father's custom of getting fresh meat for Pesach, but how? We had a friend, Chaim Lecht, who owned a *shlachthaus* outside Pawtucket, Rhode Island. He always used to tell me, "Whenever you need meat, I'll give you a *teletzke.*" A *teletzke* was an older calf, whose meat was somewhere between veal and beef. It would be just the right size for our needs. Even better, Mr. Lecht had just hired a new *shochet* from Europe, a religious Jew and reportedly a "big *talmid chacham.*" Of course, learning about cows and knives in books is a lot different from handling them in real life, so I wasn't 100 percent sure how the new scholar-*shochet* would work out. Still, it was certainly worth a try; so off we went to Pawtucket.

When we got there, Mr. Lecht told us to wait until he got some calves ready. This gave me a chance to see the new *shochet* in action. He was a fine-looking, distinguished Chassidic gentleman with a long white beard. It was my first visit to a large *shlachthaus,* and I was fascinated. The *shochet* seemed serious enough, but he certainly had to put up with difficult working conditions. He was getting ready to *shecht* a large cow, when one of the coarse workers threw a piece of bloody intestine at him from a distance, knocking off his hat! The marksman and his cronies began to snicker and laugh; it was their way of making fun of the *shochet.* I was shocked, but the *shochet* was apparently already resigned to his lot. He picked up his hat with as much dignity as he could muster, put it back on his head and went on with his work.

"Mr. Lecht," I said, "how can you let this go on in your *shlachthaus?* Don't you know what these people are doing?"

"Sure, but with the war on, I'm lucky to get anybody. *Shlepping* bloody carcasses isn't easy work. I know that they are the lowest of the low, but I can't start up with them or they'll walk right out. I'm not the boss around here; they are!"

Finally they brought out our *teletzke*. The workers were in a hurry and things went fast — too fast. They already had the calf down on the floor by the time the *shochet* gave me his *chalaf* (knife) to check. Even the smallest nick in the blade could make the entire slaughtered animal *treif*. I ran my finger over the blade. There was nothing obvious, but one spot seemed suspicious. I was afraid it might be a problem. Meanwhile the animal's head was already in the collar and his neck was stretched. "No problem!" said the *shochet*. "I checked it; it's fine." He took the knife and ran off to do the *shechitah* before anyone could say "Wait!"

Of course the *shochet* was under pressure, the workers were impossible, time is money, and so on. That was all true, ... but I was concerned about the knife, and felt uneasy. Meanwhile, they were already hanging the slaughtered animal for an internal inspection.

At this point the *shochet* had to stick his hand deep inside the animal to check the lungs. If he found the slightest adhesions or bumps on the surface of the lungs, the animal would not be "*glatt*" (smooth). Although further tests could prove that the animal was indeed kosher, those who keep *glatt kosher* won't eat meat from an animal that fails this first test. So I offered a rather unusual *tefillah* (prayer): "As much as we need this animal for Pesach, please let them declare it not *glatt!*"

If the *shochet* declared that the animal was *glatt*, we had a difficult problem on our hands. To refuse it because of the knife would embarrass the *shochet*. To take it would saddle us with (possibly) questionable meat. Both options were unthinkable. The *shochet* slowly checked the outer membrane of the lung, inside and out. Each minute seemed an hour. Finally he shook his head. No. The animal was not *glatt*...

Grateful and relieved, I waited anxiously to see what would happen next. Would we have meat for the Pesach *seder* after all? Mr. Lecht came out, heard the verdict, and immediately said, "Don't worry. We'll bring out another one." The process began all over again. The *shochet* resharpened his knife and gave it to me to check. Again, something just didn't seem quite right. Again the rush, with the animal stretched on the floor; the *shochet* grabbed the knife and the second one was slaughtered.

By now there was a third *teletzke* waiting in the wings. Even before he checked the lungs of the second one, the *shochet* resharpened his knife for the third. This time the knife was perfect, and the *shechitah* was done in the best possible manner.

Now came anxious moments as both calves were taken to be checked. Suppose calf number two's lungs were *glatt* and number three's were not? It would be the same dilemma all over again.

There was nothing to do but offer another *tefillah*: "Ribono Shel Olam! Please let's not embarrass this *shochet*. Please have calf number three declared *glatt* and have number two declared not *glatt*!"

The animals were hoisted up and the checking began. After a tense pause, the *shochet* came over and reported just what we needed to hear: Number three was *glatt*, number two was not! I only wish that our more serious *tefillos* were as easily answered.

The third *teletzke* was soon loaded in the car, with thanks all around, and off we went to play our respective roles at the *seder* table. In fact, that *teletzke* provided meat for all of *Yom Tov* for us and our many Pesach guests.

Ki Sisa

*Make a laver of brass ... and Aharon and his sons
Shall wash their hands and feet from it ...
So they won't die when they approach
The altar to serve.
(Exodus 30:18-20)*

In Jewish tradition, water symbolizes Torah, purification and humility. Just as water seeks out the low places, washes out stains and stirs dormant seeds to life, the Torah gives spiritual life and purity to the humble. Thus before beginning their Divine Service, the Kohanim had to wash their hands and feet with water from the huge brass laver that stood near the altar, right in front of the Temple building itself. On Yom Kippur the Kohen Gadol immersed himself five times, and purified his hands and feet from the laver ten times.

The Torah often requires the total immersion of the body in water to reestablish the close relationship with Hashem that can be disrupted by tumah, a physical contamination with spiritual consequences. Tumah is usually associated with death, the opposite of water and life. This immersion requires a mikveh, a natural pool of standing water or a natural spring. Creating an artificial pool with the same spiritual powers is complicated, but possible. It usually involves filling a storage pool (bor) with rainwater, which must flow without direct human intervention, and then connecting the bor to the pool (mikveh) used for actual immersions.

The mikveh still plays an important role in Jewish life. It is essential, under Torah law, for maintaining family purity and is often used by men seeking an extra level of purity before performing special mitzvos. In fact, we are told that if a community is short of funds, their first priority should be to build a mikveh. However, an attractive, functioning mikveh is not always easy to arrange, as the Rebbe soon discovered.

❦ *The Snow Mikveh*

Wherever we lived, Father was always particular about having both a *mikveh* and a small *shul* in our home. In Williamsburg, our *mikveh* fit into a 6-foot-by-6-foot area off our kitchen, but it was still a *mikveh*. The *bor*, the compartment where the rain water was stored, was on an outside balcony, on the other side of our kitchen wall!

Nowadays, many Chassidic Rebbes and *shuls* have their own *mikvehs*, but at that time, a home *mikveh* was an unheard-of luxury. In fact, ours was the first private *mikveh* in Williamsburg. Everyone else used the community *mikveh* at the *Poilishe Shtibel*. When people asked why we needed our own *mikveh*, Father would say, "How much does a *mikveh* cost? $500? People buy a bedroom set or a dining room set for $500. Why not a *mikveh*? That's certainly more worthwhile than fancy furnishings."

When our family moved back to Boston in 1944, we had to do a lot of work renovating the old "Haunted House." Father had never lived in the house; but he did come back from New York once to inspect it. He began measuring various sections of the basement, and finally pointed to a certain corner and said, "That's where the *mikveh's* going to be." Following his wishes, we told our contractor to construct the two *boros* and the *mikveh* just where Father had specified.

The building wasn't habitable by Rosh Hashanah; but we could hold High Holiday services there — our first in Boston. It was very exciting; but what about the *mikveh*? It was unthinkable to blow *shofar* on Rosh Hashanah morning without first going to the *mikveh*. On *erev* Rosh Hashanah one could drive over to the city's communal *mikveh*, but the distance was too far to walk on Rosh Hashanah itself. On the other hand, when Rosh Hashanah arrived, our *shul mikveh* wasn't fully ready. It was still untiled, with only bare cement walls, and we could fill it only with tap water. This was only good enough for a man's largely symbolic immersion, but we were still excited. Our own *mikveh*!

The next morning we went down to immerse before going to services. What thoughts, what expectations we had. But when we opened the door to the basement we found, much to our surprise, that the *mikveh* was almost empty! The cement the contractor had used was not watertight, and all but a few inches of water had disappeared into the ground. This could be fixed later; but Rosh Hashanah and *shofar*-blowing wouldn't wait. What could we do? Even with all the faucets opened full blast, it was a close race between the water flowing in and the water draining out. Just before *davening*, the water was still only about 15 inches deep.

It could not be considered a kosher *mikveh* by any stretch of the imagination, but it was was all we had. We couldn't immerse standing up, or even sitting down. The only viable option was to lie flat on the ground, like the prostrations on Yom Kippur, *pishut yadaim v'raglaim*, hands and feet outspread. In so little water, this was anything but easy; and it had to be tried again and again before it worked. Finally, *baruch Hashem*, after quite a struggle, we succeeded. That was the first *tevilah* at 61 Columbia Road, Dorchester.

After Rosh Hashanah we had the cement sealed, and started working on the next problem. To be truly kosher the *mikveh* needed 40 *se'ahs* (a Biblical measure) of natural, unpoured water in its *boros*. Where could one get that much unpoured water? There used to be a company nearby that sold huge blocks of natural pond ice; but they had gone out of business. There was a similar company in New Hampshire, but that was too far away. Finally, just after Succos, Boston was hit by a gigantic snowstorm, which covered everything under huge mounds of snow. This seemed an obvious solution to the problem — natural, unpoured water delivered to our doorstep!

The special requirements of a *mikveh* made the work more arduous. The snow couldn't be shoveled with a *kli*, a finished tool, so the puzzled non-Jewish work crew we hired had to dig out the snow with wide, flat wooden boards. The snow had to flow by itself, so they used large tabletops to make ramps from the snow-buried lawn, through the basement windows, to the airspace over the *bor*. It was hard work, but they eventually filled both *boros* 3 feet above their brim. We were ecstatic. After the snow melted we would have not only a "symbolic" *mikveh*, but a kosher *mikveh*.

Several days later we came in and found our *boros* filled with ... 6 inches of water! Snow is relatively light because it is almost all air; the amount of water it contains is minimal. It was clear that we weren't going to fill our *mikveh* using snow, at least not before Pesach!

Finally, we turned the roof of our house into a giant rainwater collecting area and ran tubes down the side of the building, so the rainwater could flow into the *mikveh* under its own steam. This worked out just fine, *baruch Hashem*, and the New England Chassidic Center of Dorchester finally had a 100 percent kosher *mikveh* all its own, another first worth celebrating.

Mikvaos in America were a much misunderstood institution, partly because of memories, or hearsay based on memories, of the appalling *mikvaos* in the dirt-poor villages of Eastern Europe. The Rebbe's glistening private *mikveh* in Boston, and the larger new public *mikveh* that followed it, were the realization of his father's dream to bring beauty and life to traditional Torah observance in America. It also reflected his father's firsthand experience with the unaesthetic aspects of many European *mikvaos*. He was literally immersed in the subject.

❧ *The Torker Mikveh*

During our 1929 trip to Europe, our family spent the High Holidays in Torka, where my mother's father had been Rebbe. Torka was a workingman's town. It was rough country, where everyone literally lived by the sweat of his brow. The townsmen worked as day laborers, woodcutters, haulers and so on.

Father was a frequent *mikveh*-goer, but much to his regret, the *mikvaos* of the small towns in Eastern Europe were always in terrible shape. Some were springs that could only be reached by digging deep into the ground, so deep that one had to climb down thirty or more steps to reach the small, cold pool of dirty water below. These *mikvaos* were not only hard to reach, but almost impossible to clean, even if the poor *shtetlach* (towns) they served could have afforded it. This was one reason why many immigrants to America had such negative ideas about *mikvaos*.

R' Yechiel Michel of Torka, the Rebbe's maternal grandfather

Father's custom was to go to the *mikveh* five times on *erev* Yom Kippur, just as the *Kohen Gadol* used to do in the *Bais HaMikdash* on Yom Kippur day. In Torka this took strong determination. All the heavily sweating townsfolk went to the *mikveh* on *erev* Yom Kippur, straight from their jobs. By the time Father went to the *mikveh* for the fifth time, just before *Kol Nidrei*, he almost fainted from the filth and the smell. Such was the difficult life and incredible poverty of our Jewish brothers in the Poland of those days. Father managed to do what he had to do, but the ordeal made a lasting impression.

Nine years later, Father suffered a massive heart attack which left him unconscious. As he began to recover, while he was still semi-delirious, he began talking about *mikvaos* — the need to build beautiful *mikvaos*, *mikvaos* with sparkling clean tile walls, *mikvaos* that would encourage people to strive for purity. He had apparently been thinking about this for quite some time but, as with his plans for *yeshivah* day schools, he was still too far ahead of his time. (He did open an afternoon *yeshivah* in Boston, one which had 150 students at its height, but even this was eventually forced to close.)

Vayakhel

*This is what Hashem has [already] commanded ...
All the wise-hearted among you,
Should come and do all that Hashem has commanded...
And all those wise in doing work [came] and made the
Mishkan.
(Exodus 35:4,10, 36:8)*

In Parshas Terumah, Hashem commanded the Jews in the desert to bring their terumah contributions to build the Mishkan (Sanctuary). He also commanded them to make the ark, the altar and the various other parts of the Mishkan, and provided detailed instructions on their construction. Then Parshas Tetzaveh provides more detailed instructions; and Ki Sisa, still more. Now, in this week's parshah, Moshe repeats the commands yet again, and work is finally begun. In next week's parshah, everything is completed "just as Hashem had commanded Moshe" (Exodus 39:32). The original intent is realized at last.

Our Sages say that hachanah, preparation, is often even greater than the ma'aseh, the deed itself. The actual completion lasts but a moment; the hachanah can take months, years or even a lifetime. That is one lesson of these parshios which describe Israel's preparations for establishing an abode for the Divine Presence in this world. In a broader sense, this whole world is but a hachanah for the next; our finite lives, but a hachanah for eternity.

Sometimes one can spend his whole life in hachanah, without

even realizing what he is being prepared for. But Hashem's Will is ultimately realized, and so is a tzaddik's, even many years after the preparations began. The Rebbe is fond of telling this story of one such example.

∞ A Tzaddik After His Passing

It was always Father's wish to be buried in Yerushalayim, where he was born. In fact, when he turned 21, he purchased a burial plot for himself on Har HaZeisim, the Mount of Olives, next to the tziun of his father, R' Shmuel Shmelke. When Father passed away in 1941, however, World War II made this impossible. Instead, he was buried in the Tzelemer community's cemetery on Long Island, with the explicit condition that he would be reburied in Eretz Yisrael as soon as possible.

The war was over in 1945, and I immediately started trying to get all the documents and approvals needed for the reburial. It took considerable effort, and a little politics, to convince the authorities that Father's aron (coffin) had to be on the very first boat that left America for Eretz Yisrael. Finally, Senator David I. Walsh of Massachusetts managed to arrange for a priority number that assured my passage on the Loma Victory, the first freighter from the United States to stop in Israel after the war's end. So in 1946, at age 25, I sailed across the Atlantic to accompany Father's aron back to Eretz Yisrael.

The preparations for the journey were quite elaborate. U.S. health regulations required digging up the wooden coffin intact and placing it unopened in a larger metal coffin, which was sealed before delivery to the boat. The local *Chevra Kaddisha* was afraid that, after four-and-a-half years in the ground, the wood of the coffin might have rotted. We were all very relieved to find that it was still whole.

Then came the trip itself. There were only 12 passengers, four of us Jews: one openly committed, one compromising, one compromised and one hiding his Jewishness as best he could. It was just like the Four Sons of the Pesach Haggadah! We represented all the Jews of that time in

> **United States Senate**
> COMMITTEE ON NAVAL AFFAIRS
>
> DAVID I. WALSH, MASS., CHAIRMAN
> MILLARD E. TYDINGS, MD.
> RICHARD B. RUSSELL, GA.
> HARRY FLOOD BYRD, VA.
> PETER G. GERRY, R. I.
> CHARLES O. ANDREWS, FLA.
> ALLEN J. ELLENDER, LA.
> JOHN L. MCCLELLAN, ARK.
> JAMES O. EASTLAND, MISS.
> WARREN G. MAGNUSON, WASH.
> FRANCIS J. MYERS, PA.
> CHARLES W. TOBEY, N. H.
> RAYMOND E. WILLIS, IND.
> C. WAYLAND BROOKS, ILL.
> OWEN BREWSTER, MAINE
> EDWARD V. ROBERTSON, WYO.
> LEVERETT SALTONSTALL, MASS.
> WAYNE MORSE, OREG.
>
> M. E. GALLAGHER, CLERK
>
> 5 June 1946
>
> Grand Rabbi
> Levi I. Horowitz
> 61 Columbia Road
> Dorchester 21, Massachusetts
>
> My dear Rabbi Horowitz:
>
> I have taken up with the State Department your inquiry concerning a return passage from Palestine in connection with your contemplated trip to the Holy Land to have the remains of your late father interred in Jerusalem. When I have some report I shall let you know.
>
> Hoping to be helpful, and with kindest regards,
>
> Sincerely yours,
>
> *David Walsh*

The letter from Senator David Walsh promising his aid in securing the Rebbe's passage to Israel (1946)

microcosm. One would eat ham and eggs. One would eat non-kosher meat, but wouldn't drink milk after it. One would eat only "vegetable soup," without asking why there were bones in it. And one wouldn't eat anything, except the matzah and sardines he brought with him.

The trip was supposed to take 16 to 17 days, but the captain decided to eliminate the other stops and proceed directly to Haifa. We reached *Eretz Yisrael* two days sooner than expected, only to find that a dock strike was in progress. Our freighter was anchored quite far from the shore, and the tugs refused to dock her or to ferry cargo ashore, not even Father's *aron*. The captain allowed me to stay on the boat to guard the body, but the *aron* had already been placed on the deck. The fiercely hot summer sun beating down on it was sure to speed decomposition; but there was nothing I could do about it.

Two or three days later the strike ended and the *aron* was finally ferried ashore. Although I had considerable family in Israel, only a few people were on hand to greet me, since no one knew how long the strike would last. It was just after the war and private vehicles were hard to find. Someone had arranged for an old pickup truck — "ancient" might be a better word for it — to take me to Yerushalayim. I sat in the front with the driver and put the *aron* in back. The trip was a long, jolting one, over bumpy roads. The truck had little in the way of suspension, and we were shaking and bouncing the entire way. I couldn't help thinking, "I can barely take this treatment. What's happening inside the *aron*?" But I couldn't do anything about that either.

When I finally arrived, I reminded one of the people helping organize the funeral arrangements about an incident that had occurred during our family's last trip to *Eretz Yisrael* in 1934, a few years before the war. That year Father's maternal uncle, R' Alter Biederman, the Sosnovitzer Rav, passed away in Europe (he had officiated at my brother's *chasunah* in Zydatchov in 1932). After half a year's delay, his *aron* was sent to *Eretz Yisrael* for burial.

R' Pinchas Dovid's *tziun* on Har HaZeisim, next to that of his father, R' Shmuel Shmelke (to his right). The *tziun* of the Rebbe's paternal uncle, R' Avraham Horowitz, is to his left.

The Yerushalayim *Chevra Kaddisha* didn't want to open the casket, since they were afraid of what might have happened inside. They tried to convince Father that displaying a broken, decomposed body would be *bizayon hameis* (disrespect to the deceased); but Father was adamant. "You can't bury him in *Eretz Yisrael* in a coffin. He has to lie directly on the ground," for such is the age-old custom in *Eretz Yisrael*. When the *Chevra Kaddisha* refused, Father called out, in the spirit of Moshe *Rabbeinu*, "*Mi laHashem eilai!*" Whoever is on Hashem's side, come help me! One of our relatives volunteered, followed by a few other men. Together they opened the casket and buried the body properly in accordance with *Yerushalmi* custom.

The job was delicate, since the body had to be kept intact. Father told everyone what to do in great detail: First put the casket down on two stiff rugs. Remove the top and sides of the casket and then slide the bottom out from under the *meis* (deceased)... Father told us the story of the burial and its procedure over and over again throughout the years, and he used to conclude, "If I only came to *Eretz Yisrael* for this, it would have been worthwhile!" Of course, as children, this story wasn't a particularly welcome one. We didn't want to think about death, not our relative's, and certainly not our father's; but Father kept impressing it on us anyway.

Now it was my turn to stand with the Yerushalayim *Chevra Kaddisha*, some 12 years after our last visit; and now I understood why Father had repeatedly told us about that burial in such detail. Now his body was coming from *chutz la'aretz* (outside Israel) to Yerushalayim for burial, and now I had to know what to do. I told them, "No burial in a box!" I could see what they were thinking. "Of course, he is the Rebbe's son and he would like to do what his father did, but this case is totally different."

Indeed it was. Father's body had been buried in the ground for four-and-a-half years. It had traveled across the Atlantic, been left out in the broiling summer sun for days and had then been subjected to spine-jolting bumps all the way from Haifa to Jerusalem. "Better leave it alone and bury it unopened," they said.

I stood my ground, and insisted that they remove what was left of the body for burial, following the procedure Father had rehearsed with us for so many years. The *Chevra Kaddisha* went to work, and soon one of them came running over, shocked beyond belief. The body was intact! In fact, they picked it up, as if he had died but yesterday, and carefully laid it onto the ground of the grave. Word of the miracle quickly spread, and it was the talk of Yerushalayim for many days thereafter. Father had returned to his birthplace the way he had left it, whole and in peace.

I was very grateful to have shared in fulfilling Father's wish. His miraculous burial recalled the words of our Sages, "*Tzaddikim* are even greater in death than in life."

※

> *[Bring] gold, silver, copper, sky-blue wool,*
> *Dark red and crimson wool, fine linen, goat's wool,*
> *Red-dyed ram skins, tachash skins, acacia wood ...*
> *(Exodus 35:5-7)*

The Mishkan could only be made of the finest materials, a reminder that the very best we have comes from, and should be offered to, Hashem. Fine linen and brightly dyed wool, as you can see from this week's parshah, were the most sought-after fabrics in Biblical times. In the Eretz Yisrael of 1946, the front-runner might have been ...

※ *Nylon!*

When returning to Israel in 1946, I naturally took along gifts for our many relatives. Since the freighter had limited cabin space, these gifts had to be nice but small, and a dozen or so Parker 51 pens, very much the pen to have in those days, made an excellent choice. Right after World War II few "fancy" consumer goods of any kind were available in *Eretz Yisrael*.

At the appropriate time, I presented a pen to one of our relatives. His eyes lit up and he uttered a somewhat unusual exclamation of

Shemos ※ 159

thanks and delight ... "Nylon!" A second relative opened his gift and he too proclaimed ... "Nylon!" I was puzzled, but too polite to ask.

Later some of my relatives were discussing a recent purchase and one, who heartily approved, called it good, fine, fantastic — in fact, "Nylon!" Then all was clear. Nylon, the first synthetic fabric, had first come to Israel during the war, and was touted as a modern material that could do wonders. Israelis soon picked up the term and used it to describe anything new, exciting and extra-special.

Pekudei

> *Then the cloud covered the Tent of Meeting,*
> *And the Glory of Hashem*
> *Filled the Mishkan.*
> *(Exodus 40:34)*

Every Jew lives at the intersection of two worlds which coexist in different dimensions, a physical world and a spiritual world. It is the tzaddik's job to link these two worlds, bringing man closer to Hashem and, so to speak, Hashem closer to man. Thus, in the verses of Chronicles I, 29:10-13, which allude to the seven Sefiros (Aspects of Hashem), the sixth, Yesod, corresponding to Yosef HaTzaddik, is described as, "All in the heavens and the earth." Yosef, the archetypical tzaddik, represents the two together, and must bind them together. That is why it says in Proverbs (10:25): "The tzaddik is the foundation (Yesod) of the world."

The purpose of the Mishkan was to bring Hashem's Presence into this world: "Build Me a Mikdash (Sanctuary) and I will dwell among you" (Exodus 25:8). In this week's parshah the task is completed, and the Book of Shemos reaches its triumphant conclusion. The Jewish people had been slaves in Mitzrayim, caught up in its uncleanliness and spiritual limitations (meitzarim). Hashem freed them, both physically and spiritually, and gave them the Torah. Now they could make themselves and the Mishkan a place where Hashem's Glory could dwell.

The innermost point of the Mishkan was the space enclosed by the outstretched wings of the Keruvim (Cherubim) on the cover of the Ark. From there, the gateway between the two worlds, the voice of Hashem emanated to Moshe. Perhaps this is the meaning of the tradition that the Ark, when inside the Holy of Holies, occupied no space [in our world].

Although the Ark and Mikdash are temporarily no longer with us, the contact between the two worlds has never been completely severed, and tzaddikim in every generation can, at times, still span the gap and grasp whispers that other men cannot hear. One such tzaddik was Rav Aharon Rokeach (1880-1956), better known as Reb Areleh Belzer, who miraculously escaped Nazi Europe and transplanted Belzer Chassidus to Eretz Yisrael.

❧ The Curfew and the Belzer Rebbe

During my 1946 trip to accompany Father's *aron* to *Eretz Yisrael*, I made a special point of visiting my *alma mater*, Yeshivas Torah V'Yirah, where I had gone to school as a *bar mitzvah bachur,* 12 years before. I spoke for a while with the *Roshei Yeshivah,* and it brought back wonderful memories of my stay.

Once back outside, sirens went off. This was British Mandate times, during the violent ferment that led up to "the Partition" and the creation of the State of Israel. The Irgun, headed by Menachem Begin, later prime minister of Israel, had just blown up the British headquarters in the King David Hotel, overlooking the Old City walls. In return, the British immediately proclaimed a 20-hour-a-day curfew. Henceforth no one in Jerusalem could be outside except between the hours of 7-11 a.m., and then only to buy food.

I was living with a long-time family friend, R' Mordechai Eisenbach, and his family in the Bais Yisrael section of the city. R' Mordechai had visited Father frequently, and had later been helpful during my own first few years as a Rebbe in Boston. He was a cheerful person, with a lovely voice and a persistent desire to help others, even when he had little of his own.

The Eisenbachs' "apartment" consisted of one large room, which served as dining room, living room and multiple bedrooms for them and their eight children. There was also a small "kitchen" out on their narrow back porch. It had all the necessities: a Primus kerosene stove, which had to be pumped ... and that was it. There was no refrigerator, freezer or washing machine. Almost no one in the old Jewish neighborhoods of Yerushalayim had one in those days.

R' Mordechai Eisenbach, the Rebbe's host during his 1946 trip

There was also no indoor plumbing. Instead, one had to go down a big, outside staircase to the ground floor, where everyone shared an old-fashioned outhouse. This wasn't usually such a problem, but what about the curfew? One wasn't supposed to be outside from 11 a.m. each day until 7 a.m. the next morning, and the British were very strict about enforcing the regulations. The locals were pretty used to being harassed by the British, but what was a poor American visitor supposed to do? Few people had specific advice, but everyone agreed that I should take my American passport downstairs with me. Even if caught, Americans would get better treatment than the average "native."

Days passed, and my departure drew near, but I still had not visited the Belzer Rebbe, Reb Areleh Rokeach. In 1914, when Father was representing the Jewish community of Yerushalayim at a *din Torah* (court case) in Galicia, he had visited many prominent rebbes to discuss the issues involved. During his protracted stay in Belz, he became the chavrusah (study partner) of Reb Areleh, who later became the next Belzer Rebbe. They learned Talmud together every day before daybreak. Surely Father would have wanted me to see him and pay my respects; but this was difficult to arrange. Although Reb Areleh woke up early, his prayers were exceptionally long. He obviously wouldn't see me before davening, but I had to be back at the Eisenbach's apartment before 11:00 a.m., because of the curfew.

I contacted my cousin, R' Zysha Brandwein, who was himself a great *tzaddik*. In fact, when the Belzer Rebbe had a difficult problem, he would call for R' Zysha and send him to Meron to pray at the *tziun* of R' Shimon bar Yochai, the great *tanna* and mystic who authored the *Zohar*. The Belzer Rebbe asked R' Zysha to take his *kvitlach* to Meron so often that R' Zysha was often called the "*Gabbai* of R' Shimon." If anyone could get me a special appointment with the Belzer Rebbe, it was R' Zysha.

R' Areleh Rokeach, the Belzer Rav, a chavrusah of the Rebbe's father

This plan worked out fine. R' Zysha came back and told me that the Belzer Rebbe would see me the very next morning. In those days, it was a long trip from my haven in the Bais Yisrael section of Yerushalayim to where the Belzer Rebbe was staying near Bayit Vegan. Because of the curfew, there were only two people in the Rebbe's anteroom, the *gabbai* and the Rebbe's brother, R' Mordechai of Bilgoray, the father of the present Belzer Rebbe.

Before I entered Reb Areleh's room, his *gabbai* asked, as was customary, if he could help me write a *kvitel*, a brief note asking for the Rebbe's *brachah* or prayer on my behalf. That put me in an awkward position. Father had been my only Rebbe. Would writing a *kvitel* to another Rebbe imply that I was accepting his authority? I politely said no, and the *gabbai* ushered us in.

The Belzer Rebbe was very kind. He invited me to sit down, and began to ask the usual polite questions. My references to Boston didn't mean anything to him (he knew Father before he left for America); but he recognized Father's name at once. We briefly discussed my new *rabbanus* in Boston, and he was supportive; but we could exchange only a few more sentences because time was very limited. I had to go all the way back to the city before the curfew was reimposed.

During his 1963 trip to Israel, the Rebbe (R) delivered this sefer Torah to Merkaz HaRav Yeshivah in Jerusalem. The Torah is being held by his cousin R' Zysha Brandwein, "the Gabbai of R' Shimon bar Yochai."

When leaving, "to be remembered" (sort of an oral *kvitel*), I mentioned my name and my mother's name: Levi Yitzchak ben Soroh Sashe. This is, of course, precisely the same name as R' Levi Yitzchak ben Soroh Sashe of Berditchev, one of the most famous of all Chassidic Masters. As soon as he heard the name, Reb Areleh stood up and said, "A *heimishe nomen*," a familiar name. He left me standing there, and started pacing the room, back and forth, from the table to the window, from the window to the table and back again. He was clearly experiencing or maneuvering something in a world far beyond

The Rebbe being hosted by R' Yissachar Dov Rokeach, Shlita, the current Belzer Rebbe, nephew of R' Areleh Belzer

our ken. He continued pacing and then came back to the table and told me, "Say the name again!"

"Levi Yitzchak ben Soroh Sashe." Off he went again, back and forth, from the table to the window and back. The atmosphere in the room was incredibly charged. It is impossible to describe the experience itself, but it was powerful, unique and unforgettable.

I had no idea what was going on. Obviously the Belzer Rebbe had absolutely no need to impress a young Chassidic rabbi he hardly knew. Something was happening, on some spiritual level, with the great Berditchever Rav's name, something special, something important, but it was beyond me. I was only 25.

Finally Reb Areleh came back and gave me a *brachah*, a good strong *brachah* — although I cannot remember a word of it. I was still too shaken and excited by my encounter. His *gabbai*, who had been standing in another part of the room, was also almost in a trance. It was clearly something very out of the ordinary, even for him.

Once in the anteroom, I tried to ask the *gabbai* what he thought about the whole affair, but he had rushed out to beat the curfew home. I told the Belzer Rebbe's brother, Reb Mordechai, that I now wanted to submit a *kvitel*. He wrote it out and went in to deliver it; but Reb Areleh was busy washing his hands. This was an elaborate procedure with him, one that could take some time. Reb Mordechai told me to rush back home before the curfew began, and promised to give the *kvitel* to Reb Areleh later.

To this day, on Reb Areleh's *yahrtzeit*, the present Belzer Rebbe (Reb Mordechai's son) often asks one of my children to repeat this story, and sometimes he tells it himself, the story of the Belzer Rebbe and R' Levi Yitzchak ben Soroh Sashe.

Vayikra
The Book of Leviticus

Getting Down to Work

The Heavens and Earth were completed. The Jewish people were completed; and their work on the Mishkan was completed. The adolescence of Am Yisrael was over. It was time to get down to work.

And what was the work of Am Yisrael? Serving Hashem through Torah (study), Avodah (the sacrificial services) and gemilas chasadim (kind deeds). We readily relate to the first and last of these. They are down-to-earth, familiar parts of our daily lives. In contrast, the Avodah, especially so many centuries after the Temple was destroyed, seems unfamiliar. Yet magnificent synagogues, bar mitzvahs and fund-raising dinners — all the usual "necessities" of modern Jewish life — are not even mentioned in the Torah, while the construction of the Mishkan and the sacrifices to be offered inside it are recorded in great detail for all generations to come. Collectively they occupy a large fraction of the entire Torah. Where we would have emphasized philosophy or science, the Torah emphasizes the sacrifices. Clearly Hashem has His own priorities for man.

Although this is not the place for a detailed treatise, one should note that the word korbanos (sacrifices) comes from the same root as *korav* (draw near), and that their purpose was to bring man near to Hashem. This can be understood on several levels. On the symbolic level, man must sacrifice the animal within himself to Hashem. His *ruach* (soul) must rise Heavenward, like the altar smoke, as a *rei'ach nichoach*, a scent pleasing to Hashem. On the experiential level, the sights of the Mikdash, altar and *korban*, the sounds of the Levites singing and the odor of the incense and the burning sacrifice entered man's senses to produce an intense, purifying impact on the individual, one stronger than anything we can now imagine. On the educational level, the sacrifices helped man realize: Since I sinned and acted on the animal level, all that is now being done to this animal should have been done to me. There are also many deep Kabbalistic explanations.

Although much of the true meaning and impact of the sacrifices will remain hidden from us until the Temple is rebuilt (speedily in our days!), three things, at least, are clear. First, there is no comparison between the closeness achieved through the Temple Service, a *kaparah* (atonement) that shook man to the roots of his *neshamah* and recast him anew, and the effects of sitting on a padded synagogue bench for an hour or so before lunch. At the very least, the sacrifices jolted man out of his anesthetized existence and told him: "Religion is a matter of life or death!" Second, in our inexperience, we can't adequately gauge the terrible loss of those sacrificial *mitzvos* which Sefer Vayikra describes. Third, those "thoroughly modern" souls who decry the "waste" of animal life required to achieve the spiritual goals of the *korbanos*, and who then go home to eat a corned-beef sandwich that they will soon turn to refuse, are revealing their own attitude toward physical versus spiritual priorities, not the Torah's.

Although many *korbanos* were brought by individuals, others were brought by the community as a whole. As a young new rabbi in Boston in the 1940s and '50s, the Rebbe learned a lot about the sacrifices, of both descriptions, required to shake a community out of its habits and to help it strive for religious standards no longer out of reach.

Vayikra

And He called to Moshe, and Hashem spoke to him.
(Leviticus 1:1)

The Voice went and reached [Moshe's] ears;
But all [the rest] of Israel did not hear.
(Rashi)

Or if he touch the uncleanness [tumah] of man, and all such [spiritual] uncleanness ... and sin
(Leviticus 5:3)

In many places, young children begin their study of Chumash with Vayikra, which deals largely with issues of atonement and purity. The reason, says the Gemara, is: "Let those who are pure occupy themselves with purity." The spiritual purity and closeness to Hashem achieved by the korbanos (sacrifices) requires physical purity (taharah) as well. The opposite of taharah is tumah, a state which leaves man unable to assume the full range of his relations with the Divine. For example, a person who becomes tamei (unclean) cannot enter the Temple Court and cannot eat sacrifices, terumah and other sanctified foods before he is purified.

Although a dead body is a primary source of the most intense tumah, it has always been the custom to "purify" the bodies of the Jewish deceased to prepare them for their final rest. This was the *special duty of the local Chevra Kaddisha (burial society), who were among the most respected members of the community. Their efforts were considered a chessed shel emes (true charity), since the deceased cannot repay the kindness shown him.*

Given the traditional Jewish concern for purity and the proper care of the dead, one wonders why these matters are not fully addressed and appreciated in many communities today. However, it is hard to blame individuals without first asking why the organized community has shirked its responsibility. Finally, in defense of the community, one must turn to its leaders. This is not unfair, as we learn from Rashi on the opening verse of this week's parshah, "but all Israel did not hear." Communities on their own rarely hear or realize the full implications of the Divine command. It takes sensitive community leaders and other special individuals to hear and to mobilize the community as a whole.

Fifty years ago, Jewish religious facilities in most places in America were lacking, and Boston was no exception. Once settled in his Dorchester home, young Rabbi Levi Yitzchak Horowitz wasted no time in mobilizing self-sacrificing "hearers" to help.

ೀ *Jewish Boston-1944*

Father would hardly have recognized the Jewish Boston of 1944. For example, wearing a beard in those days was considered outlandish. When I walked down the street, people actually stopped to stare; they thought I was one of the Smith Brothers, whose bearded visages graced the boxes of a popular brand of cough drops! One of my first ports of call in Boston was the office of Mr. Moses Parsons, a *shomer Shabbos* lawyer, who was to help us with our Dorchester *shul*. When I walked through the door of his office, he took one look at me and remarked with a smile, "I see you are a Protestant."

"What?"

"A Protestant — you are protesting against the prevailing norms of your environment."

PORTRAIT OF A CHASSIDIC RABBI — TORAH VODAATH STYLE

It has long been recognized that the Chassidic rebbes with their unique approach towards Judaism and its people have revitalized our religion and instilled in it a joy and warmth. Their wise counsel, humaneness, religious zeal, and closeness to the people have done much to enhance the status of Judaism throughout the world. Nowhere is such an approach more needed than in the United States, and a new crop of young, dynamic, English-speaking chassidic rebbes, who with an intimate knowledge of the American scene, are quickly assuming spiritual leadership in the reactivation of a lifeless and distorted American Judaism.

One of these young chassidic rebbes is Torah Vodaath-trained Rabbi Levi I. Horowitz of Boston. Rabbi Horowitz is the son of Grand Rabbi P.D. Horowitz of blessed memory, one of the first chassidic rebbes to settle in America. After receiving his secular education in the Boston school system, Rabbi Horowitz left for Israel to pursue an intensive training in talmudic and chassidic lore. Upon returning to the United States in 1936, he entered our Mesivta Torah Vodaath where he studied under Reb Shlomo Heiman, of blessed memory, who ordained him in 1944. Heeding the call of his father's followers, he returned to Boston where he became the spiritual leader of Cong. Beth Pinchas and its chassidic center, an institution unique in the American way of life. The center acts as headquarters for many vital religious activities affecting the entire Boston Jewish community. It also houses a *mikveh* and a special oven for the baking of hand-made *shmure* matzohs. Few Jews residing in or visiting Boston miss an opportunity to come to the center to seek a spiritual uplift. From Rabbi Horowitz they receive information and guidance in the same religious spirit and warm personal manner that made his sainted father beloved by all.

Rabbi Horowitz has been active in all phases of Jewish community life. He has especially dedicated his efforts to the support of all institutions that promote traditional Judaism. He has also used his exalted position to influence others to join in the support of religious enterprises. He is a pioneer in the field of *taharas hamishpocho* and was instrumental in the erection of a $35,000 ultra-modern *mikveh* claimed to be the most beautiful in America, and as president of Daughters of Israel, the local *Mikveh* organization, he is conducting an intense educational program on *tahara*. He was also the coordinator in the construction of the $20,000 Chelsea *mikveh*, and directs the activities of the newly organized *Chevra Kadisha* of Greater Boston, which he helped to establish.

Rabbi Horowitz has many "firsts" on his record. He is the first Torah Vodaath alumnus to become a chassidic rebbe, the first American-born chassidic rebbe, and the first rabbi honored to become the New England representative of the Union of Grand Rabbis, Agudath Israel, and president of the Massachusetts region of the Rabbinical Alliance of America. Torah Vodaath is the only American yeshiva where such much-needed chassidic rebbes are trained. Rabbi Horowitz is its first such product but by no means its last.

Rabbi Levi I. Horowitz

Rabbi Horowitz and followers baking shmure matzoh

A private mikveh at the chassidic center

Updating Boston's communal facilities in the 1940s and '50s was anything but easy. Here the Torah Vodaath Alumni News for 1955 describes the Rebbe's success organizing new mikvaos and a Chevra Kaddisha.

His words basically summed up the situation, although the culture clash did occasionally have its humorous side. Once on a train a secularist Jewish passenger came over and began to harangue me about my hopelessly "archaic" dress. I pointed to two black-habited nuns sitting a few seats away and told him, "Why pick on me; why not pick on them instead?"

Such externals as dress and personal appearance were, unfortunately, far from the only areas in which Jewish Boston had changed. The strict observance of Shabbos, *kashrus*, *tefillah* and *taharah* were also widely regarded as old fashioned in many circles.

The Rebbe and his sister Faigie, just after the family's move back to the West End of Boston in 1944

The prevailing decay in individual religious observance had already affected communal observance as well. For example, every *shul* once had its own *Chevra Kaddisha*, but the original members had aged and many died, leaving no replacements. When only one or two old men were left, they could no longer take care of their own, and the local undertakers began to take over. As commercial concerns, their attitudes, in those days, were often distinctly unhelpful: "What do we need a *Chevra Kaddisha* butting in for? We can do it all ourselves." Their non-Jewish staff did the *taharos* (ritual washings) mechanically, without the requisite prayers and religious sensitivity — if they did *taharos* at all! This was the tragic state of affairs when we arrived.

This was definitely not a "glamorous" issue, and it was difficult to get people involved. Fortunately, we soon found that reestablishing a proper *Chevra Kaddisha* had long been a goal of a local resident, Mr. Philip Aronson, although his efforts to date had been unsuccessful. To help him, we called a city-wide meeting between the Jewish undertakers and the Orthodox rabbinate; but almost no one showed up! One influential individual even told a prominent undertaker: "Don't bother with it; they're not going to do anything anyway!" It was easy to see Mr. Aronson's problem.

How could such things happen? Times were hard, and a sizable portion of a synagogue rabbi's "living" came from conducting funerals for funeral directors. Most Boston Jews were no longer affiliated with a specific synagogue or community. Usually a man would sim-

Vayikra ❦ 173

ply show up at a funeral home and say that his father had died. The following brief dialogue would then ensue:

"To what *shul* do you belong?"

"Don't belong."

"Who is your rabbi?"

"Don't have one."

"In that case, we'll arrange for a rabbi to officiate."

"Fine. Thank you very much."

Being on the undertaker's "approved" list of rabbis could mean numerous funerals and considerable extra income, often exceeding a rabbi's meager synagogue salary. It was no wonder that no one, other than a young, idealistic newcomer, would be brash enough to stand up to the establishment. Father had encountered similar problems with *kashrus* in Boston in the 1920s (see *Torah Luminaries*, ArtScroll, 1994). However, neither of us were the type to give in.

Our Bostoner community eventually formed its own *Chevra Kaddisha*, mostly older people, recent refugees from World War II Europe. The trend grew, younger people began joining, and Mr. Aronson's dream finally became a reality.

In its later chapters, *Sefer Vayikra* describes several ways to cleanse oneself from *tumah*. All involve immersion in a *mikveh* (ritual bath) at some stage. The *mikveh* is thus both a symbol of purity and the means to achieve it. Despite the temporary suspension of the Temple service (which required *taharah*), men still often go to *mikveh* to achieve extra purity. Married women are, even today, required by Torah law (*Lev.* 15:19-24) to go to the *mikveh* to fulfill the laws of family purity. In the 1940s Boston's *mikvaos* fared no better than its *Chevra Kaddisha*. In both cases, "hearers" were in short supply.

Shortly after our arrival in Boston, I was visited by a delegation from a newly formed women's organization. Their group had one major goal and they came right to the point: "Rebbe, thank goodness you are here. You have to help us build a new communal *mikveh*."

I told them, "That's certainly an important priority, but I am only 23; and you have plenty of older, more established *rabbanim* in Boston to choose from. Wouldn't you do better to involve them in building such a *mikveh*?" "We tried," they said, "but it just didn't work out." Since a proper *mikveh* is crucial, I agreed to check out Boston's existing *mikvaos* to see what could be done.

Unfortunately, *mikvaos* in those days were located in the most awful and unappealing places imaginable. The Boston City Mikveh, for example, was located inside the Roxbury Turkish Bathhouse complex! In fact, the *mikveh*-bathhouse combination was more the rule than the exception in those days. Outside, in the dilapidated courtyard, there were tremendous logs of wood to be burned in the *mikveh's* boilers. The entrance was as filthy as a place could be, and the whole idea of *tznius* (modesty) — was completely impossible. When entering and leaving, the women had to go right past all the men using the Turkish Bathhouse.

One Shabbos, a group of religious women, in total frustration, had burst into the men's section of their *shul* and wouldn't let the men *lein* (read from the Torah) until they promised to build a new *mikveh*. As dramatic as these protests were, nothing changed; and Boston's Daughters of Israel organization was formed to address this intolerable situation in a more effective way.

We were even more shocked to find that, over time, serious halachic (Jewish legal) questions had developed concerning the *kashrus* of Boston's old *mikvaos*. For example, a *mikveh* is supposed to be filled with 40 *se'ah* of rain water. One can, however, take one *mikveh* of rain water, called a *bor*, and put it beside another one filled with regular tap water. By opening a hole between the two, which allows the two waters to touch — a procedure known as *hashakah* (kissing) — the regular-water *mikveh* also becomes valid. That way the active *mikveh* can be filled, used, emptied, cleaned and refilled time and time again, with a brief *hashakah* after each filling, a procedure which keeps the water used for the actual immersion clean and fresh.

In one *mikveh,* we found that the tap-water *mikveh* was filled properly but that the water level in the *bor* was far below the level of the connecting hole. *Hashakah* was impossible! One could only hope that the problem was a recent one; but we obviously halted the *mikveh's* use, until the *bor* refilled with rain water and other essential improvements were made. Most important, we helped the Boston community organize a campaign for "a nice *mikveh* in a nice neighborhood."

Mr. Marx Spitz, a religious Boston real-estate lawyer and a loyal *Chassid,* went to work and bought one of the nicest buildings on Seaver Street, the fanciest street in Dorchester, for the new *mikveh*. In those days, this exclusive neighborhood was quite the place to be. The *mikveh's* future neighbors welcomed it in time-honored fashion: They sued the organizers in court! They claimed that having a *mikveh* next door was no better than having a slaughterhouse next door! After lurid descriptions of "what goes on in a *mikveh*," the judge ruled against us, and we had to look for a new site. Finally, we settled on a building on Columbia Road, right next door to our own *shul*. At least the "neighbors" were sympathetic.

The building was completely remodeled and the new Boston Community Mikveh was beautiful indeed. Unfortunately, it operated for only 13 or so years, unfortunately, because the neighborhood changed. Once the bulk of the Jewish community had moved from Dorchester to Brookline or beyond, the *mikveh* had to move as well. During those 13 years, however, the Dorchester *mikveh* introduced a whole generation to the beauty and importance of observing the laws of *mikveh* and *taharas hamishpachah* (family purity).

Tzav

Every meal-offering baked in the oven,
Or made in a pan or griddle, shall be for
The officiating priest [to eat] ...
The fat of a dead [unslaughtered] animal or
A torn (treif) animal can be used for work,
But not at all eaten.
(Leviticus 7:9,24)

Having dealt with the purity required for sacrifices, in this parshah the Torah goes on to deal with the purity required for the food we eat. The ingestion of food and the use of its energy to perform mitzvos is another way — in addition to being offered on the Temple Altar — that plant and animal life can contribute to a higher spiritual realm. Indeed, Rabbi Akiva held that in these days, when we lack an Altar, the table in every Jewish home can take its place: shulchano shel adam mechaper, a man's table can provide atonement. That is only if all the mitzvos, blessings and requirements associated with eating are strictly observed and the meal is enriched with words of Torah and guests. With so much at stake, assumptions and probabilities just won't do. The world plays too many tricks on the unwary.

∞ The French Bakery

On the Jewish holiday of Pesach all leavened food products are strictly forbidden. To emphasize that the Divine command is the only reason we give up all *chametz* (leavened) foods, *Chassidim* deliberately eat such leavened goods early in the morning of the day before Pesach and again just after the holiday. It's as if to say, "See, we do appreciate such fine leavened foods, but we are willing to give them up to observe Hashem's command."

During the 1930s, Father's *Chassidim* would go out right after Pesach and buy beer, which is also *chametz*, at a non-Jewish store. They would bring it back to our house and use it for *havdalah*, the ceremony that marks the transition between *kodesh v'chol* (the sacred and secular) and, in this case, between the time when *chametz* was *asur* (forbidden) and *mutar* (permitted).

Since I don't drink that much beer, and since *havdalah* requires drinking a large cup, that particular *minhag* (custom) was allowed to lapse. Instead, during the late 1940s, I would go out with our *Chassidim* on the night after Pesach to buy freshly baked bread. This was fairly easy because Boston's West End had plenty of reliable non-Jewish bakers to choose from (Jewish bakers would need to dispose of their *chametz* before Pesach, introducing various complications).

Of course, we couldn't just go out and buy non-Jewish bread. We first had to check out the baker, his ingredients, his utensils and all that. Furthermore, we only ate *pas Yisrael* (Jewish bread). That required finding a baker who would let us help him bake the bread by, for example, adding wood to his wood-fired oven and then supervising the baking.

After a brief search, we found a nice Italian bakery where they were happy to oblige and, every year after Pesach, we went down to that bakery to bake our bread. It was a "big production." I would throw a piece of wood into their oven, and they would mix the flour and water and knead the dough and, by 11 or 11:30 p.m., we would have delicious hearth-fresh, 100 percent kosher Italian bread.

Our annual visit soon became a tradition. The baker's sons prepared well in advance and their old father would personally come to the door to greet us. Being a devout Catholic, filled with respect for the clergy, he regarded it as a privilege for us to come and "bless" his bakery with our annual bread baking. You could see that they really looked forward to it. When they eventually bought an electric oven, nothing changed. They simply let us turn everything off and back on again, as our "contribution" to the baking process. Things went smoothly year after year, loaf after loaf; but eventually they moved, and then we had to find a new source of post-Pesach bread.

We eventually found a French baker who was also very accommodating, and began going there. Everything was fine for a while. Switch off, switch on, mix the flour and water ... hot bread. Then one year, I began my usual walk around the bakery to check things out while they were mixing the dough. The room was full of stacks of bags and cans of all kinds. Things seemed much the same as the year before until I found a new can clearly labeled "fat." Although no fats at all were used in our bread, I immediately began checking the can's ingredients. The first ingredient was lard! I was shocked beyond belief, since the bakery had always used only flour, water and yeast, and nothing else, in all of their breads.

When I confronted the owner, he explained that they had just started making a new type of special bread a few weeks earlier. Although that bread also contained no fat, they had to grease their pans so the bread would come out of the pans more easily. He pointed out that this had nothing to do with our bread, which wasn't baked in a pan at all, but rather right on the hearth. That was true but, as soon as we heard that their oven had baked pans containing non-kosher ingredients, we thanked him warmly, apologized profusely, wished him well, and began edging towards the door. Alas, from that day on, we had to give up our annual treat of tasty hot French bread.

In fact, I became so concerned that we couldn't control every facet of the baking that I gave up the custom altogether, until we moved to Jerusalem. There, several major bakeries bake fresh

Vayikra ❦ 179

bread the night after Pesach (and for a week or so thereafter) with *Pesach* flour which, had it not been made *chametz* during the bread-making process, might even have been used to make *matzos*!

※

This certainly isn't the only such *kashrus*-related story the Rebbe tells; there are many dozens of them. Now, for example, let's move along from our first course, the baked meal offering, to an innocent bowl of ...

※ *Vegetable Soup*

*T*oday, *baruch Hashem*, Boston has a nice variety of kosher restaurants — *fleishig, milchig,* Chinese, even a pizza parlor — but in the 1950s there was nothing, or almost nothing. There was one "strictly vegetarian" restaurant downtown where some religious people would eat. This was particularly true of businessmen, who couldn't go all the way back to the suburbs to eat lunch at home.

A businessman friend of ours, despite our dire misgivings, checked out this vegetarian restaurant and came away convinced that it was all right to eat there. They used absolutely no meat products, animal fats, derivatives and so on. The premises were as meat-free as the inside of a turnip. In short, he soon became a regular customer for lunch. The restaurant's ample menu included vegetable soup and, since he was particularly fond of vegetable soup, that's how he began his lunch every day.

Things went along just fine — another day, another soup — for some time. Then, one day, he came in, gave everyone his usual greeting, and sat down at his usual table. He made himself comfortable, put his napkin on his lap, and eventually the waiter arrived with his bowl of steaming hot vegetable soup. A full spoonful was on the way to his mouth, when he noticed something suspicious on the spoon. What was it? A fragment of chicken bone ... A CHICKEN BONE!

He called over the waiter. "What's this? What's this?"

"It's all right," the waiter said, "we won't charge you extra. We ran out of vegetable soup and, since you are such a good regular customer, we went out and got you a bowl of hot soup from the restaurant downstairs."

That was, unfortunately, his last hot lunch downtown; but at least he knew that Hashem was watching out for him. What if there *hadn't* been a bone in his soup!

Shemini

And you shall distinguish between the holy and non-holy,
Between the impure and the pure ...
And these animals you may eat ...
All those with cloven hooves and ...
That bring up their cud.
(Leviticus 10:10;11:2-3)

The Torah continues its discussion of purity with regard to holy things, sacrifices and food. The constant repetition and preoccupation with mikveh, kashrus and other means for assuring purity might seem odd, were it not that even with all this repetition these areas usually do not receive the attention and concern they deserve.

Like many other devout Jews, Chassidim always seek to go beyond the minimum requirements of the law. For the Rebbe's family that meant observing, among other stringencies, drinking only cholov Yisrael, milk supervised from its milking to guard against forbidden admixtures, accidental or otherwise. This was a considerable challenge in Boston half-a-century ago. The understandable scarcity of milk cows in downtown Boston, even during the 1930s and '40s, led the Rebbe's family to pursue alternative strategies, with some help from their friends.

❧ *Cholov Yisrael*

*M*uch of what is taken for granted as normal today was "an experience" back in the 1930s. For one thing, we couldn't just go out and buy *cholov Yisrael* milk, milk watched by a reliable Jew from the time of milking to make sure that it contained nothing forbidden. Thus, procuring such strictly kosher milk became yet another chore for Mr. Singer, our devoted caretaker, handyman and babysitter.

Where could one get 100 percent reliable milk? From a cow. Where could one find a cow? On a farm. And where were the nearest farms to Boston? In Chelsea, a suburb past Cambridge, on the other side of the river from Boston. These farms gave Chelsea a unique atmosphere, quite literally. An old-timer from Chelsea once told us: "There are two cities in New England which have by-names. There's [the very exclusive] Manchester-by-the-Sea, and there's Chelsea-by-the-Smell!"

Twice a week Mr. Singer would go out to Chelsea at about 4 o'clock in the morning, in time for the milking of the cows. There was no public transportation at that hour, and we didn't have a car; but that was no problem. Mr. Singer would go out to the corner of Poplar and Charles Streets, dressed in his dark-blue "Boston Special Police" uniform, carrying two large metal milk containers, and hitch a ride. When people saw his uniform they would stop; and eventually he would find someone going out to Chelsea. He would do the same thing coming back; but he had a real job finding someone who would let him carry two heavy, full milk containers with him!

The whole thing was a three- to four-hour affair, repeated twice a week, week after week, for years. It was a tremendous *chessed*, not only for

Bostoner Cholov Yisrael filled a crucial gap until reliably supervised milk became more readily available.

Vayikra ❧ 183

Father, but for the whole family, and even for the *meshulachim* who stayed with us. We all benefited from his labors. Without Mr. Singer, B.S.P., we simply wouldn't have had milk to drink.

※

When we returned to Boston in 1944, Mr. Singer returned with us. He occasionally went to outlying farms to get milk, especially in the beginning, but by then commercial, pasteurized *cholov Yisrael* could be obtained with difficulty from New York. Still, this was no way to encourage a higher level of *kashrus* in the general Boston community, so we went to work.

There were already several stringently kosher families in Boston and, with their help, we started a campaign to distribute *cholov Yisrael* on a regular basis. The farms in Chelsea had long since closed, a victim of urban sprawl, but there was a reliable accommodating farm, Weiss's Farm, out in Stoneham. They were willing to help, but they needed a sizable, regular minimum order to make it all worthwhile.

We didn't have nearly enough people who really cared about *cholov Yisrael* to guarantee anything, but the daughter of a friend of ours started making telephone calls to convince people to sign up "for the good of the community." The general response wasn't exactly enthusiastic. Some people even misunderstood what we were trying to do ("Why does the Rebbe want the few extra pennies that go to the grocer?"), but others were pleasant and understanding. Many people agreed to give us part of their milk order, not out of conviction, but so that the people who really wanted *cholov Yisrael* would have the opportunity.

Soon it became a reality. Many of the original *"Bostoner Cholov Yisrael"* bottle caps are still around to prove it! It demonstrated what a community could do for itself, once it set its mind to it. In fact, the operation continued until large amounts of commercial *cholov Yisrael* became readily available from other sources.

One positive result of the "campaign" was raising the consciousness of people — even rabbis — to the importance of *cholov Yisrael*. The prevailing view that "the government checks all ingredients" simply didn't bear close scrutiny. Mislabeled milk led, at most, to a $50 fine; and the regulations were nearly impossible to enforce. We actually spoke to the state inspectors who performed spot checks on loaded milk trucks; and they told us that they only checked the bacterial count and total fat content of the milk. For that reason, those respected halachic authorities who did permit regular milk used a variety of other considerations as well. Furthermore, they usually ruled only on the permissibility of such milk, not the advisability of using it.

Public education was an uphill battle. Once someone asked how we could keep our *cholov Yisrael* fresh. Actually we were very proud that, since the big commercial dairies trucked their milk in from New Hampshire and Vermont, whereas Stoneham was relatively nearby, Bostoner milk reached its "customers" sooner. We proudly informed the man, "Rest assured, *Bostoner cholov Yisrael* milk is much fresher than regular commercial milk."

He remained unconvinced. "I don't know, Rebbe. How fresh can it be, if it comes all the way from Israel?"

෴ R' Isaac Herzog

Other people needed no convincing, and they were in good company. In 1949, shortly after Israel's War of Independence, R' Isaac Herzog, the Chief Rabbi of Israel and a great *talmid chacham* (Torah scholar), came to Boston. He and his entire retinue stayed in the Statler Hotel, the fanciest hotel in Boston, and his list of appointments included the most influential Jewish leaders in America.

R' Issac Herzog, First Ashkenazi Chief Rabbi of Israel

During his first night in Boston, the New England Chassidic Center received a frantic late-night call from R' Herzog's suite. "The Chief Rabbi says that he won't eat or drink anything unless it is personally approved by the Bostoner Rebbe."

"We would be glad to help. What does he need?"

"The main thing the Chief Rabbi needs now is milk. Is there any way we can find reliable *cholov Yisrael* milk in Boston?"

We offered them some of Boston's own *cholov Yisrael*, and they immediately sent over a driver to pick it up.

Then the Chassidic Center started preparing all of R' Herzog's food for the next day. During his entire stay in Boston, he basically refused to touch anything except what we sent him. It was a fine example of his uncompromising care and outstanding *mesiras nefesh* (self-sacrifice) for *mitzvos*.

❧ Just Take a Look

At the other extreme, especially with our college student *baalei teshuvah* in the 1960s, we had to explain everything, even the most basic requirements for physical purity, and its effect on their spiritual potentials. Typical was the college student who came to see us, wanting to become religious. I asked him where he was "holding" now; and he replied proudly: "I go to *shul* on Shabbos and recite *Kiddush* every Friday night."

"That's good. Making *Kiddush* is a big step forward. But are you making *Kiddush* over a kosher Friday night meal?"

"No, I haven't really taken that on yet."

"I see. But how could you make a *brachah* to thank Hashem for giving you a *treif* (non-kosher) meal?"

"Well, maybe I *could* take that on ..."

One thing led to another, and soon he and his wife were spending a lot of time at the Chassidic Center, making great progress, until we reached the issue of *taharas hamishpachah* (family purity). Then things came to a screeching halt. His wife wouldn't even discuss it. We tried to convince her that it was a moving experience, a link to the past, a beautiful way of bringing *kedushah* (holiness) into marriage — no argument was of avail. This was by no means uncommon, due to widespread unfamiliarity, hearsay and the awful *mikveh* conditions of earlier days (modern *mikvaos* simply look like small, tiled swimming pools; they even have chlorine, warm water and hair-dryers!)

The month dragged on with no progress in sight; something dramatic had to be done soon. During one of our sessions, I suddenly changed tactics. Picking up the telephone, I called a startled *mikveh* lady during the middle of the day (women immerse only at night) and told her to meet us at the *mikveh* in 10 minutes. Then I told the young man and his wife, "Come, let's get my *gabbai* and go take a look; you'll see it's not anything like you think." It was a rather unconventional tactic, but it worked. The family is now quite religious and, in fact, are now *Chassidim,* albeit of a different Rebbe.

Tazria

When a woman conceives and bears a boy,
She shall be tamei [ritually unclean and separated]
For seven days, as she is during the days
Of her monthly separation.
(Leviticus 12:2)

At first, the conjunction seems unusual. The birth of a child, the happiest day of the parents' lives, is followed by a period of impurity. But this is to give a couple the opportunity to reflect and appreciate what they have been granted.

Volumes could be written about the specialness and sanctity of Jewish marriage, which creates a unity so profound that it is likened to the relationship between Israel and the Torah, and Israel and Hashem. It is a unity based not on the identical nature of the two partners, but on their ability to complement each other. Jewish wives and Jewish husbands have unique roles; and the Midrash describes Adam and Chavah (Eve) as two distinct halves of one complete being. This sense of balance between male and female, and between the "other" and "self," assures that the couple's lives stay on course and bear fruit. As Rashi comments on the verse "I will make for him a helper opposite him": If he is worthy, she will help him; if he is not worthy [and veers off course], she will oppose him [and bring him back to center].

The choice of a marriage partner is thus one of the most serious choices one can make. It is a choice that will affect generations of Jewish children and the adults they become. Parents, rabbis and counselors, with their wider experience of married life, can help with their advice, but it is ultimately a choice each person must make for himself. This is hinted at in the Torah itself: "A man shall therefore leave his father and mother and be united with his wife" (Genesis 2:24). Despite this, Jewish weddings have traditionally been family affairs, in which the parents and grandparents and, when available, great-grandparents all play an integral part. Of course, there are exceptions ...

❦ *Made in Heaven*

Ideally, a person visiting a Rebbe follows a certain protocol. He checks in with the *gabbai* (attendant) in the outer office. The *gabbai* writes a brief *kvitel*, a note with the visitor's request, and then goes in to ask the Rebbe when the visitor can enter. Of course, a Rebbe in Boston, which has over 150,000 college students, has to be considerably more flexible, accessible and informal. Still, there are limits to what one expects.

One day a breathless young man dashed into my office unannounced. He ran up to my desk and said, "Rebbe, I have a special *mitzvah* for you. We need you to be the *mesader kiddushin* (officiating Rabbi) for a *chassan* and *kallah* (bride and groom). You simply must do it; you can't turn me down!"

"What *chassan*? What *kallah*?"

"They are sitting in a car outside and want you to marry them!"

I was rather taken aback. Jewish weddings just aren't done on a "drive-in" basis. If this fellow were at all religious, surely he would know that a Jewish wedding requires all sorts of prior arrangements.

"Wait a minute! We just don't do things that way. What do you mean they are here waiting in a car? Who are they and what made them decide to get married all of a sudden?"

Jewish weddings are usually a solemn, as well as a joyous, occasion. Here the Rebbe (center) leads his eldest son, R' Pinchas Horowitz, to the chuppah.

The young man had an answer for everything. The *kallah* was from a religious family — in fact, her father was a rabbi — while the *chassan* was a *baal teshuvah* from a non-observant family. They wanted to get married, but the *chassan's* father had been vehemently opposed. Finally they decided to get married without his father's consent and had come to Boston, with a carload of friends and well-wishers, to do just that.

Legally, under both Jewish and American law, they were within their rights; but I still couldn't quite accept the idea. Was I just supposed to marry them off on the spot, without parents or preparation? Their advocate went through their whole story again. The couple had sincerely tried to get the consent of his parents; this would be a big *chizuk* (encouragement) for the *chassan*, it would help him stay religious, and so on. Finally I said, "All right, we'll talk to them. But send them in so we can talk to them directly, without a middleman."

In they came, and repeated the same story. Finally I asked the prospective *kallah*, "Granted that his parents don't agree, but what about your parents?"

"Oh, mine are all in favor of it. If you marry us they will be quite happy."

"Still, agreeable or not, most parents would want to be at their daughter's wedding. Did they say it would be all right for their daughter to run off and get married without them?"

"Oh, they really don't mind."

"Can I verify that? Can I call them long distance and ask them?"

"Sure, if you want. Here, I'll give you their number."

Things were now beginning to look quite different. Having one side on board would be a lot better than having no side at all. Still, was her claim really true? It was hard to imagine a father wanting his daughter to marry without his being there. Then there were all the practical problems.

"As a religious person, you must know that you have to make certain preparations before getting married."

"I know, and I already took care of them."

My surprise was complete when she pulled out a note from her pocketbook and handed it to me. It was an official certificate, signed by a well-known *mikveh* lady on the East Side of New York, attesting that this young woman had undergone all necessary preparations for her forthcoming marriage. This made things much more serious indeed. The girl was obviously not just someone off the street; and this was definitely not a last-minute decision. The whole elaborate effort had been carefully planned, well in advance, in full accordance with Jewish law. They were evidently committed to going through with it. Furthermore, she said that her father agreed. I called the number she gave me and said, "Hello, this is Rabbi Horowitz, the Bostoner Rebbe. Your daughter is here in my office with her *chassan*, and she says that you agree to my marrying them in your absence."

"Oh, *Baruch Hashem*," said the relieved voice on the other end of the line. "*Baruch Hashem*! I am so happy. I didn't know whom they would ask to be *mesader kiddushin*, but the Bostoner Rebbe ... a *brachah auf dein kopf* (blessings on your head). I am agreeable, and I want it, and it's good ..." When I asked why he didn't want to attend personally, he just said that he "had his reasons," and hung up amidst further expressions of *brachah* and relief. Well, that settled

Being misamei'ach the chassan (gladdening the groom) is an important mitzvah. Here the Rebbe dances with R' Chaim Frankel, his grandson.

that — at least after we called the telephone company and verified his number (one can't be too careful!).

Now things were really serious. We had an agreement, at least on one side, a *mikveh* note, a *chassan* and a *kallah*. Still, there were numerous other details to straighten out. First, we needed a *minyan*. The original go-between, who had wandered back into my office, volunteered: "No problem, we brought along some friends from New York. We just need another three or four people."

"And what about the wedding meal? There has to be something to celebrate with."

"Oh, don't worry about that. We have that in the car too."

Then what about *unterfirers*, the married couples (usually the parents) who traditionally lead the *chassan* and *kallah* to the *chuppah*? Their friends were all young and single. Where would we find two married couples in the middle of the day, when everyone was usually at work? The Rebbetzin got on the phone and called a few elderly retired couples who lived nearby.

"I have a treat for you," she said. "We want you to be *unterfirers* at a wedding. When? Right now! You'll come, see the whole thing ..." We brought a few people from the *shul* for the *minyan*. The *shamash* found the *chuppah*, while we wrote out the *tenaim* and *kesubah* (marriage contract). In short, we worked it all out, and started the wedding.

Finally it was done. *Mazel Tov!* The crowd started dancing; they were so very happy! It was a most unusual scene: the drive-in *chassan* and *kallah*, their young "*mechutanim*" from the back seat — happy, jumping up and down — all singing and dancing with the 80-year-old *unterfirers,* who were characters to begin with. If it weren't that the *chassan* and *kallah* were so sincere and serious (and they were), we would have burst out laughing. For them, this was the *simchah* of the century. They said thanks, *mazel tov,* and then they all got back in the car and took off for home again.

Years later, I was called to sit on a *bais din* involving a rabbi at a local Talmud Torah (religious school). In accordance with Jewish law, the two litigants each picked a qualified judge. Then the two judges sat down to pick a third judge to form a "*bais din* of three." At first they had trouble agreeing on a mutually acceptable third judge. Finally both sides found that they trusted the Bostoner Rebbe, and they asked me to be the third judge. We went, listened to both sides, and handed down our decision. Both sides were happy.

As I was leaving, a short, elderly gentleman came over and said: "Rebbe, you did a great job on the *din Torah*; but you did a terrible thing to me." I was taken aback, since I try to be particularly careful about my relationships with others. His problem? "I had an only son, and I waited so many years to be at his wedding, and you married him off without me."

I thought for awhile, but nothing came to mind. Still, I felt terrible; how could such a thing have happened? As the old man gave more and more details, the whole episode suddenly came back to me.

"Wait a minute. Didn't your son call you that very morning, and didn't you say again that you would never agree to his marriage?"

"True, that's true, I did say so. But you never know, I might have changed my mind later anyway."

"Well, what's the situation now?"

"Fine, fine. He's still religious, I'm still not, but we are on good terms."

"Well, that's good."

In short, he "forgave" me, and started coming around to visit us, becoming more involved in *Yiddishkeit*. Later we moved to Brookline, not far his home. Proximity helped, and he began coming around even more often.

One day his son, by then a prominent out-of-town physician, came by to say that his father was seriously ill and that he had asked me to officiate at his funeral when he passed on. The young man's mother kept up the contact with us; and the son now has, *Baruch Hashem*, a large family of his own. As they say, "All's well that ends well."

Metzora

This is the law of the metzora (leper),
On the day of his being made tahor (clean),
The priest will command to take, for the one being
cleansed,
Two live kosher birds, cedar wood, scarlet and hyssop.
(Leviticus 14:2,4)

Since such plagues come from malicious talk...
Babbling birds were required ... What is his cure?
To lower himself from his pride [the cedar]
And become lowly like the [scarlet] worm or the
hyssop.
(Rashi)

Tzara'as, often mistakenly translated as leprosy, was actually a spiritual disease with physical manifestations. It came from speaking lashon hara, malicious gossip designed to belittle others. The Torah's tikkun (spiritual repair procedure) similarly utilized physical manifestations of the spiritual root cause. It symbolically involved recognizing the dangers of arrogance and the importance of submerging it in humility. Although, in our time, the soul and body are no longer so closely linked as to make tzara'as possible, we are still keenly aware of the need for both a "refuas hanefesh" and a "refuas haguf," both a spiritual and a bodily cure.

This is not to belittle the role of modern medicine. Judaism has always had a positive view towards medicine; since all life and health come from Hashem, man has a duty to actively preserve them. Similarly the Mishnah teaches that, "He who saves a life saves a whole world." Still, there is more to healing than treating the patient's body. One has to support his — and his whole family's — neshamah (spirit) as well.

This person-to-person connection and communal concern, the opposite of the enforced isolation of the metzora, is one of the key elements of the Rebbe's ROFEH medical support organization. Several events and personal experience catalyzed the founding of ROFEH, but none was more memorable than ...

❧ Ornstein's Refuah

*I*n 1949 a close friend of ours, R' Mordechai Berkowitz, was appointed the rabbi of a synagogue in Providence, Rhode Island, and we attended his installation. After the ceremony, a Jew from Yerushalayim, R' Ornstein, came over to me and said, "I was going to come see you about my brother, who lives in Israel. He has a serious heart condition, and I want you to help him make arrangements with a Boston doctor that the Chazon Ish [R' Avraham Yeshayah Karelitz, zt"l, one of the leading Torah scholars of our century] has recommended. Without a formal invitation from an American hospital, the U.S. consulate won't give him a visa."

"Fine," I said, "drop by tomorrow morning and we will try to help."

When he arrived, we asked which doctor the Chazon Ish had recommended. He said, "Dr. Dwight Harkin." I had lived in Boston almost all my life, but we had never heard of any Dr. Dwight Harkin. How did the Chazon Ish, who lived in Bnei Brak, know Dr. Harkin? I called the doctor's office, and a man's voice answered.

"Hello, is this Dr. Dwight Harkin?" I asked.

His reply was a curt, "You bet it is!" I was stunned. Here I was calling to discuss a very serious heart operation — this was long before the age of open-heart surgery — and this surgeon didn't sound all that serious himself. Still, he was recommended by the Chazon Ish, so I pressed on, undeterred.

"Dr. Harkin, I have a request from someone in Israel who wants to undergo heart surgery."

"Oh," he said in the same bantering tone, "that Israeli patient of mine is making me famous! You know there was this girl from Haifa. I operated on her successfully, and I guess she went back to Israel and told everyone about it. What can I do for you?"

"To get a visa, this patient needs a letter from your hospital confirming that they will admit him, and confirmation that you will do the operation."

R' Avraham Yeshayah Karelitz, the Chazon Ish

"No problem. I'll go right to work on it."

We gave him the details and waited and waited; but Dr. Harkin never called back. Instead, one Friday afternoon, we got a telegram from Israel: "Ornstein arriving tomorrow [on Shabbos]. Please finalize arrangements."

Flights were scarce, and apparently the only flight he could get arrived on Shabbos, when we would be unable to meet him at the airport. I immediately called Dr. Harkin, who said not to worry. He had already taken care of everything; a hospital ambulance would meet Ornstein at the airport.

All Shabbos afternoon the telephone rang and rang. Finally, after *havdalah,* we took the call. It was the hospital; Ornstein had arrived; but he was very nervous, and no one there could even talk with him, since Ornstein spoke only Yiddish. Could we please send someone over right away to help?

We rushed right over and set up a rotation of Yiddish-speaking volunteers to be with Ornstein 24 hours a day. He needed 24-hour service because what good was the hospital's night shift if they couldn't communicate with him?

Community support helped, but Ornstein was still terribly anxious about his surgery. Finally, after considerable observation and examination, Dr. Harkin informed us that the operation would take place on a certain day. That seemed like good news, but we got an immediate call from Ornstein's attendant saying, "It's the end; it's the end for Ornstein!"

The problem was that the operation had been scheduled for the Thursday before *Tishah b'Av*. That was all Ornstein had to hear. The Nine Days leading up to the destruction of the Temple are considered inauspicious for Jews, and Ornstein was beside himself. He had no intention of allowing any doctor, especially a non-Jewish doctor, to cut him open then!

I diplomatically called Dr. Harkin and mentioned that we were having a "little problem" with Ornstein. "I know," he said. "I guess that Thursday must be the worst day in the whole Jewish calendar. But I want to tell you something, Rabbi. If we go through with this operation, it is going to be the greatest day in the life of Ornstein!"

"Still, you scheduled the operation for Thursday, and *Tishah b'Av* is on Sunday, only three days away. Can't you do the operation on Monday instead?"

"No," he said, "I am leaving on Monday, and I want to be around for a few days after the surgery, just in case there are complications. And another thing I'll tell you, Rabbi, I am sure that G–d will be with me on Thursday, just as He would be on Monday." Well, that did it. I told him, "Look, Dr. Harkin, if you are taking G–d into the operating room with you, then you have my blessing. Good luck."

Next it was Ornstein's turn. I told him, "True, Jewish tradition says you shouldn't go into judgment with a non-Jew during the Nine Days; but here we are dealing with the *Ribono Shel Olam* (G–d, Master of the Universe). The doctor said he is going to take the *Ribono Shel Olam* into the operating room with him on

Thursday; so it's all right!"

It must have been all right because, the very night before the operation, a telegram arrived from the Chazon Ish in Bnei Brak. We hadn't been in contact with him because communication with Israel was poor and infrequent in those days (a telegram was an occasion). Although he couldn't possibly have heard about our discussions and decisions, there was the Chazon Ish's telegram on my desk saying: "The operation should be with *hatzlachah* (success)."

Ornstein's operation was only the 91st of its kind. We remember the number, because Dr. Harkin had tried to reassure us: "In the 90 operations of this type that we have done so far, only nine patients have died." I couldn't help thinking: What kind of reassurance is that? Why tell me how many patients died? A religious Jewish doctor would have told me how many had lived!

In any case, the operation was, *baruch Hashem,* a great success. Despite his eccentric manner, Dr. Harkin was a top-flight surgeon and a fine person to boot.

ROFEH, the Bostoner Rebbe's medical support and referral organization, has expanded over the years. Here is ROFEH House, a facility providing temporary accommodations for the families of patients.

The Rebbe maintains close contact with medical professionals in America and Israel as part of his ROFEH medical support and referral organization and as an expert in medical ethics.

He had pioneered cardiac surgery while in the U.S. Army Medical Corps during World War II, and was a thorough, no-nonsense professional. In one case we sent him, he postponed a serious heart operation time after time, because he thought the patient wasn't ready. He didn't care what the family or the hospital said. He also was very good-hearted, refusing to take any payment from the poorer patients we sent him.

Finally Ornstein went back home to Israel with a repaired heart and several trunks full of clothes, linens and household goods. Rabbi Moshe Cohn, and his wife, who had helped coordinate the volunteers, saw to that.

Somewhat later the hospital wrote up the whole story of how Boston's Jewish community had set up 24-hour translator shifts, which encouraged several other ethnic communities to set up their own health support services for patients who didn't speak English. In fact, this experience was instrumental in our own decision to start ROFEH, the Bostoner community's support service for out-of-town hospital patients and their families.

Religious patients continued to come to Boston for treatment and the Rebbe, when asked, took a personal interest in them and their families. Most just needed spiritual and emotional support, translators and a place for their families to stay, but some needed....

∾ *Even More*

This story begins with an Israeli patient who came to Boston in the late 1940s, stayed with us, underwent his treatment and then returned home. A few years later, we received a call from him. His 20-year-old daughter was coming to Boston, and he wanted us to help her get settled. She arrived as planned and stayed at the New England Chassidic Center for a while. Although her family was very traditional, we could see that she was already somewhat "modern." Still, she said that she wanted to be *chareidi* (strictly religious) and remain part of the religious community, which was fine with us.

She began looking for a job, and finally found one in New York City...as a secretary for a non-Orthodox men's divinity school! She came back to Boston to discuss the issue. Could she take the job if she didn't "get involved"? Despite her question, she had already just about made up her mind. In fact, she already had made an appointment to return to New York and sign the contract!

We were quite concerned. If an attractive young woman of marriageable age goes to work in that kind of environment, with all the eligible young men there, what are her prospects for starting a religious Jewish family? So I told her, "Why don't you wait a few weeks? It's now just after Rosh Hashanah. Wait until after Simchas Torah and, if you still want to make this decision, we will discuss it again." She seemed a bit reluctant, but she accepted the advice.

First came Yom Kippur, then Sukkos and finally Simchas Torah, when we take all the Torah scrolls out of the Ark and dance with them. There is always a great crowd of people inside and outside of our shul, accompanying the *hakafos* (processions) with enthusiastic singing and dancing. On such occasions, the *mechitzah*, the curtain that separates the men and women's sections of the *shul*, comes down a bit so the women can see what is going on.

Somehow, during the evening, our secretary-to-be happened to meet a nice young man who had also come to celebrate Simchas Torah. Although what they said to each other is unknown, just one day later, right after *Yom Tov*, she and her young man came in to see us. They wanted to get married! He was a very bright young man, from a religious family, and was studying at Yale.

They were well matched. Both the girl and her *chassan*, although religious, might have been unable to withstand the pressures of secular society on their own. Together, *Baruch Hashem*, they complemented each other well, each offering the spiritual and personal strength the other needed. After a few short weeks, they became engaged and then married. They are now living happily somewhere down South, where he is a Jewishly committed college professor. I can't even begin to guess what would have happened to her alone in New York.

Years later, on a visit to Israel, I saw her father again. When he came running over to speak to me, I assumed that it was to discuss his previous medical problem, but he had something else on his mind. "Do you have any idea what you have done for me?" he asked. "When we make a *misheberach* [prayer for the sick] in *shul* we ask for a *'refuas hanefesh, refuas haguf'* [a spiritual healing, a bodily healing]. You did a *refuas haguf* when you saved my life; but you did even more, a *refuas hanefesh*, when you saved my daughter."

Acharei Mos

And Hashem spoke to Moses
After the death of Aaron's two sons...
(Lev. 16:1)

Why does [the Torah] mention their death
In connection with Yom Kippur? To teach that
Just as Yom Kippur atones for Israel,
The death of the righteous atones for Israel
(Jerusalem Talmud, Yoma, 1:1)

In parshas Shemini (10:1-5) we read about Nadav and Avihu, the two eldest sons of Aharon, after they "offered strange fire before Hashem." In this week's parshah their death is mentioned again, seemingly gratuitously, before a lengthy discussion of the Yom Kippur service. Beyond the surface differences in subject matter, the Jerusalem Talmud, quoted above, sees a deeper connection: The death of the righteous also leads to atonement.

Although there are several different explanations of the young priests' dramatic death, one traditional interpretation sees both the "strange fire" they offered and the Divine fire that killed them as symbols of spiritual enthusiasm. Nadav and Avihu were particularly righteous and sought union with Hashem on a particularly high level. Not yet able to achieve such heights on the strength of their own fervor, they resorted to artificial means (perhaps, based on verse 9 in Shemini involving wine) to reach the required level of ecstasy.

The "strange fire" they engendered was too powerful for their physical bodies to contain, and their souls burst forth from their earthly sheaths, merging again with their Divine source. Their dead bodies were left, our Sages say, burned only within, not without. Yet their well-meant, if improper, self-sacrifice was not without its reward, for "the death of the righteous atones for Israel." When we learn from what the righteous lived for, and were willing to die for, we can indeed transform our lives and transcend our previous failures.

Although the custom of kindling small fires (yahrzeit candles) on the anniversary of someone's death is a well-known Jewish custom (based on Proverbs 20:27), the kindling of large fires at the death of the righteous also has a long history, one going back to Onkelos the Ger, the author of the Targum. The Jewish practice of burning articles of value at the funeral of Jewish kings, as a sign of respect, is mentioned in the Prophets (see Jeremiah 34:5); but Onkelos insisted on holding a similar hadlakah (burning), one valued at 70 Tyrian manahs, to honor the passing of R' Gamliel HaZaken (Avodah Zarah, 11a). He apparently based himself on the far-greater importance of a Torah leader, than a king, to the Jewish nation.

These themes — the death of the righteous, their yahrzeit, the power of their "fire" to affect our lives for the good, the hadlakah for kings—and much more besides are all intertwined in the ancient custom of celebrations around bonfires on Lag B'Omer. That day is the yahrzeit of R' Shimon Bar Yochai, the righteous author of the Zohar, the holy mystical text whose very name means "shining." For the last 500 years, great Jewish mystics, such as the Ari HaKodesh and the Ohr HaChaim HaKodesh, have made annual Lag B'Omer pilgrimages to the hadlakah in Meron, the burial place of R' Shimon. This tradition still draws huge crowds of modern Israelis of all levels of observance, as many as 250,000 a year, to the small town of Meron in the Galilee hills near Safed (Tzfas). The old Jewish community of Tiberias (Teveriah) also used to hold a special hadlakah on Lag B'Omer eve, at the tomb of R' Akiva, the righteous sage and teacher of R' Shimon. This tradition had lasted for many years until early in this century. Then it lapsed...until the Rebbe arrived.

ॐ *Amar Rabbi Akiva*

The universal custom in *Eretz Yisrael* is to light large bonfires on the eve of Lag B'Omer, the 33rd day of the seven weeks between the second day of Pesach (when a special *omer* of barley was offered in the Temple) and Shavuos. In our Har Nof neighborhood of Jerusalem, the local children begin gathering wood from nearby forests and empty lots weeks before, creating literally hundreds of tall pyres, 15 to 20 feet high. At nightfall, these *medurot* spring to life, as families visit one after another, sing "Bar Yochai" and enjoy the beauty of that holy night. Some of the more practical minded even throw foil-wrapped potatoes into the coals and have an impromptu evening cookout.

Whether mystical or merry or both, the Lag B'Omer bonfire is a uniquely Israeli tradition, one which my father brought with him to America. We, in turn, always observed it in spirit but, because of Boston's strict antifire laws, our "bonfire" was limited to a pan of burning olive oil with thick cloth wicks. Our *Chassidim* gathered around it in our *sukkah* and we all sang *Bar Yochai* with great gusto. The constant turning in all directions was not only an expression of our *hislahavus* (burning enthusiasm), it was also part of our effort to make sure that our enthusiasm was all that was burning.

The next morning the three-year-old children in our community came to *shul* for their first haircut *(upsherin)*, a beautiful ceremony remembered fondly by young and old alike. In *Eretz Yisrael* this ceremony is usually performed near the *tziun* (burial place) of a great *tzaddik*, especially that of R' Shimon Bar Yochai in Meron, where the bonfire custom originated.

Our first year after moving to *Eretz Yisrael*, we decided to go to the Galil with some of our *Chassidim* and spend Lag B'Omer in Teveriah (Tiberias), which also has an old Jewish community and many special burial sites. We were afraid that Meron would be too crowded and, since they already had an established set of important rabbinic visitors, that I might be intruding. To my surprise, however, after evening services in the local Chassidic *shul,* R' Avraham Auerbach,

The Rebbe was zocheh (privileged) to reestablish the old Israeli tradition of a Lag B'Omer bonfire (hadlakah) by the Tiberias tomb of R' Akiva, the teacher of R' Shimon bar Yochai. Here he lights a 20-foot-high pyre of wood, accompanied by the Rav of Tiberias.

Shlita, the Rav of Teveriah, lit his bonfire in a nearby empty lot. Why there and not by the tomb of one of Tiberias' great *tzaddikim*?

R' Mendel Brandwein, a cousin of mine, and one of the Elders of Teveriah, told me that things were not always this way. Back at the turn of the century the Jewish community of Teveriah, following an ancient tradition, had ventured far outside the old city limits to the tomb of R' Akiva, the great *Tanna* and teacher of R' Shimon Bar Yochai. Arab pogroms had made the trip too dangerous, however, and the custom had not been practiced since.

I decided on the spot that we would reestablish the old *minhag* of a *hadlakah* by the tomb of R' Akiva, which was now just beyond the edge of the much-expanded town.

We arrived to find the site silent, deserted and pitch black. I had the cars face each other and shine their headlights into the center. There we arranged the wood we had brought, while others searched the hillside for more. We lit the fire and danced around it singing *Bar Yochai* and *Amar Rabbi Akiva*, with all our might. We were very happy; the old tradition had been reestablished. The flame was small, but it would grow.

The next year we came well prepared, with trunkloads full of wood; and the city arranged a few makeshift lights. We used a chartered bus to ferry people from R' Auerbach's *shul* to the *tziun* and back, and a few curious locals dropped by. By the next year, the Tiberias Municipality had realized that the *hadlakah* by R' Akiva was a nice idea, and the local vendors quickly recognized its economic potential. The site was well lit by long strings of lights; and stalls selling ice cream and drinks lined the once-deserted way.

Year after year the crowds and preparation have grown. Now Lag B'Omer night by R' Akiva's *tziun* is a major attraction, with thousands of people and a huge roaring bonfire. We still light the fire and dance around it with our *Chassidim*, but a new custom has been added as well: a *peiros tish*, where we hand out apples from the stacks of crates provided by the municipality to the long lines of people celebrating this very special event.

The hadlakah in Tiberias is now a major municipal event, which ends with the Rebbe distributing apples to a crowd of thousands.

To accommodate the crowds, the municipality has now leveled the top of the hill to create a beautiful stone-paved plaza in front of the holy graves and a large flat area to accommodate the bonfire and visitors beyond. If you look carefully, you might even find a small plaque commemorating the reestablishment of this old custom on the dark, lonely night so many years ago.

I have been *zocheh* to do many special things in my long career, but few have ever given me as much satisfaction as restoring the ancient custom of the Lag B'Omer *hadlakah* at R' Akiva's tomb.

Vayikra ∞ 207

Kedoshim

You shall be holy,
Because I, Hashem your G–d, am Holy.
(Leviticus 19:2)

In Hebrew the word holy (kadosh) also has connotations of being separate and distinct from the ordinary (chol). A Jew is set apart from others by his speech, his clothes, his behavior and, most intimately and irrevocably, by the sign of circumcision on his body itself. First commanded by Hashem to Abraham (Genesis 17:9-14), this bris, literally "covenant," marks a Jew forever as a servant of Hashem, one sworn to (and capable of) the high standards of self-control the Torah demands. Since this bris is at the very root of the Jewish concept of holiness (kedushah), the circumcision is called "bris kodesh."

As in the days of Abraham, the bris is performed on the eighth day after an infant's birth. "Why is a bris needed?" asks the Sefer HaChinuch. Answer: to complete the human body and make it perfect. If so, why was man created incomplete, lacking this perfection? The Chinuch says that this is to remind us that just as the perfection of our bodies is within our power, so is the perfection of our souls.

With this background, one can readily see that entering the Holy Covenant of Abraham through a bris bears no relationship to a mechanical "minor surgical procedure" performed in a hospital. Unfortunately, 40 years ago, not everyone in Boston saw it that way.

❧ A Hospital Bris

Back in the '50s, *bris milahs* (circumcisions) in Boston were done in the hospital 95 percent of the time. In those days, women usually stayed in the hospital for nine to ten days to "regain their strength," so babies were rarely brought home before their *bris*.

Boston's hospitals would not let religiously trained circumcisers (*mohelim*) perform a *bris* on their premises. The only *"mohelim"* they allowed were two licensed doctors. They didn't exactly fit the image of a kindly *tzaddik* who, with great fervor, inducted one's son into the sacred Covenant of Abraham. In fact, one was married to a non-Jew and the other played golf on Yom Kippur afternoon! This was a big problem for religious Jews, and even for those Jews on the periphery, who wanted a "real" *bris* but were afraid to leave the hospital a day or two early. We had to work on a case-by-case basis, and every hospital *bris* we tried to arrange or avoid was a great, and not always successful, challenge.

Finally we heard that Boston's Beth Israel Hospital, a "Jewish" hospital funded by local Jewish philanthropists, had just opened a maternity ward. We also learned, through the grapevine, that they already had their first Jewish baby boy. His *bris* was only days away.

This called for immediate action. Precedent is very important in hospitals, and if Beth Israel had its first *bris* under the same unfortunate conditions as other Boston hospitals, we would have a hard time of it thereafter. With the help of various contacts, we arranged a meeting between myself, the Director of Beth Israel Hospital and R' Arnold Wieder, a highly qualified religious *mohel*. We explained that a Jewish hospital should surely provide an opportunity for parents to arrange a kosher *bris* with kosher *mohelim*, if that is what they wanted. Of course, a *mohel* would have to conform to the highest medical standards; however we objected to a hospital rejecting accomplished *mohelim* whose only "disqualification" was that they were not physicians. We also pointed out that Beth Israel Hospital would gain patients, if it was the only hospital in the Greater Boston area which let real *mohelim* perform an in-hospital *bris*.

The good doctor, an older gentlemen, was less than convinced by our arguments. We then tried a public relations tack ("How would it look, a Jewish hospital...") and finally, after a heated discussion ("We won't take this lying down!"), we convinced him to appoint a panel of doctors to examine Rabbi Wieder. Needless to say, Rabbi Wieder passed inspection easily, and was promptly placed on the hospital's official list of qualified circumcisers together, of course, with all the usual "candidates." They even put "rabbinically certified" by Rabbi Wieder's name; although they de-emphasized the fact by adding some other kind of "certified" by the other names.

Now that the *mohel* was arranged, we needed a baby! After some detective work, we found out how to contact the new parents. We wished them *mazel tov*, and told them what a great thing it was to have the first boy born in Beth Israel Hospital. Since their son's *bris* would be a great event for the whole Boston Jewish community, we wanted to make sure that it would be done properly, in the best possible way. We had already contacted Rabbi Wieder, the hospital's rabbinically certified *mohel*, who was also medically approved. He had agreed that this first *bris* was going to be "on the house," at no charge to the parents.

They couldn't easily refuse an offer like that, since a *bris* usually cost $50-$100, quite a sum in those days. Later, Rabbi Wieder also spoke with them, and told them how honored he was. Then he mentioned that, since the Bostoner Rebbe would be attending the *bris* as a representative of the community, it might be nice to offer him the honor of being *sandek* (the one who holds the baby on his lap while the *bris* is performed). They were more than agreeable; and the *bris* went off without a hitch, completely kosher. The honor of being the first *sandek* at a Beth Israel Hospital *bris* was, perhaps, part of our reward — that and the fact that hundreds of other kosher *brissim* followed.

Do not make gashes in your skin for the dead...
Keep My Sabbaths, and revere My Sanctuary,
I am Hashem. Do not turn
To those who speak to the dead.
(Leviticus 19:28, 30-31)

Respect for parents and the deceased have long been hallmarks of Jewish family life. Thus a son publicly says the Kaddish prayer several times a day during the year (actually 11 months) following a parent's departure. By sanctifying the Divine Name, he shows that the Torah ideals that the deceased stood for continue on. Still, Judaism has always been life-, not death-oriented. As this week's parshah states, overemphasis on death and over-demonstrative mourning practices are to be avoided. Instead, a Jew's emphasis should be on constructive, life-affirming observances, such as keeping Shabbos, learning Torah and praying with the congregation in shul (our current equivalent of the Sanctuary).

Still, especially during the '30s, '40s and '50s, the only Jewish observance many Jews kept religiously — often their only contact with a shul — was the recital of Kaddish for their deceased parents. As for Shabbos, it was sort of a...

❧ *Shabbos Shivah*

It was a long summer Shabbos afternoon in Dorchester, and I was giving a *shiur* (class) in *Pirkei Avos* to some of the elderly men who gathered in *shul*. In the middle of the *shiur*, a young man dressed in work clothes entered and asked, "Can I ask the rabbi a question?" Even if a Jew is not dressed for *Shabbos* and even if he interrupts a *shiur*, he is still someone who needs an answer, so I told him, "Ask."

He had just lost a parent a few days before, and he was still in the middle of sitting *shivah*. Just before Shabbos, however, someone had explained to him that on Shabbos you don't sit *shivah*, since mourning is inconsistent with Shabbos joy. Was that right?

"Yes, that's true. On Shabbos you don't sit *shivah*."

"Well, then," he naively asked, "can I go in to my Saturday job as usual?"

The innocence of the question, asked without hesitation in front of so many people, was heartbreaking. *Shivah* he had heard of, but he hadn't the vaguest idea what Shabbos was all about. He typified an entire generation of lost American Jews. Their next generation, unfortunately, didn't even know what *shivah* was all about.

Emor

A woman divorced by her husband
[A kohen] may not marry,
For he is set aside to his G–d.
And you shall sanctify him.
(Leviticus 21:7,8)

Even against his will, for if he doesn't want
To divorce [his forbidden wife, the court] beats him
And punishes him until he divorces her.
(Rashi)

A Jewish marriage is a very serious thing, and it can only be terminated by the husband giving the wife a properly written "get" (bill of divorce, see Deuteronomy 24:1-3). Until a get is issued, the couple is still married under Torah law, even if they obtain a hundred civil divorces. Worse, any attempted "marriage" by the wife to another man without first having been issued a get would have the halachic status of adultery, a serious crime. It is to the offspring of such an illicit union, or of an incestuous union, that the Torah applies the term "mamzer." This is a terrible tragedy, for a mamzer can never marry a full member of the Jewish community, and his or her disability is transmitted forever to any offspring. While a "forced get" is invalid, rabbis do not hesitate to use the strongest measures allowed by Jewish law to ensure that recalcitrant husbands promptly give their wives a get, when a rabbinic court requires it.

In these days, when families are fragmented, populations are mobile, ignorance is rife and Jewish observance is often haphazard, the problem of assuring a proper Jewish divorce looms tragically large on any rabbi's agenda. The Rebbe has certainly seen his share of such cases, but some situations take even him by surprise.

❦ Undone in Dorchester

One morning a man came to the Chassidic Center with his *kallah*-to-be. He introduced himself as Mr. A., the son of a man we knew from a certain *shul*, and then he stated his case: "I have a little problem. I want to remarry, but you know how *frum* my father is. He insists that I must first give a *get* to my previous wife, before I marry again."

This requirement is very real. Although under Biblical law a man can have many wives, a ban by Rabbeinu Gershom, *Meor HaGolah* (c. 960-1028), forbade Jewish men in Ashkenazic countries from being married to more than one woman at a time. Rabbeinu Gershom also forbade divorcing a woman against her will.

"Is your first wife willing to accept a *get* from you?"

"How should I know, Rebbe? We split over 12 years ago!"

"Still, in order to proceed, we need your first wife's consent."

"That's a real problem. She was adamant; she refused to accept a *get*."

"Well, in that case, you are in trouble. We need both parties to agree."

"Please, isn't there any condition that could make it possible?"

"Well, yes, there is; but I don't know if it would apply to your situation. What happened to your first wife after your civil divorce? Did she remarry?"

"Yes, yes, she did. Why?"

"Well, if she remarried, she is actually an adulteress, and you are *forced* by Torah law to divorce her. Then you don't need her consent. Can you go to the Registrar's Office and get a copy of the marriage certificate for her second marriage?"

"Of course, I will bring it straight to you."

"Fine, but still, before we give a divorce by default, we usually call the other party and ask them once again to accept the divorce."

"Aw, forget it. Don't call her, she won't come. It's a waste of time."

"Still, I must call her."

"No, don't call her. I'll get you the papers."

"Still...."

"O.K. I'll write down the number for you, but it's a waste of time."

After he left, I picked up the telephone and called his ex-wife. As usual, I tried to explain things in a way that helped both sides.

"Mrs. X, this is the Bostoner Rebbe calling. Your former husband came to see us recently, and he wants to arrange to give you a proper Jewish divorce. He mentioned that you previously didn't want to accept it; but it really would be to your own advantage to do so. Besides, since you remarried, he is really entitled to give you a *get* by default."

"But my second husband has already died."

"Even so, that wouldn't change anything. Remarrying without a Jewish divorce is in itself grounds for allowing a husband to give a *get* by default and, in any case, you yourself would benefit by having an official *get*. In that case you could marry again."

"No, I have had enough. I am not going to marry again."

"That is quite unfortunate. Still, we wouldn't want this to benefit only him and not you. We will notify you when we get together to issue the *get*."

"Wait a minute. Are you going through all this just because I remarried? What about him? He remarried too!"

Well, that was news! Still, I had to tell her, "That's a surprise, all right; but legally he can still issue his divorce by default."

"Well," she said, "you seem to be a reasonable person, and I like the way you talk. So, just because of you, I am going to come and pick up that divorce."

I was glad to have been successful with one party, but now I had to find out about his remarriage.

When our two-time husband came in the next day with his papers, I asked him to sit down. "Listen, Mr. A., you said that your first wife remarried. That's just awful; but what about you?"

Vayikra ❦ 215

"Uh, me? I didn't remarry."

"Well, your first wife says that you did, that you lived in Hartford, and...."

"Oh, that. That wasn't a real marriage."

"But she said that it lasted for some time...."

After some argument back and forth, he said, "Excuse me a minute; I would like to make a telephone call." He went out into the hall and, the next thing we knew, he was talking to his lawyer! After finishing his consultation, he returned and sat down.

"You know," he said, "it was only a civil marriage; and it was ended with a civil divorce."

"So what? Civil marriage or no civil marriage, you lived with that woman publicly as your wife. You have to give her a Jewish divorce."

"Well, you said that if the woman remarries without a *get*, I can give her a divorce by default. So, fine — my second wife also remarried!"

"*Gevalt!*" I thought, "This is a fine kettle of fish!"

Still, there was nothing else to do but go on with it.

"Sorry," I told him. "We still have to talk to her and ask her to accept a *get*."

"Rebbe, she won't listen. It's a waste of time..."

"Maybe, but we still have to try and get all the facts."

"I don't know. The first one's husband is dead; this one's husband is still alive. In fact, they live right around the corner from here. I wouldn't risk it if I were you."

I called anyway, with the same story: "Mrs. Y., this is the Bostoner Rebbe.... given that you have remarried, a proper Jewish divorce is critical for you and your future children..." There was a slight pause, and then a deep man's voice came on the line. He said a whole lot of uncomplimentary things, ending with a firm, "Mind your own business!" and a sudden bang as he slammed down the telephone receiver.

Insults or not, one has to do what one can. We asked our marriage-prone visitor for another set of marriage certificates, this time for his second wife. Once all the documents were in hand, I called up the Boston *bais din* and told them to get ready for a case one doesn't see too often these days — in fact, not since the time of Rabbeinu Gershom 1,000 years ago — a man divorcing two of his wives on the same day!"

Why didn't this three-time *chassan* want to mention his second marriage? He had to show his poor old father, and the unsuspecting poor old rabbi handling marriage number three, that he had a proper Jewish divorce. That meant that he needed a document from the *bais din* saying that he had divorced his first wife. However, after he presented his first *get*, no one would ever think to look for a second one. *Gittin* are complicated documents that can cost a lot of money; and this fellow was apparently just trying to save the expense! Hashem was very good to us — and to the rabbi officiating at the third wedding — by making sure that we didn't fall into that fellow's trap.

As for the first wife, the one who "spilled the beans," she never showed up after all. Still, I did what I could for all of them, preventing any further halachic problems from their previous marriages. It is all a sad commentary on the lack of a serious approach to Jewish marriage and divorce in our times.

Behar

And if your brother becomes poor,
And his hand fails among you,
Then you shall strengthen him.
(Leviticus 25:35)

The concept of charity is central to all Jewish ethical behavior. It is a broad, encompassing concept which can include giving money (tzedakah), help, words of encouragement or even the benefit of the doubt (dan l'chaf zechus). As a mitzvah, a Divine Command, it transcends the spontaneous emotions of compassion to become a religious act, subject like any other mitzvah to the external demands of halachah. If it is Hashem's mitzvah, then Hashem, not man, defines its priorities.

One such ranking focuses on how carefully the donor preserves the self-respect of the recipient: where neither knows the other, only one knows, or both know. Another halachic ranking system focuses on the donor's proximity and implied responsibility: his own family, his own city, state, country. Elsewhere, priority is given to the cases of most extreme need, the highest of all priorities going to pidyon shevuyim (the freeing of captives), unfortunately an all-too-real need during many centuries of victimization.

Of course, every Jew, no matter how lowly, deserves help in getting back on his feet, and in interpreting his failings in the most positive light. It is, however, not always easy to give such aid. Sometimes the recipient's cause seems so unworthy that it takes a religious genius, on the highest spiritual plane, to see through the obscuring dust to the faltering soul inside. Such a religious genius was ....

❦ Rav Kalmanowitz

Rav Avraham Kalmanowitz, the legendary head of the Mirrer Yeshivah during its escape from Europe through Shanghai to America, came to Boston in the early 1950s to perform the *mitzvah* of *pidyon shevuyim*. A poor immigrant rabbi, a very fine and giving person, had once yielded to temptation and had tried to smuggle valuables out of the country. He was caught in Boston and the judge, once he found out that he had a clergyman on his hands, asked his friend, a local Reform rabbi, what to do with him. The Reform rabbi, perhaps more embarrassed than compassionate, said, "Throw the book at him!" and the judge gave him a lengthy sentence at a local penitentiary.

Rav Kalmanowitz certainly did not condone this man's actions and the *chillul Hashem* they caused; but he could not bear to let a fellow religious Jew sit for years on end among common criminals. He called me and insisted that we visit the judge's friend together, even though that meant going into a Reform temple. There our host treated the Mirrer *Rosh Yeshivah* and myself to descriptions of the great level of religiosity in his "temple." They wore *tallaisim* without *yarmulkes*, whereas a rival Reform congregation wore *yarmulkes* without *tallaisim*, and *tallaisim* are more important! Rav Kalmanowitz sat through this nonsense without flinching, and his host finally agreed to help.

Next, we arranged an appointment with the judge in his chambers. Given that we were representing a convicted smuggler, I couldn't imagine what kind of "defense" Rav Kalmanowitz could offer; but he met the issue simply and head on.

He drew himself up to his full, imposing height, with his long white beard flowing from his majestic face, and told the judge, "Your Honor, the facts you know; but you also have to know why this man did what he did. He lived in Austria. When the Nazis arrived during the *Anschluss,* he was one of the Jews they bullied and degraded, making him clean the public streets. He tried to escape. This meant smuggling himself through one hostile border after another. To him, smuggling meant survival. To him, smuggling, since it saved his life, didn't seem much of a crime."

Rav Avraham Kalmanowitz, head of the Mirrer Yeshivah during its historic escape from Europe, via Shanghai, to America

The judge was impressed by this line of argument and, after an appropriate interval, the prisoner's sentence was indeed reduced. That was the length to which Rav Kalmanowitz would go to help a fellow Jew. It also gives us some inkling of the lengths to which Hashem, Who is All-Compassionate, goes to have mercy on us for our failings.

⚘

As a stranger and a settler
He shall live with you.
(Leviticus 25:35)

*M**aking the poor comfortable in your home, maintaining their dignity and self-respect, is an important, if difficult, mitzvah. The Rebbe's family always ran an open house, in which they hosted a continuous stream of meshulachim (traveling charity collectors) and others. The Rebbe, like his father, always tried his best to make their "drop-in" guests feel at home; but only in the late 1950s did he learn how well he had succeeded.*

❦ *At Home, Away From Home*

*T*hroughout the 1950s we lived in a big, rambling four-story house in Dorchester. The *shul* was on the ground floor, the *mikveh* in the basement, and our room and a variety of guest rooms were upstairs. We basically had an "open door" policy. This meant that religious travelers and guests who needed temporary lodgings and strictly kosher food were welcome to just show up and see if there was room for them. In short, our house was usually full to overflowing. This was true even during the summer months, when we spent our days and weekends in Nantasket, a seaside resort near Boston.

Our summer schedule was somewhat unusual. Every weekday evening we drove back to Dorchester to spend the night! That was the only way we could *daven* with a *minyan* early the next morning, since there was no daily *minyan* in Nantasket. Usually we came in quite late, 11-11:30 at night, so we could take advantage of the sea air until the very last minute.

One fine summer evening, as we pulled up to our Dorchester home, we saw a *meshulach* on our front porch, enjoying the cool night air. He was slowly pacing the porch back and forth, back and forth, with the easy self-confidence of a man very much at home. One would never have guessed that he was one of our self-invited guests, who had arrived while we were out and had made himself welcome. We felt good that others, whom we had never met, could feel so at ease in our house, and could derive such benefit and satisfaction from what we had to share.

As we walked up the path to the porch, he calmly stopped his pacing and gave us a kindly "*Shalom Aleichem.*" It was just as if he were the master of the house, welcoming unexpected, but not unwelcome, guests.

"Nice evening, isn't it?" he said. "Where are you from?"

And then .... "Who are *you* collecting for?"

❦

Proclaim freedom to the land...
And return every man to his inheritance.
(Leviticus 25:10)

Freedom in the non-Jewish world is largely the dropping of restraints, a freedom "from." Freedom in the Torah world is an enabling force, a freedom "to." The most basic freedom of the Yovel year is returning to one's inheritance (family fields).

The Torah is called our inheritance, Morashah Kehilas Yaakov, the Inheritance of the Congregation of Jacob; and we must learn to see our "free time" as a freedom to learn, not a freedom from learning. That was one of the driving forces behind Camp Mesivta, another pioneering effort on the part of R' Shraga Feivel Mendlowitz, the saintly founder of Yeshivah Torah Vodaath. There, behar (literally: in the mountains), the Rebbe learned many unanticipated lessons, including one which, years later, returned yet another Jew "to his inheritance."

❧ The Home Run

Towards the end of our first year at Mesivta Torah Vodaath, R' Shraga Feivel Mendlowitz, invited our class to go to Camp Mesivta, a *yeshivah*-oriented summer camp he had started in the Catskill Mountains of New York State. This was a radically new idea in those days, and most of us had no idea what the experience entailed. The camp had actually opened on a smaller scale one or two years before, but ours was the first year of full-scale, fully organized operation.

There we learned to cope with a whole new series of challenges, including how to stay on the good side of Mrs. Lock, the devoted head of the camp's kitchen. She was very helpful in meeting the special needs of some boys for *glatt* meat and *cholov Yisrael* milk, both now standard but then often considered a far-out *chumrah* (religious stringency). We boys used to take turns going out to a farm and help-

In the early years, Camp Mesivta was something new on the American scene. Here the Rebbe (L) accompanies his teacher R' Shlomo Heiman, Rosh Yeshivah of Torah Vodaath.

ing bring back big cans of milk clearly labeled PM, our code word for "private milk." This was poured into PM pitchers for those who needed it.

Shabbos came and the camp *ruach* (spirit) was something very special. But here too, things took some arranging. Although we had fish with our Shabbos evening and morning meals, at *Shalosh Seudos* on Shabbos we found ourselves fishless. *Chassidim* are particular to have fish at all three meals; but we obviously couldn't just go out fishing! Help came in the form of a special young man, a "newcomer" from Vienna, who had escaped with his parents just before the *Anschluss*. He ran back to his bunk and soon returned with a small can of sardines his mother had given him for just such emergencies.

We were all excited. All eight or ten of us gathered around while he carefully cut each sardine into pieces (the can was *very* small, as were the sardines). It reminded us of the way the *Kohanim* divided the *Lechem HaPanim* (Showbread) in the Temple on Shabbos afternoon, each getting only a bean-sized bite — but our *minhag* was intact. This very special young man, R' Yaakov Thumim, later became the Altstedter Rav of Brooklyn, and the husband of my sister Faigie.

Unlike some modern American camps, Camp Mesivta usually had comparatively little time for sports. There were, however, some notable exceptions, one of which was particularly memorable.

One day the administration announced, "Today we are going to play baseball." Not having the vaguest idea what this was all about, I decided to just watch quietly from the sidelines. Unfortunately the teams were exactly one man short; and soon I was surrounded by eager classmates.

"Come on, we need you."

"But I don't know how to play."

"Don't worry, you'll learn fast."

I soon found myself in the outfield waiting for a ball to catch. It soon occurred to me, however, that once hit, baseballs travel at great velocity, are quite hard and could cause considerable pain to a young, inexperienced *yeshivah bachur* without a mitt. So my first and only baseball game passed more in a state of high anxiety than fun. I couldn't help but wonder, "What did I need this for?" Later I found out.

Thirteen or so years passed and we were spending the summer in Nantasket, a beach resort near Boston. One day the non-religious son-in-law of a *Chassid* of ours offered me a ride into town. I hadn't really spoken to him before, and my attempts at conversation during the ride were painful failures. We simply had nothing in common to talk about. Finally I gave up trying to reach him and our non-conversation lapsed into complete silence. Then he turned on his car radio to listen to ... the Sunday baseball game.

A few minutes went by and then I commented on a play. His mouth dropped open. It was as if the steering wheel had suddenly started speaking. He couldn't believe that a Chassidic Rebbe in *Chassidic* garb could know anything about baseball. So we talked baseball most of the way to Boston, and soon began to talk about other subjects as well. He started coming by, became religious and eventually became a *Chassid* of ours.

In fact, he later became an important local Jewish leader, both within the New England Chassidic Center and within the broader Boston Jewish community. Then I understood how one can make *neshamos* even with baseball: A home run can become a run home.

Bechukosai

*But the firstling, the first born to Hashem
Among [your] cattle...belongs to Hashem.
(Leviticus 27:26)*

*Do not work with your firstborn ox;
And do not shear your firstborn sheep.
(Deuteronomy 15:19)*

The Torah has special rules that apply to a bechor, a firstborn male, whether human (bechor adam) or cattle (bechor beheimah). Both categories still apply with full force today. A bechor adam is "redeemed" for five shekels of silver at a special pidyon haben ceremony. This is a big simchah, a festive occasion for the whole family. That is hardly the case with a bechor beheimah. Once born, a bechor animal cannot be worked or sold. Instead, it must be kept until it can be offered as a sacrifice in the Bais HaMikdash, the Holy Temple in Jerusalem. This is rather difficult, just now, since we temporarily don't have a Bais HaMikdash and we won't until Mashiach comes (speedily in our days!).

Meanwhile, however, the laws of bechor still apply. Thus a firstborn animal must be fed and maintained, while it continues to grow bigger and bigger for a decade or more, a substantial loss for its owner. That being the case, religious Jewish cattle dealers — and these are a rare breed themselves — take all kinds of precautions to avoid being caught with a *bechor.* There are plenty of loopholes but, as you'll see, no system is foolproof. Then, come what may, a Jew must do what's right.

The *bechor* of the following story belonged to the Maels, a fine family who lived in Millis, Massachusetts. Mr. Joseph Mael, the patriarch of the family, had been a Chassid of R' Pinchas Dovid, the Rebbe's father; and he later became one of the present Bostoner Rebbe's closest followers.

❧ The Bechor

In their many years of cattle-raising, the Maels never once got caught with a *bechor.* They always checked whether a calf they were buying was a firstborn, and whether a cow they were buying had already given birth. They sold their own cows with first-time pregnancies to non-Jews, who would have no particular responsibilities towards a *bechor.* Everything was fine until once, after one of their new cows had already given birth to a little calf, they found out that the new arrival was, in fact, a *bechor.*

That meant they were stuck. About all they could do was wait for the *Bais HaMikdash* to be rebuilt. Meanwhile, they would have to give this calf silk-glove treatment. There was only one other way out. They could hope that one fine day their precious charge would develop a *mum* (blemish). If a *bechor* loses a limb, or even has a permanently split ear or lip, he can no longer be sacrificed on the Altar, and all the special restrictions vanish. Until that happened, our friends were in trouble.

Now if a calf is eating and not working, and if it spends all its time safely dozing in the barn, there is scant chance that it is ever going to get a *mum.* Instead, it is going to grow by leaps and bounds into a very big bull, one who eats even more, and grows even bigger. Soon it is going to be an extra big, one-of-a-kind bull, the kind no farmer in his right mind is going to want to be anywhere near!

In the Maels' case, there was only one realistic hope, short of the bull's being hit by lightning, and that was the official Massachusetts State Medical Examiner. Every year he came around to inspect every bull and, at the end of his inspection, he affixed a numbered tag to each bull's ear. Now, although we couldn't tell this to the examiner, if the hole he made in the bull's ear went through the ear's cartilage, that would constitute a *mum* and the *bechor* bull's protected days would be over.

That first year the calf became a bull, albeit not the world's biggest bull. After the State Medical Examiner conducted his yearly inspection, Mr. Mael asked me to come out to Millis to determine if his bull had a valid *mum*. I told him that nowadays no individual rabbi can examine a *bechor* by himself; instead, we would have to organize a *bais din* of three rabbis.

Of course, in the ordinary course of its deliberations, a Boston *bais din* has very few opportunities to head off to the countryside and check on the *bechor* status of bulls. So it was with some excitement that Rabbi Abraham Rose, a fine, elderly *talmid chacham* and a close personal friend, another rabbi and I drove the 30 miles or so out to Millis. At the farm, sure enough, we found a corral with the untouchable little bull. Only he didn't seem all that little when we approached to examine his ear.

As we crossed the corral, we kept glancing back at Mr. Mael, who stood safely on the other side of the fence, for reassurance. Actually there wasn't really all that much he could have done for us if the bull had decided to act wild; but it made us feel somewhat better. The closer we got, the less safe we felt; and the more often we glanced back. Once within goring range, we had to approach one at a time to make our check. Courteous as always, we gladly yielded to Rabbi Rose, the elder rabbi, the distinct honor of being the first member of our *bais din* to approach. In fact, we deferred to him without the slightest twinge of regret or hesitation! He slowly approached the bull, checked the ear and slowly headed back.

The verdict? No luck! The examiner's hole had missed the cartilage by a half-inch or so, and only went through the soft part of the ear. Looking into the face of Mr. Mael, we saw that this was not good news. It would be another year before the examiner returned. Meanwhile, there was both the expense of the feed, and the problem of controlling an increasingly large, dangerous farm animal. From Mr. Mael's description, we had visions of a huge monster bull breaking right through the door of his barn and walking off with it. We thus looked forward to our next visit with more than a little anxiety.

Another year went by. The Massachusetts State Medical Examiner returned; but this time he was also worried about this menacing oversized bull, who was being raised for no apparent purpose. As soon as the examiner left, Mr. Mael picked up his telephone, and soon the Boston *bais din's Bechor* Inspection Team was once again headed for Millis.

As we walked back towards the corral where the bull was located we saw this huge...well, we felt a lot differently than we had the year before! The three of us were soon facing a truly tremendous bull, a towering hulk who looked capable of almost anything. Stories of bulls goring, trampling and otherwise annihilating unwary humans raced through our minds. Then a chilling thought: We not only had to get

Mr. Mael lived to be over 100 years old. Here he holds matzos freshly baked in the Rebbe's Dorchester matzah oven in the late 1950s, surrounded by (L to R) the Rebbe, then 38 years old, R' Pinchas, R' Naftali (below), Nathan Friedman (the baker), R' Mayer and Mr. Singer.

in there with this bull, and go all the way over to him, we couldn't just say, "Hi!" and run back. We somehow had to get him to stand still while we held and carefully inspected his ear! Unfortunately, this cannot be done from 60-80 feet away.

I can't recall if Rabbi Rose's face changed color; but we all gallantly insisted once again that the first honor was his. Fortunately we could not see our own faces. In fact, about all any of us could see was this monstrous bull, that no one else on the farm dared get near. He seemed to be waiting for us.

Finally, we inched forward, closer and closer. Rabbi Rose made it there first, made his check and soon began inching back. He nodded affirmatively. This time the hole seemed to pierce the cartilage!

Then it was our turn. We slowly inched forward, felt the ear between our fingers and heartily agreed. The third rabbi did so as well. We now had only one question left — how to get away as quickly as we could before anything disastrous could happen.

We stepped back — well, maybe that was an understatement, since we soon found ourselves 30-40 feet away — and then we were happy, very happy, in fact overjoyed. If there was a special *Shehecheyanu* (a blessing for joyous events) for safely completing a *bechor* inspection, we would gladly have said it.

Mr. Mael was overjoyed as well, and soon the hulking bull was in a truck *en route* to market. Everyone breathed easier. It does show, however, the lengths to which one must go to observe all of Torah Law, even today; and maybe that's enough reason to justify the whole story of the Bull of Millis.

Mr. Mael himself lived to be 100 years old. He lived to see his children become *talmidei chachamim* and Jews of distinction; and they too lived into their 90s. The third and fourth generation are, *Baruch Hashem*, following in their parents' footsteps. Such is the power of *mesiras nefesh* for *mitzvos*.

Bamidbar
The Book Of Numbers

In Full Production

The Book of Bamidbar bustles with activity. First, there is a census of the entire Jewish nation and all 603,550 adult males are assigned to their appropriate families, tribes and positions around the Mishkan (portable Sanctuary). Specialists are created: The Tribe of Levi is separated, exchanged for the firstborn of each tribe, and each Levitical family is assigned its special task. The Mishkan is erected, and the princes of the Tribes each bring their offerings. Rebellions against authority are met and overcome and, after the ensuing punishments, all 601,730 Israelites are counted again. There are meticulous accounts of the annual holiday offerings in the Sanctuary. There are wars and detailed lists of the spoils and the 42 stops and way-stations Israel passed during its 40 years of wandering. It was in this busy factory of the spirit that the Jewish people was forged and came into the full possession of its powers.

Bamidbar begins in the second year of the Exodus in the Sinai Desert and ends in the 40th year. Despite the space *lavished on the first two years and on the last, almost nothing is recorded or known about the intervening 37 years of wandering. It is almost as if the Torah doesn't have words to waste on such trivialities. Yet the Torah uses 72 verses (Numbers 7:12-83 — repeating the same 68 words again and again (except for names) — to record the seemingly identical offerings of the princes of each of the Twelve Tribes: "A silver dish, 130 shekels in weight, a silver basin of 70 ..." Why not just lump them all together, or say, "And he gave the same." A single "extra" letter in the Torah, a vav or a hei, can form the basis of a complete drashah and imply important new laws. What can the Torah mean by the thousands of "extra" letters used here, in seemingly useless repetition?*

Perhaps that's the point. People are not the same, and what they can offer of themselves and their lives is not the same. The dish offered by Nachshon may have superficially looked like the dish offered by Nesanel, but each gift represented completely different things to the donor and his tribe. Just as each and every one of the 603,550 men counted in the desert had his own special place in the camp, centered around the Mishkan, so too every Jew has his own task in this world, one which no one else can accomplish. We may superficially seem the same but, in truth, we can each contribute something unique. Bamidbar teaches full production, not mass production.

For the Rebbe, the 1960s were also busy years of full production. After his move to Brookline and "discovery" by a searching generation of college students, literally thousands of students and baalei teshuvah came to the Shabbatons, classes, services and other events at Boston's New England Chassidic Center. But there too, the Rebbe insisted on treating each person as an individual, as unique, as "family." Perhaps that's why he succeeded where others failed.

Bamidbar

And Hashem spoke to Moshe saying...
When the Mishkan is to travel,
The Leviim shall take it down,
And when it is to be pitched,
The Leviim shall set it up.
(Numbers 1:48,51)

The Mishkan and the camp moved from place to place in the desert (bamidbar), departing when the Divine Cloud went up, resting when the Cloud stopped. They stayed for only a few days at some places, and at Kadesh Barnea they encamped for almost 38 years. At each stage of the journey the Leviim (Levites) were responsible for transporting the pieces of the Mishkan and setting it up to function as the spiritual center for the Jewish people. Each stage was a step upward towards their ultimate goal — Eretz Yisrael, a holy land for a holy people.

Wherever it camped, whatever its external circumstances, the Jewish community retained its internal structure. The Torah, represented by the Two Tablets of Stone in the Ark, were in the center, surrounded by the Mishkan. This was, in turn, surrounded by the Leviim who were surrounded by the rest of the nation, grouped into encampments (degalim) and tribes. Thus, all eyes faced inward towards the Torah, the center of our people in that era of wandering and in every wandering thereafter. The externals change; the internals remain. People still are born and still die —

now as then. There are still men and women, meetings and marriages, and children to raise. We still eat and breathe, get sick and, hopefully, recover. Not much has changed over the ages. Dress, transportation, appliances? Nothing that ultimately matters.

This is true of our individual lives as well. We grow and, especially in America, we move as we continue to pursue our various goals. On this journey too we must carry our Mishkan with us to maintain our Torah-directed home-camp intact, despite external change.

The Rebbe's father grew up in the Holy City of Jerusalem, his home for 37 years. Then he moved to New York, to Boston, back to Jerusalem, back to Boston and finally back to New York. Yet few men have been less changed by their external circumstances. The Rebbe also had his share of moves: from Boston's West End to Eretz Yisrael, back to Boston, to New York and then to Dorchester. The disintegration of the Dorchester Jewish community, under the pressure of the changing neighborhood, seemed to be the painful end of so much that the Rebbe and Rebbetzin had struggled to build over the previous 17 years. Yet their move to Brookline at the beginning of the turbulent '60s marked a new beginning, an expanding circle of baalei teshuvah and communal service.

ॐ *Boston Comes to Brookline*

*I*n the early 1950s Dorchester and Roxbury, Boston's largest "Jewish neighborhoods," began their rapid decline. Blacks moved in and the Jews moved out, taking their communal institutions with them. The Hebrew Teachers' College left Dorchester in 1953; and most of the big Conservative temples left a year or two later. Most of our friends and congregants moved to Brookline, a refined upscale neighborhood that was closer to the city center. Once home to many of Boston's finest families, Brookline's streets are still lined with elegant old townhouses and fine old trees.

The Rebbe recites Birkas HaChamah (the blessing over the sun) outside the current New England Chassidic Center at 1710 Beacon Street in Brookline, Massachusetts. The frieze of the Kosel Ma'aravi (Western Wall) is made from stones specially imported from Jerusalem.

This exodus increasingly left us with black Baptist neighbors who, while not threatening, had no particular interest in forming a *minyan*, and couldn't have helped us if they had tried. It was sad to contemplate leaving. Every inch of progress — the *mikveh*, the *shul* — had cost so much effort and was so full of memories. Still, after eight more years of holding on, there really was no other option. The Cloud had gone up and, in 1961, the New England Chassidic Center followed it to Brookline. It was, in retrospect, *hashgachah*, a gentle "nudge" from Divine Providence.

The Chassidic Center's new location was a large four-story townhouse on Beacon Street, Brookline's tree-lined main thoroughfare, and 34 years later, it is still there. The fine old oaks are older, as are we, but the college students, quite different now than in the tempestuous '60s, still come.

Harvard, M.I.T., Boston University, Brandeis — Boston is culturally a large college town, with some 150,000 college students, of whom about a quarter are Jewish. They are a transient, searching community, with a rapid turnover of both populations and ideas. When, in the early 1960's, a few students wanted to learn with us during the evenings, they rented rooms upstairs so they could stay nearby. This helped everyone, since student apartments are very hard to find in Boston and, as relative newcomers, the Chassidic Center needed help in making a *minyan*. Soon their friends began dropping by, and then their friends.

Our house was soon chock full of student guests every Shabbos; and the overflow had to be farmed out to nearby families. The Shabbos atmosphere and Boston's personal approach — we treated every student guest as "family" — began having its effect, and we soon found ourselves at the center of an active student-oriented, and partially student-run, *baal teshuvah* movement. The weekends became "Boston Shabbatons," with communal suppers, speakers and programs for 50-100 students at a time. Still, we tried to find time to talk to each student privately, either before *Kiddush* or after a meal. It wasn't easy remembering 1,000 or so new names and faces a year; but we managed.

The students' problems, doubts and needs were superficially quite different from what a Chassidic Rebbe is used to but, on a deeper level, they were much the same. We found a special openness, honesty and rapport, and tried to help them all. *Baruch Hashem*, many became "regulars," sincere *baalei teshuvah* and close friends. They are now raising lovely religious families and a whole new generation of "Bostoners" from Israel to Switzerland to Australia.

The Bostoner college calendar was a full one. Not only were there weekly Shabbatons, there were also all the holidays of the Jewish year. A particular favorite of the college community was Purim, not only because of the partying and outrageous costumes that are allowed, if not actively encouraged, but also because they could conveniently ride *en masse* to Brookline (on most major Jewish holidays, work and riding are forbidden).

During our first year in Brookline, a group of our college student friends got together and announced that they wanted to organize a "real" Purim celebration, complete with skits, music and *grammen* (witty improvised songs). That first year several hundred college students packed our *shul* on Beacon Street for the festivities. This obviously couldn't continue, so the next year the Chassidic Center rented the cafeteria of Brookline's largest public high school, put together a live band and catered full *glatt* kosher meals for the 600-700 people who came. The students even reestablished the old custom of having a Purim Rav, a sharp-witted Rabbi-for-a-Day, who mercilessly mimicked the community's notables and everyone else in sight. The highlight of his performance was his *drashah,* a spoof on all the local and national problems of the day, liberally sprinkled with outrageous puns, quotes and (especially) misquotes from Jewish sources.

The annual Bostoner Purim *seudah* quickly became a popular Brookline tradition; one year the *Boston Advocate,* the local Jewish newspaper, ran a banner headline "Rebbe and Purim Come to Brookline High!" It was a great way to reach out to marginally committed people, especially during Jewish Boston's crucial "growing years." Later, *Baruch Hashem,* the increasingly established members of our community became more religiously sophisticated; and many people who used to come to our communal *seudah* began saying,

Here, suitably attired as Purim Rav, R' Meir Wikler enlivens the proceedings at the annual Boston Purim tish (circa 1980). Nowadays, the tradition continues, although the Rebbe himself usually spends Purim with his community in Har Nof.

"Why don't we have a Purim *seudah* of our own!?"

The singing and dancing at the New England Chassidic Center on Simchas Torah was even more popular, with several thousand adults and students coming and going and filling the nearby streets. This is still a local tradition, providing a good public demonstration of the Chassidic emphasis on serving Hashem with joy and the lasting impact such joy can have on one's life.

Another "open house" activity was *matzah*-baking before Pesach. The professional wood-fired baker's oven in our basement was especially designed for the occasion. Now a common pre-Pesach outing, our public *matzah*-baking was unique in its time. Thousands of children came in large buses from all over New England just to watch our community bake *matzos*. We sang, explained things and taught the children how to bake *matzos*. It all made quite an impression.

One year a woman came over and introduced me to her 10-year-old daughter. "I'm here," she said proudly, "because 20 years ago, when I was a little girl, my mother brought me here to see the *matzah* baking. Now I want my daughter to see it, too." Another young woman came and was so impressed by what she saw — how personally involved everyone was, not wasting a moment lest the dough's potential be lost — that she asked if she could spend the next Shabbos with us. In fact, she is now spending the rest of her life "with us" as an observant Jewess. Enthusiasm for *mitzvos*, with joy and without apology, is definitely contagious.

❧ Anything but ...

One earnest young man, who came to a Bostoner Shabbaton, seemed to be looking for something more in his Jewish observance. His father, a prominent physician, attended a Conservative temple, but his son was still searching. It was a nice Shabbaton, with lots of singing and activities and speakers; and this young man was quite impressed. Back on his college campus, he rapidly began moving towards traditional *Yiddishkeit*.

Naso

When a man or woman vows to be a Nazir,
He must abstain (yazir) from wine and strong wine ...
He must grow long hair on his head ...
And [upon completing his vow] ... shave off his hair.
(Numbers 6:2,3,5,18)

In every society, there are those who seek to live beyond that society's norms and social conventions. Judaism channels this tendency, as it does all human drives, into serving holiness. The nazir took upon himself the extra restrictions of abstaining from all wine and grape products, a major limitation in a society in which almost all public and private celebrations included wine. In defiance of common fashion, especially in close-cropped Roman times, he grew his hair long. Men with long, matted hair are nothing new to Judaism; but there was a spiritual rationale for the nazir's rejection of a "normal" lifestyle, a yearning for more (not less) purity and more (not less) self-control.

Even so, the nazir's "extreme" stance, as well motivated as it might seem, was treated with some unease. The tendency was to limit the vow in time — the typical nazirite vow was only 30 days — and the Torah itself insisted on the nazir going to the other extreme, shaving off all the hair on his head, once his nazirite period was over.

Most telling, the nazir was required to bring a sin offering. Some commentators say it was to atone for the nazir's leaving his

A few weeks later we received a polite thank-you note from him, as we do from so many students. Then he started coming by quite often and soon became a committed *Chassid*. I was *mesader kiddushin* at his wedding, and helped him make many key business and personal decisions. He is now raising a fine observant family, and we still see each other quite often. He davens a Chassidic *davening (Nusach Sefard)* and wears a long black Chassidic coat. His children have Chassidic *peyos* (long side-curls) and go to Chassidic day schools and *yeshivos*.

Not long ago, while cleaning out an old file cabinet, I came across a long-forgotten folder labeled "Letters From Students." Leafing through the old letters, I found the long-forgotten thank-you note from this same young man; but now its self-confident wording made me smile. It read:

> Dear Rebbe,
>
> Thank you very much for a very nice Shabbos. I really enjoyed it. It meant a lot to me...but one thing I want to make clear: Yes, I have an interest in becoming more involved in Judaism; but one thing I can promise you: I will never become a Chassid!

ultrahigh level to return to the mundane world; but others say that, on the contrary, it atoned for his having left the mundane world and having rejected Hashem's gift of wine. The Torah prefers a balance between limitations and freedom. It is all too easy for the superhuman to become the inhuman. As one Chassidic Master put it: When Satan wants to seduce a man, he encourages him to become too pious!

Pursuit of the mirage of absolute control has continued to our own day and was a prominent feature of many of the extremist, Eastern "cults" that sprang up in the '60s. During that tumultuous era, the Rebbe certainly got his share of long-haired young men looking for paranormal experiences. Some were sincere, some were under great stress and some were just strange. The Rebbe did what he could — and succeeded beyond all expectations with many — but, tragically, some were too far gone to return. These two stories of "failures" emphasize three important points: (1) Cults are incredibly dangerous just because they take away the individual's ability to choose and to change; (2) one is not free of his obligation to help fellow Jews just because success seems unlikely; and (3) one must not become discouraged, but rather one must continue to try. The effort is in our hands; the success, in Hashem's.

❧ Hari Krishna Versus Shabbos

The '60s were a time of spiritual and emotional turmoil in Boston's large college community. Many Jewish students reacted to the spirit of the times by seeking their own "roots," and soon all kinds of students began coming over for Shabbos. Some were rather odd, some had problems, and most knew nothing about *Yiddishkeit*. We had, *Baruch Hashem*, great success with many of them. That was not usually the case, however, with those Jewish students already into the various "cults" — some exotic, all coercive — that flourished at that time. Once young people had accepted their abnormal cult lifestyles as normal, there was usually little we could do. Two particularly sad cases come to mind, and typify the dangers of cult movements as a whole.

One day a friend of ours called to say that a younger cousin had become involved in the Hari Krishna movement. This was a pop-version (and perversion) of Hinduism. Its adherents went around in public with shaven heads and orange robes, chanting *mantras* and collecting money from passersby. Being that far outside prevailing social norms may have been an exhilarating ride, but it was also generally a one-way trip. Our friend wanted to know if I would invite her cousin over for a Shabbos and "talk to him."

I agreed and he came over for an initial chat. He seemed rather uptight, but we had a fairly reasonable conversation about all kinds of topics ... except one. He was, as the Talmud says, a *shoteh l'oso davar* (selectively insane). He really couldn't objectively discuss his involvement with his cult.

Of course, I didn't attack his cult movement directly (although there was much to attack). Instead I concentrated on, "Why not look into your own roots first?" I invited him over for Shabbos, and he accepted. Maybe the special fellowship, atmosphere and *kedushah* (holiness) of Shabbos would rekindle the Jewish soul within him.

He came, stayed for the *davening*, and heard us sing our beautiful *Lecha Dodi*. Then he came upstairs for *Kiddush*, and sat down among our many other college-age guests for the Friday night meal. He seemed content enough, but one thing puzzled me: He was mumbling to himself. In fact, all through the meal he kept on mumbling and mumbling. After the meal I quietly asked a student who had been sitting next to him what had been going on. What had he been mumbling? It turned out that he had been sincerely impressed, which worried him. So he had been mumbling his cult's *mantra* (a phrase repeated endlessly to induce a trancelike state) for several hours nonstop to "protect" himself from the infectious *kedushah* of Shabbos!

Clearly no one was going to reach him just then. However, that one Shabbos may have had an impact after all, since he eventually did quit the movement and is now living a comparatively normal life. Unfortunately, he was far from the only Jewish student who was searching for spirituality, and who "found" it in a very wrong, dangerous way.

❦

Another case involved the relative of a particularly fine American Jewish family. He became a practicing Buddhist, and eventually became a Buddhist monk. Finally he married another Buddhist. One day his family called to ask me to talk to him.

It was, of course, more than a little late; but that does not absolve a Jew from his responsibilities. I agreed to see him, and he came by a few weeks later. We made a rather incongruous pair. I was dressed in a black Chassidic coat and a wide-brimmed black hat. He was dressed in the robes of a Buddhist monk, incongruously topped with a big white turban (apparently a sign of rank in his particular sect). Unlike the Hari Krishna addict, who was clearly abnormal and always on edge, this fellow was relaxed and comparatively "together."

He readily agreed that, if he had come to Judaism first, he might have found what he was looking for there. As it turned out, he felt that he had already found it in Buddhism and saw no reason to change. Just because he was so "normal," he probably never changed. It was another poignant reminder of the importance of active outreach, of being the first on the scene.

❦

What attracted Jewish students, especially unstable ones, to these cults? Fellowship and acceptance may have brought them in, but strict cult discipline kept them there. Contrary to what one might think about intellectuals, what many undisciplined, disorderly, "lost" types want most is strict discipline, order and certainty. They want complete control over their emotions and actions. In the cults, all the decisions are made by others, and one simply obeys. In return, cult followers don't have to face their frightening freedom.

Judaism, despite all its rules and regulations, takes just the opposite approach. The Torah wants man to control his drives, but only in a gradual measured way that preserves the individual's complete freedom to choose at each step. Thus, we always insist on explaining everything to *baalei teshuvah*. We invariably apologize to them six times over for our custom of waiting to say *Kiddush* on Friday nights until after the hour of *"ma'adim"* (an inauspicious time discussed in the Talmud, *Shabbos* 129b). Why bother, especially when so many of them just want to be told, "Do this, don't do that. I am the Rebbe and I say so"? Because man is created free, in the image of G-d, and one neither can nor should take away that freedom.

※

In contrast to those Jews who knew nothing, and wanted to know nothing, about their Judaism, the Rebbe met many non-Jews in the Boston of the 1960s who were respectfully interested in knowing more about our heritage. If only our lost brothers, instead of trying to be like non-Jews of all descriptions, would realize how much others respect what *we* have to offer, when we respect it ourselves.

※ *A Catholic Chaburah*

Rabbis are used to receiving many requests to speak. Most are quite standard, but some can be rather surprising. One day, for example, the Chassidic Center received a call from the Head of the Divinity School of Boston College, a Catholic school. He wanted to send some seminary students over to the Chassidic Center to meet with "the Grand Rabbi." They wanted to understand why we Jews consider ourselves the Chosen People. He was quite respectful and serious, but I was in a quandary. How could one give a *"shiur"* on this topic to a group of future Catholic priests, one that honestly laid out our position without antagonizing them? Nonetheless, I agreed.

On the set day, six senior seminary students arrived and, after the usual pleasantries, repeated their question. In the best Jewish tradition, I immediately met their question with another question: "Why does it matter to you whether we regard ourselves as the Chosen People or not? After all, you can form your own opinion, perhaps one different from ours."

"It matters a great deal to us," they said, "because we also believe that you are the Chosen People. When our ancestors were still pagans, yours already worshipped the One G-d. Thus you have a unique place in our theology."

Since they had apparently come to learn, and not to debate, I easily lead the conversation to our idea of chosenness: being an example to the world, suffering throughout history to stay true to Hashem's Will, and so on. The discussion ended on a positive note, and they apparently left satisfied. It was a good reminder that we should be more constantly aware and appreciative of our chosenness.

Beha'aloscha

Make two trumpets for yourself of beaten silver,
And use them for summoning the people,
And for the camps setting out on their journey ...
And when you go out to war in your land ...
You should blow the trumpets and be remembered
Before Hashem, your G-d.
(Numbers 10:2,9)

Although the Jews in the desert saw the Cloud rising from the Mishkan, they didn't break camp and journey forward until they heard the trumpets. A single blast, a tekiah, and they all gathered together. A series of short blasts, a teruah, and the Eastern Camp (Judah) began the march, followed by all the others. Thus it is in our lives as well. Spiritually we often fall into a rut and slumber, and we need sharp bugle blasts to wake us up and get us moving again. Sometimes it is a dramatic, cataclysmic event, but more often it is a word, an experience or a memory that might seem ordinary to others, but which shakes us up, wakes us up and moves us forward.

As we go out to war against our evil inclinations and desires, we must blow these trumpets and actively seek out those experiences which can awaken and strengthen our neshamos. The Rebbe saw this happen over and over again at his Shabbos tish. College students, their Jewish neshamos hearing the special reveille of Shabbos, woke up one after another, sometimes dramatically, sometimes ever so slowly and hesitantly, sometimes only after a journey of years. The pace did not matter; the march had begun. There was no way to go back to sleep with those trumpets making all that racket inside.

☙ The Returned Tefillin

A young lady who often spent Shabbos in our community once asked us to host (and check out) a fellow college student who wanted to date her. He had a Jewish education, but he had since wandered off the beaten path. She was concerned that he wasn't sufficiently religious, although she thought that he had considerable potential.

The young man did come over for Shabbos and, during that one day, did a complete turnaround. He remembered how his grandfather had been from a prominent religious Jewish family, and how his father had carried on the tradition (albeit more weakly). He remembered his

The parchments of tefillin, like those of a sefer Torah, must be carefully written by an accomplished scribe. Here the Rebbe (L) and his son R' Naftali (R), the Rav of the New England Chassidic Center in Brookline, oversee the writing of a new Torah scroll.

yeshivah, his *rebbeim* and their Shabbos table. In short, he went straight back to his roots and became very excited about *Yiddishkeit*. I was quite impressed by the strength of his reactions and the depth of his enthusiasm.

Once Shabbos was over, he thanked me profusely for setting him straight, and then asked with an expression of deep concern, "But what can I do about tomorrow morning?"

"About what?"

"About my *tefillin*. I don't have my *tefillin* here in Boston. I left them at home and haven't used them for years. I can't go without putting on *tefillin* tomorrow. That would be awful!" "Don't worry," I reassured him. "We'll find you a pair somewhere for tomorrow. Meanwhile, why don't you call your parents now and ask them to send you your *tefillin* as soon as they can?"

He called his parents then and there. His father was so overwhelmed that he started to cry from joy. He had never expected to hear his son ask for his *tefillin* again. In fact, before his son had met our friend, he had been seriously dating a non-Jewish woman and they had even started discussing marriage. The situation had been very critical indeed.

The young man's turnaround changed all that. He started coming around quite often, attending *shiurim* (classes) and making friends in the community. A few years later he met a fine religious young lady, whom he later married. He and his family now live happily in Israel, where he teaches at a *yeshivah*. He has, *kein ayin hara*, a large lovely family, and in some ways has surpassed his father's level of religious involvement.

✥ *On the Brink*

At another Bostoner Shabbaton, as was my custom, I called in a few students to talk with them privately about "where they were holding." One girl, Ellen, came in saying that she desperately needed help. She had an important decision that she absolutely had to make that very weekend. She was seriously considering marrying a non-Jew ... and soon!

We talked about it for a while, but avoided forcing the issue. After

Shabbos, Ellen came in to say that, when she had arrived on Friday afternoon, she was "a girl on the brink." Now, after a Shabbos in our home and with our community, she felt secure. She had firmly decided to turn her non-Jewish boyfriend down.

A few days later, I decided to call her back and see how she was doing. After all, someone who had been "on the brink" often needs a little extra help. Her roommate answered and went to get her. When Ellen came to the phone, I told her that the Bostoner Rebbe was calling. Her response was rather unexpected.

"Who?"

"The Bostoner Rebbe."

"You'd better stop kidding!"

"I'm not kidding. This *is* the Bostoner Rebbe."

"You'd better stop it!"

"Really, it is the Bostoner Rebbe."

There was an ominous silence.

She seemed to be formulating a sharp retort that she would probably regret later, so I quickly added, "Remember, you spoke to me on Shabbos about being on the brink?" She suddenly realized that this wasn't a crank call — she must have had quite a few — and we continued our conversation from there. She eventually married a nice young Jewish man. She may not have become Orthodox; but she made considerable progress and was quite sincere.

Some of her theological concerns were rather interesting. She was particularly troubled that she was unable to experience Hashem directly. Of course, her expectations for direct contact were rather unrealistic. There haven't been any authentic prophets with Divine communications for over 2,000 years! I tried to explain to her that it was unlikely that Hashem would simply appear to her one night and say, "Hello, Ellen. Here I am!" Rather, Hashem is already everywhere, and it is up to us to open ourselves to Him and find Him.

As an analogy, I suggested that she imagine herself traveling rapidly along a beautiful scenic route, camera in hand. Unless she took pictures, she would never be able to capture and remember the gorgeous scenery that flashed by. To do so, her camera would have to be ready, uncapped and focused. She would have to catch split-second opportunities as they appeared.

In all our lives there are many such special moments; but often our spiritual camera is not ready and focused, and the opportunity passes by unnoticed in the general rush of things. Even when we do succeed, we are left only with a photo, a very precious photo our conscious mind can long savor, but not the split-second, unfathomable Divine "Hello" itself.

❧ Delayed Reaction

During his years in Boston, the young man of our *tefillin* story used to bring many of his college acquaintances over to the Chassidic Center for Shabbos. We particularly remember a young professor from Princeton who came by one long winter evening. In our conversation before *Kiddush*, I explained how *Yiddishkeit* tries to help a person do the right thing in this world, how a person cannot always make the right decisions on his own, and how the Torah helps us grow towards a more correct lifestyle.

I offered the example — it was at the height of the Vietnam War protests — of how people who were supposedly demonstrating for peace were yelling, "Kill the pigs!" at police officers blocking their access to the White House. What did "the sanctity of life" mean to these people? Were they really ready to kill people in Washington just to get nearer to a building, while protesting violence in Vietnam, thousands of miles away? Were their motives imbued with purity or power? The Torah doesn't allow us to kill others just because we can't have our own way. It lays down objective criteria for when we can and cannot kill, and when we can and cannot let ourselves be killed.

The professor suddenly took a personal interest and responded sharply. "What's wrong with killing? If some other guy is in your way, and he won't give you what you want, kill him! The only thing you have to be careful of is not being caught; because then you will have to suffer the consequences. Otherwise, what's wrong with killing?" I waited to see if he was "pulling my leg," or just trying to be provocative, but apparently he was not. I was still a bit unsure, but he seemed serious enough about his strident amorality.

This professor stayed the whole Shabbos, but with a dispassionate, detached attitude that contrasted with the enthusiasm all around him. Darkness fell, he said goodbye, and that was it, or almost ...

Several years later, we received a call out of the blue from this same "pro-death" professor. He needed to discuss an important matter right away. He came over to the Chassidic Center, and my surprise was complete. He had just become engaged to be married to a member of one of New York's most prominent Jewish families. They were planning a garden wedding with many important guests; but they didn't want any gifts. Instead, they wanted to put a note in the invitation saying, "In lieu of a gift, please make a contribution to our family charity fund, to be administered by the Bostoner Rebbe, Grand Rabbi Levi Y. Horowitz."

It was a fine idea to donate his wedding presents to charity, but I was rather surprised. He was still teaching at Princeton, with any number of Nobel Prize scientists and many philosopher friends. Why did he want an "archaic" moralizing Chassidic Rebbe to administer his family's charity fund? Why did he want me to be involved in this most precious moment of his life? Thinking back to all the impressive, if amoral, people who must have influenced him throughout his years as a student, instructor and professor, I decided that our one Shabbos together had not been in vain, after all.

The professor's fund is still helping others. He is now raising his family in a Jewish environment which, even if not fully observant, leaves most of his classmates far behind. In fact, he once called to ask if and how the Torah's injunction against causing pain to animals (*tzaar baalei chayim*) would apply to animals used in scientific experiments. He was in doubt because the results of his research were not guaranteed to provide direct human benefits, the usual grounds for permission.

So that's how someone who once asked, "Why not kill other people?" ended up, *Baruch Hashem*, asking to what extent one may cause pain to even the humblest of Hashem's creatures.

Shelach Lecha

They cut down a branch with a cluster of grapes ...
And pomegranates and figs ...
(Numbers 13:23)

On your holidays you should make [an olah offering],
A pleasing fragrance to Hashem, from the herd or flock ...
Of the first of your dough, you should give Hashem
As a gift throughout your generations
(Numbers 15:3,21)

Food has both physical and spiritual dimensions, a duality hinted at in this week's parshah and its commentaries. The spies cut down a branch of grapes. Rashi implies that this is just what one would expect of such materialistic individuals. Yehoshua and Caleb did not; their thoughts were focused on the higher, more spiritual aspects of the land. Yet this week's parshah hardly dismisses physicality and food. Indeed it explicitly tells us that food can be a "pleasing fragrance," an "offering," a "gift to Hashem."

The essence of food — spiritual or gross — depends on how it is used. The spies wanted to show the people that, "just as the Land's fruits are strange, so are its people" (Rashi). In contrast, the animal offering (olah) and dough offering (challah) sanctified the animal and vegetative aspects of the world and man, raising them to a higher spiritual plane.

Eating is ultimately the conversion of the external to the internal, the transformation of the nonself into self. Eating, as part of our daily avodah, involves the elevation of lower forms of life to a higher service of Hashem. We affect the food; and it affects us as well. We are, as the saying goes, what we eat. The Jewish dietary laws (kashrus) reflect this. For example, in Jewish mystical sources (such as Recanti), milk represents the birth and life of the new animal, and meat its slaughter and death; hence the inappropriateness of mixing them.

Keeping the laws of kashrus has become both easier and more difficult in modern times. There are now certifying agencies of varying degrees of strictness, but the multitude of new food additives and ingredients makes modern kashrus a complex matter indeed. The problem is greatly exacerbated in environments such as hotels and hospitals, in which one has to rely on non-Jewish or nonknowledgeable staff for food. The advent of sealed prepackaged kosher meals, originally developed for the airline industry, was a big help in solving this problem. However, these were virtually unknown in 1960s Boston, until one day ...

❧ T.V. Dinners

In the early '60s, during a visit to my brother, R' Moshe Horowitz, the Bostoner Rebbe of New York, I had an attack which required immediate, albeit minor, surgery. Friends took me right over to nearby Caledonian Hospital, where the required procedure was done. The next day I was resting in my hospital bed, when a non-Jewish nurse came by and asked, "Would you like to have a kosher dinner?" What? A kosher dinner in a non-Jewish hospital? We knew that in Boston, even in the so-called "Jewish hospitals," there was no such thing. We had to make hot meals for religious patients and deliver them ourselves.

"Kosher meals?" I asked. "Where do you get them?" "Oh, it's no problem," she said, "we have them all ready and prepackaged right

The Bostoner Rebbe (of Boston) with his elder brother, R' Moshe, the Bostoner Rebbe of New York (left), in the early 1960s

here in the hospital's freezer," and she brought me a kosher dinner prepared by a local caterer. It was, perhaps, not as fancy as nowadays, but it was for all intents and purposes a kosher T.V. dinner. Although I didn't eat it anyway (I was concerned about the *hashgachah*), I said to myself: Well, at least now I know why, after working with all those big hospitals in Boston, I ended up here at Caledonian Hospital in Brooklyn. There could only be one reason ... to discover that there are now kosher T.V. dinners available for Jewish hospital patients! I realized what this would mean for all those Bostonian *nashim tzidkanios* (righteous women) who had to cook hot soup and make, bake and take things to the hospital at all hours of the day and night.

Once back home, I began "brainstorming." How were we going to get kosher T.V. dinners to Boston? And once we got them there, how were we going to get the hospitals to serve them? And even if they agreed to serve them, who was going to pay for them? If they had to pay extra, many borderline "customers" might say, "Look, our hospital bill is high enough already!"

Some careful strategy was in order. The determining voice would be that of the chief dietitian, who had to rule on all hospital food services. Our first target was New England Brigham Baptist Hospital, because the Baptists, as Biblical fundamentalists, would probably respect kosher meals quite well. Second, not long before, R' Shlomo Twersky, a Chassidic Rebbe from Denver, had stayed in that very hospital, and people had to bring in his food every day. The hospital was in an uproar just trying to provide his meals. They just might welcome an easier solution.

Their chief dietitian received us politely, and we carefully stated our case. Patients needed substantial hot meals, not just cold vegetable salads, before and after surgery. She readily agreed. Yet, in the case of observant Jewish patients, this was difficult. Their hospital had had considerable trouble providing hot kosher meals for Rabbi Twersky. Again she agreed. "Well then," I said, "our community can help you. We can import prepackaged T.V. dinners for you from New York." She thought the whole idea made sense, so she said, "Fine, I'll take it up with our Board." After a while, we received their answer. Not only was it all right, they would even pay the extra costs involved.

Next, we went to the Massachusetts General Medical Center, one of the world's most famous hospitals. They had both Jewish patients and a number of *kashrus*-observing interns with no place to eat. We went to see their chief dietitian. She got up, came over to greet us, and then — an awkward moment — she stuck out her hand with a cheerful, "How do you do, Rabbi Horowitz?"

This was a problem, because a Jewish man may not touch women except for his wife and other close relatives (similar rules of modesty apply to Jewish women). What could I do? I was afraid that once I mentioned the problem she would feel embarrassed, and she would probably also be confused, since the hospital's Reform chaplain presumably did shake her hand. It would hardly be the ideal way to ask for a favor. Still, I obviously couldn't shake her hand.

Instead, I explained the prohibition and then smiled and tried to put her at ease. I told her, "You know, you are in good company. Jacqueline Kennedy was scheduled to visit us a few weeks ago with her husband Jack, whom we knew as a young man. A rabbi asked

The Bostoner community continued to grow and, in 1980, two of the Rebbe's sons, R' Mayer (L) and R' Naftali (R), were installed as Rav and Dayan, respectively. They now head the local Bostoner communities of Jerusalem and Boston, respectively. Reb Moshe Mir z"l, then President of the New England Chassidic Center, looks on (far L).

me, 'What are you going to do if she tries to shake your hand?' 'Too bad,' I said. 'If I don't give others my hand, I can't do it for her either. A rule's a rule.'" That story broke the ice, and we soon had another approval.

We were equally successful at several other hospitals: Peter Bent Brigham Hospital, University Hospital and the New England Medical Center. There was, however, a technical problem at the old Deaconess Hospital. Their freezer was too small to store extra dinners so we would have to deliver them almost on demand (today the Deaconess has a large new building with a spacious new freezer).

Now that the hospitals agreed, someone had to bring all the dinners to Boston. None of the commercial firms we spoke to wanted to get involved. "What do you mean? I'll have to store it and wait for the hospitals to call. And how many calls will I get, and who can say when? For that I have to *patchke* and *schlepp*?" Finally we called in Rabbi Leonard Small, the owner of the original Butcherie in Brookline, and told him, "Look, this is a big *mitzvah,* and the

Boston community really needs someone to do it. Later it will spread and you'll be glad you did it too." Eventually he agreed, and even managed to combine it with Boston's weekly *glatt* kosher meat order to save on shipping costs.

The system worked just fine and, *Baruch Hashem*, to this day kosher T.V. dinners are readily available in Boston hospitals for all who need them — although I doubt if anyone connects them with my surgery at Caledonian Hospital in New York.

Korach

> *And they assembled together against Moshe and Aharon,*
> *And said to them: "You are [acting] too great!*
> *All of the community is holy ...*
> *Why do you lift yourselves up so?"*
> *(Numbers 16:3)*

In the Mishkan in the desert, Moshe and Aharon reached great spiritual levels. Unfortunately, such success always makes the Korachs of this world defensive. "Why are you putting on airs? What's wrong with us and the way we do things?" There is a potpourri of emotions churning under the surface: a sense (usually unfounded) of rejection, anger, jealousy, guilt and loss of control.

Rashi explains that Korach was upset that his cousin, Elitzaphan ben Uziel, had been appointed a prince when he, Korach, had "better" claims. Angered by the perceived rebuff, he took it out on Moshe Rabbeinu. He dressed 250 men all in blue wool, says Midrash Tanchuma, and confronted Moshe: "These robes are totally blue, and yet they still require blue tassels (tzitzis) on their corners?" He mocked the mitzvos, blaming "religion" for his own feelings of hurt, helplessness and inferiority. The issue was not piety, but power.

Korach was not alone. Many people overreact to a perceived slight or threat to their self-esteem. Baalei teshuvah, despite their best efforts to avoid confrontations with their parents, almost always trigger some bit of this every time they go home, especially in the beginning. They have to work hard to convince their parents that they are not rejecting them as people or parents, that love and contact will continue, and that they can grow more Jewish together. After a year or so of such treatment, feelings mend, relationships deepen and parents usually come to value and even admire their children's return to the Torah lifestyle of our Eternal People.

❧ *Parent Problems*

Parents who couldn't adjust to their children becoming *baalei teshuvah* were a regular part of my life throughout the '60s and '70s. Fortunately, most of the time we were able to help them become more understanding of their child's choice, but it was always a challenge.

One fellow became a *baal teshuvah* just before Pesach. He was immediately faced with all the problems of going home for that beautiful but stringent holiday, when all *chametz* (leaven) products are forbidden. What was he going to eat? His home was both *treif* (non-kosher) and *chametz*.

There was no time for gradual readjustments, so I invited his parents in to help "negotiate" some kind of arrangement they could all live with. Unfortunately, everything seemed to be a problem. For example, on Pesach, their whole family came together for a *seder, treif* to be sure, but an important family event nonetheless. They brought out all their best china for the occasion, and they couldn't face the embarrassment of everyone eating on their *treif* fine china while their son used paper plates. Then there was the food ... We can't reveal our solutions, because every case is different, but eventually everyone was satisfied. The parents even developed a respect for *Yiddishkeit* from our encounter and their son's mature behavior, although they never became particularly observant themselves.

A few years later, they showed us just how much their attitude had changed. Their younger son had become fanatically involved with all kinds of exotic groups and was heading for trouble. Although they felt that there wasn't much we could do for their younger son — we had no previous relationship to build on — they came anyway to ask: "Isn't there something you could do to make our younger son more like our older son?"

※

Another young woman told us that she could never stomach religion, because of the way her parents misused it. They belonged to one of the most exclusive temples in the United States, but only went to services twice a year: on Rosh Hashanah and Yom Kippur.

However, attending those services wasn't a religious activity for her parents, but a performance, a chance for her mother to dazzle her friends with her extravagant new clothes. Every year she would buy a new wardrobe and then make a grand entrance "dressed for the kill." As far as they were concerned, that was the whole purpose of the ritual. You could forget about prayer, because they already had everything they wanted: children, health, a yacht, a Rolls Royce, a mansion. As for a Jew's other needs, they gave them nary a thought.

When she started visiting us, and she saw how our community

Another Bostoner Shabbaton ends as the Rebbe (seated) extinguishes the traditional Havdalah candle in wine.

lived a truly Jewish life, she was very impressed. We don't know how her story turned out, but we were impressed by how much she had analyzed and had been affected by her parents' behavior. It was enough to deaden one's soul for life.

❦

The sad truth is that "the deeds of the fathers are portents for their children" in this area as well. Korach may have been the first congregant to give a Jewish leader a hard time, but he was far from the last. Years later, as the Rebbe points out, when the prophet Samuel turned over the kingdom to Saul, he told the people, "Bear witness against me .. Whose ox have I taken? Whose donkey have I taken? Who have I defrauded or oppressed?' (*I Samuel* 13:3), and the nation answered, "You have not defrauded or oppressed us!"

After an entire life of tireless communal service, the best even a prophet could hope for was not thanks, not praise, but, "Yes, you are not a *ganev* (thief)!" Given this background, rebbes, rabbis and other modern leaders don't expect a lot, and are used to complaints, argumentative types and abuse. Usually that's just the way it is; but when one gets it from someone one has just done a favor for, it still hurts.

❦ *The Adoption*

Throughout the '60s, I often received requests to help find babies for adoption, but I was never able to help very much. Locating adoptions seemed to require rather specialized connections. Once I met a particularly fine couple who were very involved in *chinuch* (education) but, unfortunately, could not have children. When they came to ask for help in arranging an adoption, my heart really went out to them. I understood how they felt when they left my office disappointed.

Two days later a young lady called who simply had to see me right away. It was URGENT! She came to my office in the Chassidic Center and introduced herself as a nurse at a local hospital. A friend of hers, a European, had just given birth to a baby, but wanted to give it up for adoption. It was a healthy, normal Jewish baby with a

Jewish mother — perfect! But the adoption arrangements had to be concluded immediately, because the mother wanted to register the adopted name with the hospital before checkout. Could we recommend someone?

Dozens of names immediately flashed through my mind. They all wanted children. Which one to choose? Somehow I felt that it belonged to the couple who had asked for help two days before. After so many years without a child to place, and now suddenly this unexpected opportunity — it must be meant for them, *min hashamayim*, a gift from Heaven.

I called them and they were very excited indeed, but there was still one more hurdle to overcome. This couple was very poor, and the relinquishing parent wanted whoever adopted her child to pay the hospital bill. The bill was modest — about $500 — but the couple simply didn't have it. Then I remembered an old lady who came by every so often, crying and crying about her late husband. They had been childless, and there was nobody to carry on her husband's name. Couldn't we find someone who would name their child after her husband? If so, she would pay anything, "even $1,000." She kept hounding us — she "needed a name."

Everything seemed to fit into place. The old lady needed a "name," the young couple needed a baby and the baby's mother needed $500. The deal was soon completed, with a *bris* thrown in for good measure.

The *bris* was held a few days later. The adopting parents were happy, the old lady was happy and we were happy. After the *bris* itself, the recitation of the *brachos* began, leading up to the climax, the naming of the baby. The old lady quietly handed me the money and was radiant as the child was named in memory of her departed husband. It was a heartwarming ending to the story.

The next day, however, I received a phone call from the old woman. She wanted her money back! She claimed that the name wasn't given and that the whole thing was a hoax.

"How could that be? You were there and heard the whole thing yourself!"

"Not true!" she said. She argued some more and then hung up.

It seemed rather strange, but old people can become a bit senile and no harm had been done. The couple had the baby, the baby had her husband's name and we were accustomed to receiving crank

Bamidbar

calls. We forgot about the whole thing until, a few days later, the mailman delivered a letter from her lawyer! She was suing us for taking money "under false pretenses." I spoke to her lawyer and asked him what on earth was going on. The *bris* was a big public affair, with almost 100 people hearing the child being named after her husband. "Sorry," he said, "but what can I do? She is claiming otherwise."

Worse, she kept going around publicly complaining about the "swindle" and generally causing no end of problems and embarrassment. Apparently she had decided that, since the name was already given and couldn't be taken back, she might as well try to get her money back as well. Her "case" was obviously thrown out of court, but it was still quite a *bushah* (embarrassment) that such a thing could have happened at all.

The whole affair was particularly traumatic for us, because we have always insisted on *hakaras hatov*, actively showing gratitude to anyone who has ever done us a favor, no matter how small. To us it had always been the cardinal principle, the underlying bedrock, of all interpersonal relations...and it still is.

Chukas

This is the law when a man dies in a tent,
Everyone coming into the tent and everything in it
Shall be tamei [ritually unclean] seven days ...
And he shall wash his clothes and immerse in water.
(Numbers 19:14,19)

And Miriam died there and was buried there ...
And when all the people saw that Aharon had died,
They wept for Aharon thirty days.
(Numbers 20:1,29)

This parshah deals with the death of the righteous (Miriam and Aharon) and the order of purification after contact with death. On the third and seventh day, the tamei (ritually unclean) person must be sprinkled with pure water mixed with the ashes of a red heifer, which had been burned with cedar wood, hyssop (a low shrub) and wool dyed with a red extract from certain worms. The water renders the tamei person clean, but renders the clean man who prepares it tamei. Thus, we begin to confront the paradoxes of dying, the interface between the life of this world and the life of the next. In the Torah's details, the paradoxes symbolically continue: Those as lofty as the cedar and as low as the hyssop meet the same physical end, in a place of worms.

Yet physical death is not the end of the story. Our Sages tell us that the righteous, those who live a life of the spirit, are even more *alive in the next world; while the wicked, who live a life of flesh, are not truly alive even in this world. The main focus of Jewish mourning and purification practices is, thus, to instruct the living, as King Solomon said:*

> It is better to go to a house of mourning
> Than a house of feasting,
> For that is the end of all men,
> And the living will take it to heart.

When a person dies, we often hear, "Oh, why did this man die?" Yet how seldom do we hear at a birth, "Why was this baby born?" Surely the two are linked. How can we hope to discover the purpose of death, until we discover the purpose of life and live it accordingly? This parshah, according to the Midrash and Rashi, gives us more than a hint of how to proceed. If you are as haughty as a cedar, become humble as the hyssop, then you can purify yourself and others.

❧ The Wandering Casket

There is a long-standing Jewish custom to immerse the bodies of the deceased, especially the pious, in a *mikveh* (ritual bath) before burial. Unfortunately, during the '50s and '60s, none of Boston's funeral homes had a *mikveh*. Thus, the deceased could be purified only by the less preferable method of pouring *tishah kabin* (nine buckets) of water on the body without pause.

Once, after our move from Dorchester to Brookline, Massachusetts, a very respected local rabbi passed away. This *rav*, a very special person, faithfully went to the *mikveh* every week during his life. Was it proper that he go to his *kevurah* (burial) without first being immersed in a *mikveh*? It was impossible to contemplate. Still, we couldn't use the regular city *mikveh*. In those days, *mikveh*-going among Boston's Jewish population was still somewhat marginal. People still wondered if *mikvaos* were "sanitary." They would certainly be afraid to go — indeed terrified — if they knew that the *mikveh* had been used for a dead body! What could be done?

I had an idea. There was an old *mikveh* in Dorchester, where we had lived before moving to Brookline. Dorchester was now largely a black community; and the *mikveh* had been closed two years before. Since our *shul* had contributed much of the original funds and users, we still had a key. My solution was simple. Precedent or no precedent, we would go to the old Dorchester *mikveh* and immerse this very special *meis* (deceased) there.

We went to the funeral home and, as if it were the most natural thing in the world, told the director, "We are going to take this body and *toivel* it in the Dorchester *mikveh* and bring it right back." Much to our surprise, although the funeral was due to start in just a few hours, he agreed. He even lent us a station wagon to transport the casket. That being arranged, Hoshea Lewenstein, a member of the local *Chevra Kaddisha*, and his team of loyal recruits piled into another car and off we went.

All the way there everyone felt good. Thanks to our joint efforts, this very special *rav's* body was going to be *toiveled* in a real *mikveh* in Boston, a city in which there was no *mikveh* for pre-burial purification. Within 20 minutes we were in Dorchester, in front of the deserted *mikveh* building. Hoshea took the key, went over to the door and tried to fit it into the keyhole, but he had no luck. The key didn't fit and the door wouldn't budge. Someone had changed the lock!

Hoshea went around the building, pried open a window and bravely climbed inside. All of a sudden, as he opened the door for us, local men began appearing from all sides — some from this building, some from that.

"Hey man, what are you doing here? You'd better leave or we're going to call the police and charge you with breaking and entering."

"What do you mean, breaking and entering? This is our building!"

"No, it's not!"

"Yes, it is!"

"No, it's not. Our community bought it."

"What do you mean 'bought it'? When?"

"I'm telling you it's been sold, and if you guys don't leave pronto, we're calling the police."

This did not seem to be the appropriate time to tell them about the dead body we had in the back of the station wagon, just waiting to come in! Still, how dare they concoct such a story and change the lock? Hoshea went around the block to use a pay phone to check things out. He called up the president of the Woodrow Avenue Shul, who was still in charge of the *mikveh*, and came back about 10 minutes later, crestfallen.

"You know, it's true."

"What do you mean, it's true?"

"The *shul* sold the building."

"Why didn't anyone tell us? After all, we helped raise the money for the *mikveh*."

"I don't know, but it's not ours anymore."

What should we do now? Some were for pushing our way through and toiveling the body, no matter what happened later. But, if the building really wasn't ours, to my mind that ended it. We had meant well and had tried, and Hashem rewards such efforts, but one simply could not take it any further. So we went back to the funeral home, without accomplishing the great *chessed* we had intended. Nonetheless, that was the beginning of our crusade to put mikvaos in Boston's Jewish funeral chapels.

⚘

This was no simple task. The local funeral home owners were not particularly religious Jews. They didn't care that much about *toiveling* the dead, and installing a *mikveh* would be quite an expense. Our approach was both simple and direct. We went to the first funeral home and told the director, "You know, no Jewish chapel in Boston has a *mikveh*. If you were to install one — and we would help you do it — you would be able to offer something to the religious community that no one else can." His initial response was hardly encouraging: "Aw, forget it, Rebbe! How many people would be interested? Almost none!"

That was "strike one." But a year or so later, the same director came over to the Chassidic Center and said, "You know, Rebbe, we are remodeling our whole operation. Now would be the time to put in that *mikveh* you wanted. Come on down, give me the measurements, and I'll try to fit it in." So we did, they did, and soon Boston had a kosher funeral home *mikveh*.

A week later, a rival chapel came over to the center and asked us to help them install a *mikveh* too. They didn't want to be left out. "But wait a minute," we said. "You aren't doing any remodeling. Where will you put it?" "Well, I've been looking around, and I think I have a place where we can fit it in." Now we had *mikveh* number two. Soon Jewish funeral chapels all around the Greater Boston area just had to have a *mikveh*! We were busy but happy. Now Boston is the only city in the United States, besides New York City, where every Jewish funeral home has a *mikveh*.

We still regret that we were not able to do that first, special *tevilah*. Still, as this story shows, no good deed — or even attempted good deed — goes without eventually making an impact on the world.

Balak

> *And the Israelites dwelled in Shittim,*
> *And began to sin with the daughters of Moab.*
> *(Numbers 25:1)*

At first glance it is hard to see how it could happen. Today, when "perfectly matched" marriages are failing at a rate inconceivable a generation ago, why would anyone even try to start their married life with someone from a completely different culture and religion, someone with a completely different present, past and future? Is it due to a lack of Jewish education and home observance, a lack of restraint or long-term perspective, a lack of concern for future children? What can they be thinking? Cases differ, but one thing is for sure: The naive approach of "she'll do her thing and I'll do mine" just doesn't work. The Torah put that canard to rest three thousand years ago (Deuteronomy 7:4).

So the battle between the religions goes on in the home, with the children lost in between. Outside the home, the battle between the religions has continued, mostly one sided, for 2,000 years, filling Jewish history with massacres, crusades, pogroms, inquisitions and the Holocaust. The persecuted marry the persecutors and disappear from history, intermarriage accomplishing what the stake could not.

The same battle also takes place inside every Jew exposed to alien cultures, especially if he has little Torah protection.

Particularly unfortunate are those whose conflict is never fully resolved. Like the embryonic Jacob, struggling with Esau in the womb (Genesis 25:22), they continue to tumble round and round, marking time aimlessly, within the womb that should have given them birth.

❧ *An Unfinished Journey*

On one of our trips to *Eretz Yisrael*, I received a call from a man named Moshe in Bayit Vegan, a religious suburb of Jerusalem. The preceding Friday morning, while learning at home with his *chavrusah*, he had received a call from a total stranger, an American professor, who was on his first visit to Israel. "I'm just calling to give you greetings from a friend of yours," he said.

"Where are you calling from?" asked Moshe.

"A Catholic hostel in the old Arab quarter."

"Are...are you Jewish?" asked Moshe, rather puzzled, since people in Bayit Vegan rarely get calls from Catholic hostels in East Jerusalem.

"No, I'm Catholic," the professor answered. "But," he added, just to make conversation, "actually, one of my grandmothers was Jewish."

"Really — which mother?"

"My mother's mother."

That was a different story. According to Jewish law, this Catholic professor was actually Jewish! Moshe felt that he had to do something, and fast. "Why don't you come to us for Shabbos?" he suggested. "You would probably find it interesting."

The professor had never been to a synagogue and had never seen a rabbi, except in the movies. A nervous feeling told him to turn down the invitation and hop a tour bus to Bethlehem instead; a much deeper and more powerful impulse told him to go to Bayit Vegan. That night, at his first *Kabbalas Shabbos* in the Gra Shul, he was deeply moved by the powerful singing and, especially, by the closed-eyed intensity of the men during the silent prayer (*the Shemoneh Esrei*).

At the evening meal, the professor told Moshe that his grandmother Sarah had been born in Lithuania and had come as a teenager with her mother Rachel to Boston in 1902. Rachel died the following year, and Sarah had converted to marry a Boston Irish Catholic. Her daughter, the professor's mother, was raised Catholic. During his youth the professor had spent seven years in a monastic setting, preparing for the priesthood, and he had come to Israel to visit Bethlehem and other Christian holy sites. Despite his prior religious commitments, during the powerful *Lechah Dodi* at the Gra Shul, something sleeping deep inside him had sprung to life. He felt a strange sense of being "at home."

While impressed, the professor told Moshe that nothing could make him convert. "Don't worry," replied Moshe. "If Sarah and Rachel were who you say they were, you couldn't convert even if you wanted to. You are *already* Jewish."

This sudden revelation filled the professor with a bizarre mixture of joy and terror. His new-found friends were also deeply concerned. They now had a full-fledged Jew on their hands. They had to do something to save his Jewish *neshamah*; so, since he was born in Boston, they decided to bring him to the Bostoner Rebbe.

The professor visited our home late one evening. He told me of his background, his feelings at the Gra Shul, his nervousness, but also his willingness to explore the implications of what he had learned. The problem was that, despite his feelings at *shul*, he also still felt an attachment to the church and rituals of his youth. He also had deep bonds to his Spanish wife, a practicing psychologist and a devout Catholic, and to their one-year-old son, born after 12 years of waiting. He and his wife had married each other in part because they did not believe in intermarriage — Catholics should marry other Catholics! So how was he going to explain his brand new *yarmulke*?

All the conflicting pieces — his unrenounced past, his suddenly transformed present and his uncertain future — just didn't fit together. I didn't quite know what to say. The religious issue might work itself out in time, but the family issue was a real stumbling block.

I told him quite frankly, "When I look at you I see the millions and millions of Jews whom we lost throughout the ages, whether in the time of the Romans, the Crusaders, the Moslem Jihads, or the Inquisition. The Christian and Moslem religions have always tried to impose their faiths on us Jews. So many of us have been lost, some forever." He too seemed saddened, perhaps less for the plight of the nation than for his own sudden personal dilemma. "You know," he said, "I'm now sorry that I just signed a contract for a position out West next year. If I had known about my hidden connection to Judaism, I would have liked to have entered that world through you and your center in Boston."

A few months later we returned to Boston from Israel, and went down to *daven* at the 8 a.m. *minyan*. To my surprise, the professor was also there, wearing *tallis* and *tefillin*.

"*Shalom Aleichem!*"

"*Aleichem Shalom!*"

"How are you progressing?"

"Well, I've been *davening* here practically every morning now, since I came back from Israel."

"What about Shabbos?"

"I have started to keep Shabbos. I stay over with religious friends here in Brookline."

"Fine! what about your wife?"

"That's more serious. Our family situation has not yet been resolved."

As an expert in languages — he had already studied about 15 — the professor picked up Hebrew in record time. He soon *davened* fluently and spent considerable time in the community. He eventually documented his Jewish ancestry with birth and death certificates, discovering in a Jewish cemetery near Boston the grave of his great-grandmother Rachel, who had indirectly summoned him back home. However, his new-found Judaism struck his Christian family like an unexpected thunderbolt, creating tension and distance. His relationship with his wife was a particularly difficult issue. They had ruled out a formal divorce, since the Catholic church would not recognize it, leaving his wife unable to remarry.

I once told him, "You know, many Spanish Catholic families have Jewish Marrano roots. Maybe your wife also has Jewish ancestors. Or maybe she would be interested in becoming Jewish."

"No," he said. "We have discussed it fully. She's not following me into Judaism. Period. We're talking about separation; but maybe you could talk to her first?"

One day she came in for a talk. If I hadn't known who she was, I might have guessed that she was a Jewish housewife from Meah Shearim. She was wearing a long-sleeved dress, a kerchief that covered every strand of hair, and in general exuded an air of modesty and refinement. We talked for awhile and finally she said, "Usually I am a very open-minded person; but this is one thing that I just cannot accept. I myself don't really know why, but I just can't do it. I fully respect my husband's choice, and I understand his need to be Jewish. If we have to separate, so be it." It was very sad.

Some time later he came in to tell me that he had just placed a deposit on an apartment near the Chassidic Center and was in the process of moving out of his house. He and his wife had only one argument, an unusual one for couples who are separating. He insisted that she keep their house and all their money, and he would start again from scratch. She insisted that he also needed resources to start over again, and wanted a 50-50 split.

How this would have worked out is unknown. Unfortunately, sudden tragedy struck as the move was in progress. The professor received an unexpected phone call from Spain informing him that three of his wife's relatives, including her brother, had been killed that morning in an accident. He rushed to his wife's place of work, broke the tragic news, and made arrangements for their joint journey to Spain. He couldn't let her face that tragedy alone. The move was postponed, his deposit on the apartment was forfeited and, to this day, the family remains together, on parallel but separate tracks.

They moved to his new position out West, to a university town without an Orthodox Jewish community. There he lives, trying to observe his *Yiddishkeit* all alone, with no Jewish community to turn to and with a Spanish Catholic wife, who understands but cannot share his Jewish observance. Both are fine people trapped in a distressing problem not of their own making. If only uncommitted Jewish parents realized the problems such situations can cause future generations!

The professor's life is still a painfully mixed bag. He *davens* daily, wears *tefillin*, observes Shabbos; he even reads the Torah for a small group of Jewish students on campus (he taught himself the *ta'amim* and script from tapes and books). But he is constantly aware that this dual life is artificial. One week while *leining* he found an error in the Torah scroll, which made it *pasul* (invalid). The reading came to a sudden halt and the scroll was rolled back up in sad silence. He later told me that this seemingly minor incident painfully reminded him of the sad duality of his own life in *galus*. It was full of words of Torah, yet as *pasul* as the scroll from which he had been reading.

He continues to maintain occasional contact with us, but his journey home is still incomplete. This story, unfortunately, does not yet have a "happy ever after" ending; the struggle goes on.

⚘

Then there are those who intermarry and who say: "Don't worry about me, I can handle it." It's enough to make one cry. Man "handles" nothing in this world without Torah. Not in life; not in death.

⚘ *The Attorney General*

Massachusetts State Attorney General George Fingold, the Republican candidate for governor, seemed poised to become the first Jewish governor of the State of Massachusetts. People, polls and papers all agreed. However, despite all his carefully laid plans, he suffered a massive heart attack and died suddenly at age 43. It made big headlines but, from a Jewish perspective, a much bigger battle was being waged behind the scenes.

Mr. Fingold's wife, a non-Jew, wanted to bury him in a non-Jewish cemetery. His old Jewish mother, of course, wanted to bury him in a Jewish one. Since under Massachusetts law the wife's wishes usually take precedence, Mr. Fingold's Jewish body was set to spend eternity buried in a non-Jewish cemetery, probably with a cross atop his head.

True, Fingold wasn't particularly religious, but he had never converted out of the Jewish faith and his mother regularly attended an Orthodox *shul* in Malden. The Malden Jewish community was in an uproar and finally arranged to have the case heard in court. The judge was well acquainted with Fingold's many representations for Jewish causes and ruled that the deceased should receive a Jewish burial.

From Boston's historic Massachusetts State House to lying in state, life has many unpredictable turnings, making Torah values more important than ever.

The funeral, coming as it did after a hotly contested court case, was extremely tense. One of the attending clergy told us that the aisle at the funeral was like a barricade separating two warring factions. The looks that went back and forth were downright venomous. "If you ever wanted to see the consequences of intermarriage up close," our friend said, "that was it."

The crowning irony was the presence, between the rival camps, of the mute body of the late George Fingold. He was, of course, unable to say what he wanted for himself, unable to protect himself even from a non-Jewish burial. He now controlled nothing, not even his own corpse, although had he lived, he would probably have controlled one of the most important states in the Union. It was not only a human tragedy, but a reminder to all those contemplating intermarriage. No matter how powerful you may think you are, your future will be totally out of your hands — your burial, your children's faith, your grandchildren's. You will have no say at all.

Of course, this argument doesn't sway everyone. I once raised the specter of being buried in a non-Jewish cemetery to one gentleman, only to learn that he had long since written a will ordering that he be cremated (in direct defiance of Jewish law). He was thus, tragically, not going to be buried in *any* cemetery!

Pinchas

> *Pinchas ben Elazar, the son of Aharon the Kohen*
> *Has turned back My anger from the Children of Israel ...*
> *Therefore, I say, "Behold, I give him*
> *My Covenant of Peace ... a Covenant of eternal*
> *priesthood."*
> *(Numbers 28:11-13)*

At first sight it seems strange. The Jews were going astray after the non-Jewish women of Midian at a dizzying rate, and Zimri, a prince of the Tribe of Shimon, brazenly brought his non-Jewish mate back to the camp. Outraged at this desecration of Torah, Pinchas grabbed his spear and, catching them in the act, thrust his spear through both of them, killing them on the spot. The plague that had been raging through the camp, the external physical manifestation of the spiritual plague raging within, ceased at once, leaving behind 24,000 dead. Granted, Pinchas' act was noble, necessary and effective, but why was it rewarded with peace? We know that Hashem rewards "measure for measure." What made Pinchas' act of violence an act of peace?

Shalom, peace, in Hebrew, also means completeness (shleimus). Pinchas' brave, self-sacrificing act — he could have been killed by Zimri or his powerful family — reestablished the peace, the completeness of the relationship between Hashem and the Jewish people, that had been shattered by their unfaithfulness. That is why Pinchas subsequently (in the time of Joshua) became the High Priest. The most basic and remarkable function of the Priest is to take a sinner, shattered by all that his sin has destroyed, and offer his sin-offering (chatas) on the Altar to bring him atonement. This is the ultimate repair (tikkun) to the damaged bonds between the sinner and his Creator.

Pinchas' ability to offer sacrifices for others thus ultimately came from his willingness to sacrifice himself. Originally it had been assumed that Pinchas was ineligible for the Priesthood, since he had been born before the Priesthood had been made hereditary. Only by passing his test did Pinchas reveal the true depths of his soul and achieve enduring greatness. So too did the extraordinary two women whose story follows.

✣ To Be or Not To Be

A young man we knew once came by to spend Shabbos with us with his potential fiancée. He was about 18 years old and had just been accepted at Yale with a scholarship. The young lady was angry at him; she wanted him to continue his Jewish education. Ordinarily this would represent a fine, if uncommon, sign of commitment on the part of the girl. In this case it was extraordinary, because the girl herself wasn't Jewish!

I asked her what she thought would be the final outcome of their relationship. She said that she wanted to convert, "to do everything right," and to marry him.

"Wouldn't all that be too difficult for you?"

"No, I am already keeping almost all the *mitzvos* anyway!"

"But why do you want to be Jewish in the first place?"

"Well, I met my boyfriend and many other Jewish people through him, and I love them. Then I started looking into Jewish philosophy and religion, and I love that too."

She was a serious girl, sincerely interested in *Yiddishkeit*, and she was clearly mature enough to know what she wanted to do with her life. But conversion? There was still a big question here. They were two wonderful people in every way, but was she really interested in *Yiddishkeit* for its own sake, or was she being swayed by her fondness for this particular person? If the latter, her conversion was problematic. When asked, she told me frankly: "I don't know. This is a question that has long troubled me as well, but I have no answer. I do know that I want to live a Jewish life, because of all the circumstances that have led up to today, but had the circumstances been different ... I just don't know."

She didn't know, we didn't know, and they wanted "to do everything right." How could one render an appropriate halachic decision? We met several more times, without making much further progress. Finally a decision, one way or the other, had to be made. I thought awhile and came up with the following test. I told her, "If you want to do things the right way, you will first have to agree to follow the decision of the rabbis of the Boston *bais din* (religious court): first, on whether you can be converted, and second, on whether you can keep seeing your boyfriend. If they say yes, fine; but if they say no, you'll have to break up, completely and finally. He'll simply have to be out of the picture."

That was a pretty heavy decision for such a young person; and she asked for time to think it over. A few days later she called back and said: "Rebbe, the one main concern in my life right now is that I become a Jewess, no matter what the consequences. If the rabbis say no, my boyfriend and I will break up." I thought of calling her back with a decision a few days later, but considering that she had already spent several days in high anxiety, I told her, "Fine. Call back this evening." When she did, I told her: "Your conversion can proceed, and so can your marriage."

She was very happy, and I was happy too. She had withstood the test. But then she said, "... and now I'll be able to call him." What was that about?

After our last meeting, she had called her boyfriend and told him about the conditions that had been set. Then she said, "This may be our last conversation together. I am not going to call you again unless they say I can." She assumed that when I said that he would be "out of the picture" if the rabbis said no, that she could not even talk to him by telephone, not even to tell him that the answer was no! She was a marvelous person. Her response made me feel particularly good about the whole thing, since this confirmed how completely sincere she was.

They are now, by the way, still happily married and raising a fine Torah-true family.

※

A similar case came my way a few years later. A Jewish young professional became a *baal teshuvah* while on a trip to Israel. He even studied there for a while in a *yeshivah* for *baalei teshuvah*. When he set out on his trip, however, he had left behind a young woman he was seriously dating, a non-Jewish lawyer. When he explained his new-found commitment to her, she was supportive, but still she was a non-Jew, and their relationship had started before all this, and she did not know quite what to do.

She started spending time in an East Coast *kollel* community, and became close friends with many of the people there. Soon she was observing *mitzvos* and progressing nicely. The time came for a decision. Her *kollel* friends were very excited about her, all the *mitzvos* she did, how committed she was. Still, could she be converted? What about her relationship with her boyfriend? It was the same question all over again. Finally, after several long telephone calls, they drove to Boston to see me.

We met a few times but, again, it was difficult to separate all the various influences and motives involved. Finally I tried the same test: "We'll move forward on the conversion, but if the *bais din* says you and your boyfriend have to break up, then you will have to separate completely."

She was terribly distraught and started crying. I told her not to try to give an answer on the spot, but rather to think it over and come back later. When she returned, she asked again if there was any other way to make their marriage possible. I told her no, that this was the

The variety of highly personal problems that enter the Rebbe's study is endless; but all receive his undivided attention and sage advice, based on his wide experience and the many hundreds of classical texts that fill his office and home to overflowing.

only way that seemed possible. It would have to be a firm, final agreement. She came back the next day, crying again, and said that yes, firmly and unalterably, she would accept the decision of the *bais din*, whatever that might be.

I told her to come back with her boyfriend that evening. When I told them that she had passed the test, and that they could get married, they were, of course, very happy. After things calmed down a bit, he turned to her and said, "Now we can cancel that reservation." When I asked what he meant, he explained that since they had come to Boston together in the same car, and since they might not be able to see each other again, they had called an airline and made a reservation for him to fly back alone! That was another detail that made a difference.

They too are happily married and religiously committed. In fact, she is now a lawyer to most of the observant community in their hometown, where her dedication is a model to others.

Of course, every case is different, and what would be an appropriate test in one situation may not be appropriate or sufficient in another. Still, we were impressed by the uncompromising devotion displayed by these two new members of our people.

Mattos

And Moses said to them: "Have you spared the [Midianite] women?
They are the very ones [who caused] the Children of Israel...
To rebel against Hashem..."
(Numbers 31:15-16)

And Boaz said to her [Ruth, the Moabite],
"...May your reward be complete from Hashem,
The G-d of Israel, under Whose wings you have taken shelter."
(Ruth 2:11-12)

The relationship between the Jewish and non-Jewish worlds has long been a double-edged association. One cannot ignore the disastrous ways in which the blandishments of non-Jewish society can sap the religious strength and continuity of our people. A single look at America's Jewish illiteracy and staggering intermarriage rate makes that point all too clear.

This week's parshah reveals that these corrupting attractions and their fatal consequences are, unfortunately, nothing new. The Torah even identifies their root cause, an improper emphasis on personal physical gratification. The Israelites began by eating from the sacrifices of their pagan neighbors and intermingled with their daughters, and the end result was their worship of the same idols that their neighbors worshipped with such zeal. The very nature of the worship of the idol of Midian (which involved bodily wastes) only served to mock the emptiness and worthlessness of such materialistic "worship," but the Jews, no less than their neighbors, became hooked.

Our Sages expand on the negative role the Midianite women played in this process. The old women stood outside the Midianite tents saying, "Bargains! Come buy excellent merchandise for cheap." Having excited their greed, they then lured Israelite men into their tents ("Even better bargains inside!") where the young Midianite women enticed them to sin. Modern secular society certainly knows how to use greed and lust to "hook" its victims as well. Not many realize until too late that it is really no bargain at all, but a terrible loss.

On the other hand, the nobility and spiritual grandeur of those non-Jewish men and women who have been able to rise above the pitfalls of their own culture, and who seek the purity and beauty of a Torah life, cannot help but elicit, as in Boaz's case, the most sincere admiration. Our Sages explain that the entire Moabite and Ammonite nations were saved only because of the "two young doves," Ruth and Naamah, who were destined to descend from them. Their comment has an important corollary: For two such righteous women, it was worth it!

The Rebbe has been deeply touched by the religious commitment of the sincere converts he has helped over the years. Their stories are numerous and varied but perhaps this one — adapted from a letter the Rebbe recently received — can suffice.

✺ Ruth in New England

"*I* lived with my parents in a small town in New England. It was a beautiful, peaceful place; but it was one place where, if you were Protestant or Jewish, you didn't bother mentioning it. The town was definitely Irish Catholic.

"My maternal grandmother was born Presbyterian, but she had to sign papers at her wedding promising to raise her children as Catholics. My mother, however, left Catholicism to become a Methodist when she was only 17. Then my grandmother converted back to Catholicism when she was in her 50s. I even went to the ceremony. I was greatly impressed, if scared, by all the pomp. Mother, however, was disgusted by the showy rituals reserved only for the priests, and forbidden to the common man.

"My parents were very ethical, moral people and I was raised as a good 'moral majority' Christian. Dating was not encouraged, although my folks gave me lots of freedom and encouragement to spend time with other female friends.

"While preparing for confirmation, my intensive Bible study made me aware of the surprising fact that the founder of Christianity had not himself fulfilled the responsibilities of his own faith. To a 12-year-old this was very confusing. All of my childhood had been involved with church activities and youth groups; but I continued my course of Biblical, increasingly Jewish-oriented, study throughout my teenage years. By 16 I had decided to become Jewish on my own. I began by keeping 'kosher,' although most of the rules were, at that time, not very clear to me. For example, I began by not drinking milk with cheeseburgers (!) and forgoing pork and ham.

"When I told Dad that I wanted to be Jewish, his only comment was a typically laconic New England one: 'Just don't tell your mother.' My school friends had changed, and slowly, over the years, I began to realize that many of my closest friends were Jewish. In college I studied ancient cultures and continued reading about recent Jewish history. After a European tour with a college choir in 1979, I went home and told my parents that I had definitely decided to become Jewish. I had dated a few Jewish boys in college and now had a much better grasp of *kashrus,* Shabbos and *Yom Tov.* (You learn fast when you are the only *goyah* at the *seder* and people seem less than thrilled by your presence.)

"I became friendly with many 'Conservadox' students at college and came to Boston to attend the Gerim institute of New England's Assembly Course. But the more I learned, the more the institute didn't seem quite the right place for me. For example, we were required to write an important term paper on Judaism to pass the course. Being *shomer kashrus, shomer Shabbos* and *shomer negiah* didn't seem to matter so much; the paper appeared to hold more weight. Then I noticed something else about my fellow students: Out of the 25 to 30 people taking the course, only two of us were not engaged to be married to a Jew! If there was neither personal commitment nor observance, what was left?

"By then I had already met the Bostoner Rebbe, and the Rebbe's approach to *halachah* had me thinking...Why convert this way when I wanted to do more? I called the Rebbe and, soon afterwards, began studying with Mrs. Yehudis Fishman at the Rebbe's suggestion.

"During my first school break home with my family, Mother, racked by an almost physical pain, closeted herself in her room for a few days and refused to speak to me. My father's wry comment on all that was, 'Well, I hope you know what's for lunch!' — another masterpiece of Yankee understatement. When Mother began speaking to me again, the canyon between us was immense. She said I didn't love her, that I was betraying everything they stood for, that I was separating myself from the family.

"During this sensitive time I tried to come home only for *'parve'* holidays, and eventually I stopped going home during the last week of December, replacing that visit with a short weekend at the beginning of the month. Often I would light my Chanukah menorah in the kitchen, with my parents' tree all set up in the living room. The heart-wrenching pain I felt each December, when I knew how much this must hurt my parents, was incredible. I stopped entering stores, didn't listen to the radio and tried to avoid any awareness of non-Jewish holidays. Hearing all the seasonal songs was especially difficult.

"During this transitional period I didn't seem to be either a Jew or a non-Jew. It was almost like leading a double life. The last time I entered a church with statues, I felt a sick feeling in my stomach. All the kneeling down and communions were already not a part of my life; but what would replace them? I was also very concerned that I might not be accepted into Judaism. Then I would be stuck in a no man's land; not able to live as a full member of either community. I knew that I could never go back to being what I was, but what about my children? It was frightening; but I felt that I had to be Jewish.

"I spent only one more Easter dinner at home, before I converted and stopped going. It was, to say the least, a tense, surreal meal. There on the table were my *matzos* and my mother's ham and hot cross buns. Then my maternal grandmother suddenly said, 'Oh look — *matzah* on the table, just like when I was a girl.' Very strange, but under the circumstances, I let it pass.

"I was finally allowed to convert and join the Jewish people. Later I met my future husband and we married. After I had been married for a year or so, my grandmother told me, 'You know, dear, my mother's grandfather, Solomon Moss, was Jewish. His wife's last name was Rothchild and she may have also been Jewish, especially since her children were named Fanny, Sarah and Rachel.'

"Why hadn't I been told before? Apparently she considered it unseemly to discuss how every generation of our family had converted to some other religion. My family has been very busy trying to get back to *Yiddishkeit*. I am glad that, despite all the difficulties, I was *zocheh* to make it."

The Rebbe often emphasizes that influences from previous generations can affect the present. Sometimes the most unlikely influences are involved — yet another example of how Hashem shows that He, not mechanical necessity, rules the world. This is not only true of non-Jewish converts; it is true of "Jewish converts" as well, as the following short glimpses demonstrate.

❧ The Road Back

A young lady from America once spent Shabbos with us in Jerusalem and came back later in the week for a *brachah*. I asked her how she had become such a determined *baalas teshuvah*. "It began," she said, "with my grandfather. He once called me in and told me: 'I want you to remember three things. Remember that you are Jewish. Remember Shabbos. And remember me.'

"His statements made a powerful impression on me; but since our home was not religious, I was rather at sea. I decided to start by lighting Shabbos candles. Every Friday night I faithfully lit my candles...week after week. And every Friday night my father just as faithfully came and put them out, week after week. So I became religious because of my grandfather...and my father."

Her words, uttered with complete seriousness, seemed baffling at best.

"Your father? The one who put your candles out, week after week?"

"Yes," she said. "He was the one who made me realize that if he could so stubbornly put them out, I could just as stubbornly keep them burning. So I became religious because of both of them, my father and my grandfather."

She had learned a great deal from her two "teachers." We can learn not only from the positive influences we encounter, but from the negative ones as well — withstanding them, transforming them and strengthening ourselves in the process.

※

I once asked the same question, "How did you become a *baal teshuvah*?" to a young man who was studying in a *kollel* in Yerushalayim.

His odyssey began in a Buddhist *ashram* (meditation center) in the American southwest. One day their little group was abuzz with exciting news: The brother of the Dalai Lama, the head of Tibetan Buddhism, was coming for a visit. Anticipation was incredibly keen until the great day arrived.

The young man waited his turn until, at last, he too was admitted for a private, face-to-face meeting. The Dalai Lama's brother calmly scrutinized him and asked him quietly, "Where do you come from [spiritually]?"

"Our family was originally Jewish."

"And do you know anything about Judaism?"

"Not really."

"Then why don't you study your own religion?"

Our young friend was stunned; but decided to try. Unfortunately, where he was located, he couldn't find anyone to advise him on what Jewish books to read or where to find them. Eventually someone recommended a book by Isaac Bashevis Singer which had become popular just then. Despite the book's worldly cynicism and pornographic veneer, our friend was moved by the underlying glimpses of the warm family life of a religious, Eastern European Jewish home. Where there is a will, there is a way. Our Sages relate *(Taanis 25a)* that the daughter of R' Chanina ben Dosa once put vinegar instead of oil into the Shabbos lamp. Her father told her: "Don't worry. He Who makes the oil burn will make the vinegar burn as well." Thus, even this "vinegar book" was enough to kindle our young friend's interest in *Yiddishkeit*.

One book led to another until he finally read Herman Wouk's *This is My G-d*. Then everything seemed to fall into place. He left the *ashram*, and moved to Jerusalem with his young family to learn in a *kollel* for *baalei teshuvah*.

After hearing his story, I couldn't help but marvel at how hidden from mankind are the way of *hashgachah* (providence). We cannot fathom the rewards that are meted out in the World to Come. One could almost picture I. B. Singer knocking on the gates of *Gan Eden* pleading, "Open up and let me in! Can't you see that *baal teshuvah* I helped make? Just look at him learning in *kollel* and raising a *frum* family in Jerusalem!"

Masei

Anyone who kills a person accidentally ...
Shall live there [in the city of refuge]
Until the death of the High Priest.
(Numbers 35:15,25)

Because the High Priest should have prayed
That there should not have been such a calamity.
(Rashi)

Prayer, Torah observance and mutual concern are the ultimate preventative medicine, both for the community and the individual. We are responsible not only for our own physical and spiritual health and well-being, but for that of every other Jew as well. Every life is so very precious that, when one person shortens another's life, even accidentally, he must leave his own normal life to seek atonement through exile in a city of refuge.

Although the Torah explicitly gives doctors permission to heal, they are constantly involved in thorny ethical dilemmas, for valiant medical attempts to prolong life can often end up accidentally shortening it. Since such treatments are active, deliberate interventions, there are no easy answers. Jewish law is full of discussions about temporary life (chayei sha'ah) and more permanent life (chayei olam) and how to weigh one against the other. In particular, the poskim discuss at length the complex problems involved in deciding how and when to risk the former for *a chance at the latter. It is encouraging that the world at large, and the medical profession in particular, is becoming more sensitive to these very serious issues.*

❧ *Medical Ethics*

One day Dr. Henry Mankin, a top orthopedic surgeon at the Massachusetts General Hospital, called the Chassidic Center and asked me to serve on the search committee for the Cheryl Chair of Biomedical Ethics at Harvard. The Harvard administration was receptive to the idea of including a Chassidic Rebbe to represent the Torah point of view. I accepted at once, since Jewish medical ethics has long been an interest, almost a specialty, of mine and I was interested in learning more about how the non-Jewish world went about addressing similar ethical considerations. The appointment would also provide useful contacts with several leading physicians who were not yet affiliated with our ROFEH health support organization.

The final committee was fairly large, about 20 people, each a recognized expert in his field. We met about 20 times to discuss both the candidates and broader ethical issues. Although the committee itself was mostly non-Jewish, they were intensely interested in hearing the Torah point of view. I didn't realize how far this went until the day the chairman came over and said, "You know, the Massachusetts General Hospital is holding a full-day seminar on Biomedical Ethics and we hope that you can come join us. Why don't you come around noon?" As a member of his committee, I felt obliged to attend, at least for an hour or so, to show my support.

When I arrived, several people greeted me in the lobby. "Please wait a few minutes," they said. "We want to seat you at the head table." That seemed somewhat odd, because the people at the head table were presumably part of the program, but perhaps committee members were an exception. The huge auditorium was packed and the speakers were impressive indeed. They were dis-

Deeply involved in medical outreach and chessed, the Rebbe here visits and comforts seriously ill children from Israel's Zichron Menachem Organization.

cussing the hypothetical case of an 80-year-old man with a punctured aorta: chance of death with surgery, 80%; without, 97%. What should one do? The chief of nursing proposed one criteria: Do what you can. A distinguished doctor countered with another: Do no harm. The arguments flew back and forth, until the session chairman brought it to a close.

"Now," he said, "let's hear what the clergy think." Relaxed, I looked up and down the table, trying to find the clergymen he was referring to. "Rabbi, what do you think?" Who, me? I hadn't prepared to speak at all, but this was obviously no time for excuses.

Carefully I explained that, from a Jewish perspective, the order in which various ethical principles are applied is very important. We start with the position that our bodies are created by Hashem and belong to Hashem. At this first level, we have no right to damage any body, for any reason — it's simply not ours to dispose of. That's why we do not permit post-mortem autopsies. But saving a life is also an important Torah principle, so surgery is allowed if a life will indeed be saved. Thus, while each case is different, if an operation is generally 98 percent successful but 2 percent unsuc-

The Rebbe (R) often discussed the halachic ramifications of medical issues with his close friend, R' Shlomo Zalman Auerbach, zt"l, (L) here seen at a meeting with R' Markovitz, Karliner Rosh Yeshivah (C). The Rebbe's oldest grandson, R' Moshe Shimon Horowitz, is seated behind them.

cessful we obviously permit it. But if an operation is rated 80 percent unsuccessful, 20 percent successful, the question is serious. Life is sacred, and our permission to act is limited. While one can never generalize, sitting passively (*shev v'al taaseh*) is usually preferable in such cases to "having blood on one's hands." Perhaps those last words were a bit overdramatic, but I was speaking extemporaneously without time to prepare a more gentle response.

A minister spoke next; he would allow such a long-shot operation. Then someone else spoke, and the discussion continued. I had to leave before the session's end. As I slowly walked by the session chairman, he quietly voiced his thanks and then asked, with a gentle smile on his face, "Does the Rebbe really think that we have blood on our hands?" I knew from our many conversations that the two of us basically agreed on the underlying issues involved, but he couldn't resist the friendly barb.

Rather than return the pleasantry, I decided to answer his question seriously. One could well have different perspectives at different times. A doctor has to decide, on the spot, what has to be done and do it. However, when a doctor later looks back and reconsiders his case, he can often see something he may have done wrong. The on-the-spot decision, if sincerely made to the best of one's ability, is in some sense *prospectively* right. However, that same decision can be *retrospectively* wrong. I suggested that physicians focus not on the question of their *post-facto* guilt, but on how they could best learn from their past experiences to make better decisions in the future.

※

> And the daughters of Zelofchad did
> What Hashem had commanded Moshe...
> They married into the families of Menasheh
> The son of Yosef.
> (Numbers 36:10-12)

What better way for Sefer Bamidbar to end than with a nice Jewish wedding!

Of coursed finding the right mate isn't always easy, and the daughters of Zelofchad are not the only ones to have spent much time weighing all the complex factors involved. And rightly so. Marriage is a serious decision, one which requires considerable siyata d'shmaya (Divine aid).

The Midrash tells us that a Roman matron once asked Rabbi Yose ben Chalafta, "What does G-d do all day now that the world has been created?" He told her, "He is busy arranging marriages" (which also creates new worlds). Not to be outdone, she paired up a thousand male and female slaves and married them all off in one day. Her cockiness disappeared the next morning when a thousand slaves, many with black eyes and bruised limbs, returned to complain: "I can't possibly live with him/her!" Then she had to admit that Hashem's chosen "profession" was beyond human abilities after all.

Our Sages say that finding the right mate is as difficult as the splitting of the Reed Sea. The Rebbe's son, R' Mayer, is fond of saying that this is because at the Sea, according to the Midrash, everyone had their special plans for what to do: some wanted to surrender, some wanted to fight, etc. Hashem, however, had His own plans, and what actually happened was the one thing that no one had anticipated: The Sea split and they were saved without recourse to any of their prior plans.

Finding one's bashert is similar. Everyone has their game plans, ideas and advice — and honest effort is in order — but one often finds one's bashert in the least expected way. One shouldn't worry unduly. Hashem knows his "business" and the world is in good hands. Indeed, as one of the Rebbe's Chassidim found out, when it comes to matchmaking, Hashem still does a spectacular job.

ೞ *The Fountains Of Rome*

There was a student who came by every so often, a well-meaning fellow who was no more (or less) mixed up than most of the college students who visited the Chassidic Center. He stayed in Boston an exceptionally long time, progressing from undergraduate to graduate student, to post-doctoral fellow, research associate and finally associate professor, remaining unmarried all the while. He had met many young women, but never "the right one."

He finally found an out-of-town job and moved to the suburbs of Philadelphia. There he dated the few Orthodox girls he could find, and then his usually active social life plummeted to zero. By this time, even he was beginning to worry about marriage, so he made some friends in the large Orthodox singles "scene" on the West Side of Manhattan and spent nearly every Shabbos there. He left work early, caught an Amtrak train to New York, dressed quickly and went to *shul*, ate, slept (often on the floor in a sleeping bag), got up, went back to *shul* ... and tried to meet people.

This young man was quite methodical and efficient. He arranged to meet young ladies at Shabbos meals with his friends and at classes on Shabbos afternoons. He arranged dates for Saturday night and for Sunday morning brunch and for a museum trip on Sunday afternoon before heading back to Philadelphia. Once he even made (by mistake) and kept (by extreme effort) two dates for the *same* Saturday night! It was hectic and draining to say the least, but he was determined.

Despite all this effort, he just couldn't seem to find "Miss Perfect." I happened to see him once at our *shul* in Boston and asked casually how things were going. He suddenly looked very serious and asked me, "Actually, can we go upstairs and talk about it?" Upstairs in my office, he poured out his heart: all the effort, the disappointments, etc., etc., while I just sat there and listened. Finally he finished and waited expectantly for the sympathy he felt he deserved. Instead, I let the silence deepen and then asked him quite frankly: "Do you have any other choice?" That quickly brought him back to reality, and the pursuit continued, until one summer...

Our friend was going to Berlin to attend one of a long series of international meetings for his firm. One of the department heads called him to ask if he would accompany him to a meeting in Rome first. "Sorry," he said. "I don't want to be away so long." This executive however, wouldn't take "no" for an answer. The meeting was relevant to our friend's work, his office would be able to cover for him and — the real reason — this particular executive hated traveling alone. Finally our friend agreed, and off they went.

The meeting went well, and our friend *davened* that Friday night in the small *shul* in the Via di Balboa near his hotel. "Tomorrow," he said to himself, "I'll get up early and walk all the way to the big synagogue in the Old Ghetto." In fact, he did nothing of the kind. He woke up late and was lucky to make it to the Balboa *shul* in time to catch services "acceptably" late.

It was the height of the 1970s wave of Jewish immigration from the Soviet Union, and immigrants were traveling through Vienna to Rome, where they waited to leave through the port of Ostia to the U.S. or Israel. When our friend went downstairs for a moment during the services, he found an American Lubavitcher *shaliach*, surrounded by a crowd of Russian emigres in jeans, asking him for various types of help. Our friend waited patiently and then introduced himself. He asked the *shaliach* if he knew the Bostoner Rebbe and, when his response was, "Of course!" they soon got to talking.

The rabbi wanted to invite him over for lunch, but our friend explained that a young Libyan fellow sitting next to him had already done so. "Don't worry," the Rabbi said, "I'll take care of that for you. Besides, he probably lives far away, while I am relatively nearby."

After *shul* the two of them began walking to the rabbi's apartment...and walking, and walking, and walking. Every few blocks — for three miles! — the rabbi kept saying, "Just a bit more now," until finally they arrived. When he knocked, an attractive young woman opened the door. She was holding a baby with one arm and holding onto a young child with the other. Our friend assumed she was the rebbetzin, but it turned out she was a frequent house guest and volunteer babysitter, a religious American Jewess who was working in Rome.

During the meal they began talking, and then they went for a walk with the rabbi's children (she had promised them and just couldn't disappoint them). That night they walked around the beautifully lit fountains of Rome. It was wonderful, but our friend still had to leave for Berlin the next morning. They agreed to meet in Madrid the next weekend, on his way home. There they walked around the beautiful Plaza de Mayor each night, with a few more fountains thrown in for good measure — courting in two of the most romantic places on earth.

A month or so later, our friend was acquiring more "frequent flyer" miles traveling back to Rome for a 10-day "vacation." He told me he had found someone "interesting," and told his father only that he was paying for this trip himself, after years of company-sponsored travel. We both immediately knew that something was up and, sure enough, a month or so later, the two of them were shopping on New York's Lower East Side for 200 embossed *benchers*.

They were married on the front lawn of their new home outside Philadelphia, and the Rebbetzin and I, and many of their Boston friends, came to celebrate with them. Our friend had been in a quandary, because his parents wanted their local rabbi, a close family friend, to officiate. At almost the last minute this rabbi's son decided to remarry on the same day (in Boston!) and so I was *mesader kiddushin*, as they had wanted, after all.

Although it was late autumn, which is usually cold and rainy in Philadelphia, their wedding day was warm and sunny. In short, it was a lovely *simchah*. Still, when someone asked why we had come all the way down to Philadelphia to marry them off, we couldn't resist telling them: "After all these years, we wanted to make sure he went through with it!"

They are still happily married, our friend and his beautiful bride, and they are now raising a wonderful religious family in Israel. His wife, a busy *baalas chessed* and the granddaughter of a Williamsburg *tzaddik*, somehow takes it all in stride. The Rebbetzin and I still see them every so often and have enjoyed seeing their family grow.

Everything that happens is *hashgachah*, the result of Hashem's guidance over the world, but this is clearer at some times than at others. This young man had planned (unsuccessfully) for years to meet his *"bashert"*; he wasn't supposed to go to Rome, or to *daven* that morning in the small synagogue, or to go to lunch with that *shaliach*. And I wasn't supposed to be *mesader kiddushin*, and it was supposed to rain ... and Hashem "supposed" the opposite, and everything turned out fine. *Baruch Hashem.*

Devarim
The Book of Deuteronomy

Casting Accounts

The 40-year journey nears its end; the young child has now become an old man. A new generation of Jews spreads out across the Plains of Moav, waiting impatiently to cross the Jordan to Jericho. The Book of Devarim teaches two lessons that the old have always tried to teach the young. First, to remember.

Devarim thus begins with a set of "snapshots," a photo album of important national events. Here we are encamped in the Aravah, here we are at the Reed Sea (Deuteronomy 1:1). This is what happened at Sinai, with the Spies, in the Wars. But all this is not mere reminiscence. It reflects an insistence that we learn from the past and live a different, better future.

That is the second main lesson of the book: to learn. Here Hashem reveals through Moshe the "real" story, the hidden spiritual story of Israel's past and its implications for the future. Again and again Moshe hammers home his cautionary vision of the future: glory, then sin, suffering, repentance and restoration. Again and again he tries to limit the future damage, recalling Hashem's love, demanding Israel's faithfulness, promising blessings, threatening curses.

His efforts reach their peak with the Song of Ha'azinu (Deuteronomy 32) in which Moshe calls Heaven and Earth as witnesses against those who would break their faith with Hashem. But, in introducing Ha'azinu, the Torah itself hints at the ultimate purpose of all remembrance and warning:

> And Moshe spoke the words of this song
> In the ears of all the Jewish people
> Until they were complete ["tumam"]
> (Deuteronomy 31:30).

The "they" of the verse does not refer to the words of the song, say the Chassidic Masters, but to the people. Moshe spoke these words over and over again until the hearts of the people were complete and perfected (another meaning of the Hebrew word tumam), and his words themselves had that power. The purpose of Torah is to change the very essence of the person.

The stories of this section are also largely recollections of different times and assorted challenges but, like all true memories, they also point to what's wrong, what's right and, most importantly, what's possible.

Devarim

*These are the words [of rebuke] which Moshe
Spoke to all Israel ...
"How can I bear alone
Your trouble and burden and strife?"
 (Deuteronomy 1:1,12)*

*If Moshe left [his tent] early, they said ...
"He probably has troubles at home,"
If he left late, they said ...
"He probably was [busy] sitting and plotting
Evil plots against you."
(Rashi)*

Running a community is not a simple matter — not in Moshe's time and not in ours. Each member of the community is an individual world and requires personal care. Furthermore, although the ikar (main thing) in life is spiritual, ours is a physical world and the world itself does not let you forget it. Everyone's thanks and gratitude for the help given them is heartwarming and appreciated, but the shul's heating system must be fixed, food is needed for the upcoming Shabbaton and the last shul appeal didn't yield the expected results.

People don't forget to share their troubles and failures with their Rebbe and community, but when it comes to sharing their successes and resources, memories tend to be a bit shorter. Yet *such strengths and successes are precisely what the community needs to help others. It is said that a Rebbe who once told his Chassid that every middah (character trait), even the seemingly worst, has its proper place, and that is why it was created. "Really?" the student asked, "But what about kefirah (heresy), denying the very existence of Hashem?" "Quite important," said his Rebbe, "for, when someone asks you for help, you shouldn't say, 'Hashem will take care of it' you should do it yourself!"*

Few people understood the needs of community, its institutions, leaders and laymen better than ...

❧ The Ponevezer Rav

During the 1940s, R' Yosef Kahaneman, the founder and head of the famous Ponevez *yeshivah* in Bnei Brak, frequently visited America to help raise funds for the yeshivah. He was an exceptional figure, a legend in his own time, and his approach to fundraising was equally exceptional.

In those days, Boston was on the itinerary of most prominent, and not-so-prominent, *rabbanim* collecting money for their institutions. As a young rabbi, just starting out, I was almost always a target of their demands. Could I give them a list of prospects, call some of our donors for them, visit prospects with them — never mind that they were the 10th such demanding visitor that week! I was rarely able to oblige, because setting a precedent could have been disastrous ("Why him and not me?").

R' Kahaneman was different. He came to pay a courtesy call — despite my young age — discussed Torah topics for a while, paid his respects and left. His *divrei Torah* (teachings) on such occasions always made a lasting impression. He never asked for help of any kind and he never went to our regular *gevirim* (wealthy members), on whom our *shul* relied for support. He visited only people on his own list, his own contacts, friends and alumni.

This uneven relationship continued for years, until I finally asked Rav Kahaneman if we couldn't help him in some way. If he would just say the word, I would join him. *"Chas v'shalom!"* he said, in his characteristically direct manner, "Collecting money is like going to a *shvitz-bad* (Turkish bath)." He saw my puzzled expression and explained:

"What happens in a *shvitz-bad?* First you have to undress — embarrassing, very embarrassing. Then you *shvitz* (sweat) in the steam room. Then you lay down on the massage table and wait for the *beder* (attendant) to come and give you a *pletze* (rubdown). And what do you

R' Yosef Kahaneman, the Ponevezer Rav, whose vision turned Bnei Brak into a bastion of Torah

think as you lie there? Here I am, a *chashuvah* (important) person, lying here without my clothes on, and this ignorant *beder* is going to come in, fully clothed, and see me in this embarrassing position. What a *bushah* (embarrassment)! But then you think: true, but that's what happens in here. In a few minutes, after I get what I need, I'll be gone and this *beder* will never see me again.

"That's what makes collecting money bearable," said R' Kahaneman. "But you, my dear Rebbe, you are staying here. You have to retain your *kavod* (dignity). I'm leaving town, but you must remain here in the *shvitz-bad!*"

> *You shall not respect persons in judgment,*
> *You shall hear out the small and great alike,*
> *And shall fear no man —*
> *For judgment is Hashem's.*
> *(Deuteronomy 1:17)*

Devarim ◦₰ 301

When it comes to making sure people do the right thing, one cannot consider one's own personal welfare, embarrassment, special relationships or "political correctness." One must be fearless, even when facing those who think themselves great and knowing, especially when they are too ignorant to know the magnitude of their potential loss, or the depths from which you have saved them.

෬ The Granddaughter

Once, during the early '90s, we received a call from Monsey, New York. It seems that a certain old woman, the granddaughter of a great European Torah giant of a previous generation, was critically ill in a Boston hospital. Although neither the old woman nor her daughter, a mathematics professor who had emigrated with her from Russia, was religious — not surprising after so many years of Communist rule — the caller wanted us to offer our assistance. When we called the hospital and asked if we could help, the daughter, who answered the phone, said a curt "No!" and slammed down the receiver. It was hardly a promising start.

The next morning we called the daughter's boyfriend to offer our help once again. He told us that would not be necessary; the mother had died during the night and her body was scheduled to be cremated, in direct defiance of Jewish law, at 9 the next morning! We immediately called the funeral home to see if they could either stop or delay the cremation, but they said that it was out of their hands. Finally, closing the circle, we called our friend in Monsey who said that the only person the daughter might listen to was a cousin who lived in Israel.

We decided to call in Judge David Knight and his wife Goldie, a very special religious couple who had befriended this mother and daughter in the past. Judge Knight and his wife went over to the daughter's house and tried to convince her to cancel the cremation. She wouldn't budge, but she did agree to try to reach her cousin in Israel. The Knights stayed with her all night.

When she finally reached her cousin, he told her, "I can't tell you what to do but, if it was up to me, I wouldn't do it." Considering the daughter's strong opposition and her cousin's rather weak response, the Knights were surprised when, on a sudden impulse, she abruptly turned to them and said: "O.K. There will be no cremation."

They continued talking to prevent her from changing her mind. Then she made another impulsive comment: "There will be no cremation, but I don't want a funeral either, or any graveside ceremony, just the two of you with me at the cemetery." The Knights agreed and called us, around 5 a.m., with the good news. At least there wasn't going to be a cremation. Judge Knight wanted to know what to do about the non-funeral, and I told him to just recite a *kapitel Tehillim*, (psalm) quietly at the grave, when no one was looking.

Later the daughter broke up with her boyfriend for "getting her into this mess," and she sent us a scathing letter for "plotting" against her. It was a letter that Nikita Krushchev, the crude former premier of the USSR, might have written. Here she was, the great-granddaughter of a Torah giant, an "educated" college professor who had never heard of *Yetzias Mitzrayim* (the Exodus from Egypt), pouring out her wrath on virtually everything her pious ancestor had stood for in *Yiddishkeit*. Still, one couldn't help but feel that her impulsive change that crucial night was Heaven's way of nudging things along at that great *tzaddik's* request.

※

Be not terrified,
Nor frightened of them.
(Deuteronomy 1:29)

Fear is a strange thing. The Israelites had witnessed Hashem's destruction of the mighty Egyptian army, the pride of the largest empire of the time, while they stood by the Reed Sea in helpless silence. Yet they were afraid of a handful of small, scattered Canaanite kingdoms. Indeed they concluded that Hashem must have hated them to have put them into such a terrifying situation (verse 27).

Fear is more a reflection of our perception of reality than reality itself. In explaining verse 25, the Sages of the Sifrei quote the well-known proverb, "What you feel about your friend, you imagine he feels about you." Our fears of the outside world are often projections and externalizations of what we feel within. Rav Nachman of Bratzlav made much the same point when he taught that people desire what cannot help them and fear what cannot harm them, for their desires and fears originate within their subconscious selves (Sichos HaRan, 83).

Fear is always part illusion; and obeying the Torah's advice to put fear aside helps us concentrate on the all-too-real challenges we face. Indeed, sometimes fear can be all illusion.

ೞ **Not Quite Kidnapped**

During the 1950s, one of Boston's top renal specialists was a certain Dr. M. of the Peter Bent Brigham Hospital. He had been deeply involved in developing the dialysis machine and other kidney-related devices and was, in short, an outstanding physician. He was also eccentric, excitable and enjoyed collecting his expensive fee.

He once charged a poor rabbi from *Eretz Yisrael* $500, an astounding sum in those days. I called to try to explain the delicate financial situation of this patient to Dr. M.'s secretary — after all, I didn't want to bother such an important doctor with mere "money matters." To my surprise, he immediately took the telephone himself and said in his solemn bass voice, "Hello. This is Dr. M. I would like to be paid the $500 in full, with another $100 as a donation to our research program. Thank you." [Click!] Apparently he felt that if one was lucky enough to get him — and he was a true expert — money should be no object.

This particular story took place shortly after the 1956 Suez Campaign, when the Middle East was still in turmoil from the British-French-Israeli invasion of the Sinai. A young Israeli with serious kidney problems had been admitted, with the help of ROFEH, our medical support organization, into Peter Bent Brigham Hospital, where King Saud of Saudi Arabia had stayed the week before. The king had been accompanied by a large retinue of Arabs who ran all around the hospital dressed in their exotic-looking *kaffiahs* (headdresses) and *galabiyahs* (Arab robes). The U.S. and Arabian Secret Service were there, too ... in short, it was a major production. And rightly so: The newspapers were full of stories about Middle East violence almost every day.

One day, while visiting our Israeli charge, we met Dr. M. in the hall. He was accompanied by about 20 to 30 students and interns who were following him on his rounds. When he saw me, he stopped and said, "Oh, Rabbi Horowitz! I just had the scare of my life!"

"Really? What happened?"

"Well," said Dr. M., "I went into your Israeli friend's room and found him surrounded by a group of Arabs in black-and-white striped robes and headdresses. I was petrified, but I tried to intervene. War or no war, how dare they kidnap a patient from our hospital!

"Just then, one of the 'Arabs' excused himself; saying, 'I am sorry if we frightened you, doctor. We just came to make a *minyan* and we are now finishing our prayers!'"

Apparently, the black-and-white *tallaisim* (prayer shawls) we Jews wear over our heads during prayer were mistaken by the good doctor for extra-long *kaffiahs!* Indeed, things sometimes are not what they seem.

Devarim ❧ 305

Va'eschanan

Observe [these commandments] and do them
For they are your wisdom and understanding
In the eyes of the [non-Jewish] nations ...
(Deuteronomy 4:6)

We Jews have been in exile for almost 2,000 years now, so the question of how to relate to non-Jewish society and "the nations of the world" is far from a theoretical one. One response, unfortunately, has been to abandon our own heritage and become more Greek than the Greeks, more German than the Germans. Far from yielding the respect and worldly advantages they sought, the intrusion and competition of these "new goyim" only fueled the resentment of the non-Jewish society. Not only were the conversos of Spain not accepted, they were actively persecuted, and hostility towards them helped bring about the Inquisition. Similarly, economic and cultural competition with the successful "Enlightened" Jews of Germany is often cited as one of the underlying causes of the Holocaust.

This week's parshah, which contains both the Ten Commandments and the Shema, the most basic fundamentals of our faith, charts another course. It condemns spiritual compromise with other religions in the strongest possible terms (7:2-6), while making a remarkable promise. Not only will an unflinching spiritual stance not fuel anti-Semitism, it alone will provide true security and respect. When Jews respect themselves and their Jewishness, others will respect them as well. As for "What will the goyim say?" the Torah itself addressed that very issue, from a higher perspective, long ago. "When they hear all these religious laws they will say: 'Surely this great nation is wise and understanding' (Deuteronomy 4:6)." Mutual respect can only begin with self-respect.

❦ *A College of Cardinals*

Unlike Judaism, the Catholic Church has a fixed hierarchy, with the cardinals ranking just beneath the pope. As would be expected, cardinals command considerable respect, particularly in the highly Catholic sections of Boston. I haven't had many public meetings with such senior non-Jewish clergy; but two near-misses did make a lasting impression.

The first began with my visit to a local Jewish funeral parlor. Usually the funeral director was a somber man, dressed in black, speaking in quiet soothing undertones. Today he came over, unable to suppress an ironic smile, and said, "Well, Rebbe, you would never guess what just happened. It's been a great day here for the clergy!"

Just before we had arrived, he had been preparing for another Jewish funeral, when in walked Richard Cardinal Cushing, the cardinal of Boston! It seems that his sister had married a Jewish man, who had retained his Jewish identity. The cardinal, as the brother-in-law of the deceased, had come to pay his last respects.

He took great care to ensure that the occasion remained private and that he caused no offense. He came without a retinue or cross. He asked for permission to read a few psalms and made no sermon of his own. It was tastefully done; but the funeral director couldn't hide his glee: "First a cardinal and now, Rebbe, you are here too!"

❦

Our next non-meeting with a cardinal involved a 1,000-person meeting of the Anti-Defamation League (ADL). They were honoring a close friend of ours, Professor William Schwartz, the dean of Boston University Law School, a religious Jew and now Vice President for

Academic Affairs of Yeshiva University. For reasons best known to themselves, the ADL had asked a recently appointed American cardinal to attend. When he walked in, via a side aisle, the crowd rose to its feet. Since I was seated on the center podium, I couldn't see who had entered and automatically stood as well. When I finally figured out what was going on, it was too late. The cardinal was already halfway down the aisle, his cross blatantly displayed.

What would I do when he reached the podium? To stand in respect for a cross was impossible. According to the *Midrash*, the reason Mordechai had refused to bow to Haman was that Haman wore an idol on his chest. On the other hand, to sit down just as the cardinal approached would be both an embarrassment and an insult. Meanwhile the oblivious cardinal kept coming closer and closer, nodding and smiling to the audience on both sides.

Once the cardinal had made the final turn, he could finally see the central podium. He immediately noticed me, dressed in my long black coat and wide-brimmed black hat, and he suddenly realized that a senior Jewish religious leader was present. Without a pause the cross suddenly disappeared under his heavy cassock, as he continued waving and walking towards the podium.

After the meeting, I was surrounded on all sides. "Did you see what the cardinal did? Did you notice? Unprecedented! What an honor!" This large group of non-religious Jews, who an hour ago couldn't have cared less about the cardinal's cross, was now suddenly proud of its *Yiddishkeit*. I was going to say something about Jews being honored by Hashem Himself at Mount Sinai and not needing the honor of human speakers at fund-raising banquets; but instead I told them what Father always said: "Once you respect yourself and your *Yiddishkeit*, others will too." It's advice still worth remembering.

Eikev

And if you will listen to these laws ...
Hashem your G-d will keep the covenant
And the mercy which He swore to your fathers...
Only in your fathers did Hashem have delight,
To love them and choose their seed after them.
(Deut. 7:12-13,10:15)

Zechus Avos, the merit of the fathers, is an important aspect of our designation as the Chosen People. Just as fathers can store and leave their descendants physical treasures, they can, if their devotion to Torah and Hashem are sufficient, leave them spiritual treasures as well. Every Rosh Hashanah, Jews all over the world still pray for Hashem to remember His love for Avraham and the sacrifice (Akeidah) of Yitzchak, and to forgive our errors for their sake. Indeed, the Shulchan Aruch states it as a matter of law. If you know that someone will grant you a favor both for your sake and for your father's sake, you should honor your father by saying, "Please do this for my father's sake."

Hashem remembers "the covenant and mercy He swore to our fathers" whenever we ourselves follow their ways ("If you will listen"); and the examples set by our fathers can themselves influence us to choose the proper path. That is one reason why we Jews have always felt very close to our ancestors and teachers (and to our rebbes), even after their passing. Among Chassidim, yahrzeits are usually celebrated with a siyum and seudas mitzvah or with a l'chaim and refreshments in shul. All convey the same message: We identify with and dedicate ourselves to what these tzaddikim stood for. A related custom is visiting and praying at the graves of the righteous. Our proximity to these spiritual giants inspires us to serve Hashem with some spark of their greatness. Such a trip also honors the Torah and Hashem, whose ideals the righteous embodied.

This practice goes back at least to the time of Calev, a contemporary of Moshe Rabbeinu and Yehoshua who, according to the Talmud (Sotah 34), went to the Tomb of the Patriarchs in Hebron to pray that he be saved from the evil influence of the Spies. Similarly, it has long been the custom of Chassidim to go to great lengths to visit the graves of their rebbes and the founders of the Chassidic movement. Unfortunately, until recently, many of these holy sites were locked behind the Iron Curtain. Even after the collapse of Communism in Eastern Europe, visiting them has not been all that easy and sometimes, as the following story shows, it requires a bit of extra help.

ೞ *Eliyahu in Nikolsburg*

As a seventh-generation direct descendant of R' Shmuel Shmelke of Nikolsburg (*ben achar ben*), I had always wanted to visit and pray at his *tziun* (grave). As long as Czechoslovakia was behind the Iron Curtain, this was impossible; but in the late 1980s, things began to open up. So, one year while visiting my *Chassidim* in Zurich, we decided to attempt a special trip to Nikolsburg with R' Danny Wormser, a Swiss *Chassid* and friend of ours.

We took a plane to Vienna where an experienced Jewish guide was supposed to meet us, since the local arrangements in Nikolsburg were rather complicated. The old Jewish cemetery was surrounded by a high wall, and the key had to be obtained from a caretaker who lived somewhere in the city. The graves themselves were also very difficult to locate.

Unfortunately, upon arriving in Vienna, we found that our guide had gone off on another assignment! Instead, he had sent an inexperienced, non-Jewish guide to drive us to Nikolsburg. Having no other choice, we got into the car and headed eastward to Bratislava, where we crossed the border from Austria into Czechoslovakia. We then circled back in a long arc to the northwest through Moravia *en route* to Nikolaev, which is what they called Nikolsburg in those days.

On the way we passed signs to the Bohemian town of Horovice (between Plzen and Prague), the city that gave our family its name, Horowitz. The family's original name was Bonvenisto but about 500 years ago, the head of the family began signing his letters "R' Yeshayahu HaLevi, Ish Horowitz." There are two traditional explanations of why he included the title *Ish*, the Hebrew word for "man." One tradition says he was the Lord Mayor (leader = "man") of Horovice; another, that *Ish* (*aleph-yud-shin*) is an acronym for Avraham Yeshayah Shmuel, the ancestors of the Horowitz line, according to family tradition.

Finally we arrived in Nikolaev. No Jews live there today, but we managed to find the old non-Jewish lady who still kept the keys to the Jewish cemetery. She also gave us a piece of paper on which there was a rough sketch that was supposed to help us find the *tziun*. The driver found the cemetery without difficulty, and left us off at the gate. Before entering I suddenly realized that my *kvitel* book, which listed all the people I wanted to pray for, was still in the car. Danny went back, but the car was already speeding off towards town.

A rebbe doesn't need all his luggage in a cemetery, but one thing a rebbe does need in a cemetery is *kvitlach*. Danny dashed off in a vain chase to stop the car as it sped away. "Don't worry," he called back. "If I don't catch up with him, I'll find him in the town."

After a brief wait, I entered the cemetery alone to search for the *tziun* using the old woman's hastily scribbled "map." It was hopeless. Nothing matched, and row after row of headstones revealed nothing even vaguely resembling R' Shmuel Shmelke. Finally I put the paper away and set off on a wider search, but in vain. No matter in which direction I turned, whether right or left, forward or back, the *tziun* was not to be found.

We had come all the way from Zurich just to pray at R' Shmuel Shmelke's *tziun*, and now we couldn't even find it! The driver was only a substitute guide, so he wouldn't know where to look, even if Danny could find him, and the old lady certainly didn't know anything. I redoubled my efforts at "detective work," but without results.

From the far end of the cemetery there was a view of a green valley and a beautiful mountain beyond. Below the cemetery wall, there were some teenage boys playing ball. Since they were not Jewish and I didn't speak Czech, there wasn't much hope that they could help, but I tried anyway. I took

His wish fulfilled, the Rebbe prays at the tziun (grave) of his famous ancestor, Reb Shmuel Shmelke of Nikolsburg.

out a pocket-sized *Tehillim* and started *shuckling* (swaying) as if in prayer. I was trying to say, "Where do people *daven* like this here?" When they didn't notice, I began *shuckling* more and more openly. "What's the matter? What else do they need? Don't they understand what I am looking for?" It seems humorous in retrospect but, at the time, the situation seemed desperate. Finally I had to accept that our quest had been futile.

I headed back to the cemetery gate, anxious because time was running out. The long drive back to Vienna would just barely leave time to catch the plane. A few minutes later, Danny Wormser came running in with the *kvitel* book. He had gone from one restaurant to the other until he had finally found the driver. *Baruch Hashem*! But I had to confess, "Danny, I can't find the *tziun*." "Don't worry," he said, running off again, further into the cemetery, "I'll find it." I watched his progress and then waited — 5 minutes, 10 minutes, 15 minutes.

Then I started to hear voices. I followed them and finally located Danny and an old Czech who had appeared from nowhere (the cemetery was walled, locked and we had the key!). He had chased after Danny yelling "Shmelke, Banet? Shmelke, Banet?" making a sign for him to follow. By the time I caught up to them they were close to where, indeed, R' Shmuel Shmelke lies buried next to R' Mordechai Banet (Panet), another famous Rav of Nikolsburg. Although the *tziun* wasn't far away, it was easy to overlook without an expert guide.

We stood before the *tziun* and said *Tehillim* and *tefillos*. It was a very emotional moment, and I was filled with tremendous gratitude that Hashem had helped us accomplish our goal. When we finished, we walked back to the gate; and there was the old Czech again. This time he was holding a container of water and a pitcher, so we could wash our hands, as is the Jewish custom after leaving a cemetery!

I was so excited that I hardly thought over this strange turn of events. The driver pulled up in the car and ordered, "Quick, get in! We have to leave at once to catch the plane." So we gave the old Czech a tip; asked the driver to tell him to give another tip to the old lady, and off we went.

While driving along, a thought came to my mind. "That's strange. We were in the cemetery for at least an hour without seeing anyone. No one came in the front gate, and there were no other gates. There was a tall wall all around the cemetery; and the gate had been locked (we opened it ourselves when entering). How did this fellow, who seemed so at home there, get in? In fact, he was coming from the *far* side of the cemetery when we met him. How did he know how to find the *tziun* of R' Shmuel Shmelke? And how did he know that we needed water to wash our hands?"

R' Shmuel Shmelke had somehow helped make sure that his *einikel* (grandson) did not make the trip to his *tziun* in vain.

Re'eh

> And you shall keep the holiday of Shavuos
> Fore Hashem your G-d ... and you shall remember
> That you were [formerly] a slave in Egypt
> And observe and do all these laws.
> (Deut. 16:10,12)

Again and again the Torah connects the prohibition against working on Shabbos and Yom Tov with our slavery in Egypt. In a sense, our slavery to human masters in Egypt, which meant working even when we didn't want to, has been replaced by a "slavery" to Hashem, our Divine Master, which means not working even when we do want to. The essence of slavery is that "it's not up to you" to negotiate your own terms. That should characterize our attitude towards all mitzvos — particularly the prohibition of working on Shavuos, the day the Torah itself was given.

❦ Commencements and the Jewish Question

Boston is a city with many universities and over 150,000 college students. A sizable number are Jewish, which enabled us to start an active young *baal teshuvah* movement on several campuses.

The big event of the year at most universities is the annual commencement ceremony, which is usually held in late May or early June. There, after four years of hard labor, the student finally gets his earthly reward ... a college degree. It is also the culmination of many years of effort, hopes and dreams for the parents and grandparents who have invested $100,000, $120,000 or $150,000 and many sleepless nights in their child's secular education. This is the parents' moment of glory as their son or daughter steps forward to accept his diploma. In short, to them, it's an important day.

One year in the early '80s, the Massachusetts Institute of Technology (M.I.T.) scheduled its commencement for Shavuos, the Jewish holiday that commemorates the giving of the Torah on Mount Sinai. For Orthodox Jewish students, this would be a disaster. They would be prevented from participating in this event, since they would be in *shul* throughout most of the day and all the previous night. Riding, writing, handling money and countless other "normal" activities would be forbidden; and the conflict in atmosphere would be unbearable. Sacrificing their commencement might be an acceptable, even noble, option for the students themselves but, for their families, it would be a terrible disappointment. In the case of the *baalei teshuvah* among them, it could even create lasting parental resentment and opposition towards their children's new religious lifestyle.

Time was limited but, *Baruch Hashem,* we had a fine group of religious students at M.I.T. and they did a lot of the preparatory work, helping contact sympathetic staff, civil liberty groups and community leaders. They pointed out that they were, in effect, being discriminated against, being forced to choose between being eliminated from the commencement or forgoing, *chas v'shalom,* their religious principles. Through these efforts, three M.I.T. vice presidents, including the one in charge of the commencement, came to my office at the New England Chassidic Center to better understand why religious Jewish students could not attend on Shavuos. After all, college commencements were usually held on Sundays, a non-Jewish holy day, without any non-Jews complaining.

I patiently explained the many prohibitions and issues involved. The vice presidents also explained their problem. M.I.T. is one of the most important schools in the country, and its alumni include many of America's top scientists and industrialists. Such people plan their calendars months, even years, in advance. In order to encourage their attendance at the various reunions and meetings that accompany the commencement, dates are typically announced several years before. M.I.T. had acted in good faith, even asking one of their Jewish administrators whether the conflict was acceptable. He had looked at "Shavuos" marked on the calendar and said: "I never heard of it; it can't be that important. Just forget it!" To change things now would be virtually impossible.

One of the M.I.T. vice presidents, Professor Walter Rosenblith, who was also Jewish, appreciated our concerns and agreed to take them up in further meetings with the administration. After several such meetings, despite the major dislocations involved, M.I.T. actually decided to reschedule its commencement, in deference to the religious needs of its observant Jewish students. It was a beautiful *kiddush Hashem* and, on M.I.T.'s part, a beautiful demonstration of the meaning of minority rights in a democracy.

So much for M.I.T. We were not as lucky with Harvard University a few years later. Their commencement exercise that year coincided with both the 200th Anniversary of Harvard, which started as a divinity school, and the second day of Shavuos. We discovered the problem quite late and, here again, the top brass of the country would be invited. Many of these attendees would be at the prime of their careers and earning power. The loss of even one company president in a charitable mood was unthinkable. For our part, we tried getting more people, including members of the American Jewish Committee and American Jewish Congress, involved in the campaign, but Harvard couldn't bear to think of trying to change everyone's schedules.

The campaign soon came up against a nominally Jewish, but not observant, Harvard dean, a distant cousin of a well-known rabbi in Israel. Unsympathetic at best, this dean felt that Harvard should ignore our arguments and stick to its Shavuos date. Just to be sure, however, he consulted an important Conservative rabbi he knew, who said that it was certainly all right for Harvard to hold its commencement on Shavuos. In fact, according to this rabbi, Shavuos is the day that Harvard's commencement preferably *should* take place. According to him, Shavuos, the day that Hashem revealed Himself amidst fire and lightning on Mount Sinai to give *Am Yisrael* the Holy Torah, was actually an "education day," just like Harvard's commencement! Thus, Harvard felt justified in ignoring this campaign on behalf of its Orthodox Jewish students, to whom Shavuos, with all its restrictions and austere beauty, had a far different, transcendent significance.

Finally, I decided to discuss the issue with an Orthodox rabbi and scholar who had personal connections at Harvard. I explained how disastrous the situation would be for Orthodox students and their families. He, however, saw things somewhat differently. The Jewish community's efforts might be misconstrued as trying to force Jewish observances and holidays on non-Jewish institutions. Harvard, by this time, had offered to organize an early *minyan* near campus. Since they were making such an effort, he felt that to ask for more might seem ungrateful.

Our respective attitudes were rather surprising, because this rabbi, although he had received a college education, seemed to be taking a position similar to that of the European *galus* Jew: "Don't upset the *goyim*"; whereas I, despite having lived in a comparatively sheltered *Yiddish* environment, was taking an American activist position: "Stand up for your rights." After all, the United States of America is a democracy which guarantees religious freedom to all of us equally, Jew and non-Jew alike.

We finally met with some of the top people at Harvard. They agreed to take Shavuos into account in the future; but this time it was out of the question. So that's how America's first divinity school couldn't accommodate religion, while a citadel of science — usually assumed to be uninterested in religion — went to great lengths to show their respect.

❧

Like most stories, this one has a sequel. Harvard may have made their decision; but they still had a public relations problem. They certainly didn't want to *appear* insensitive to the American Jewish community's needs. So that year, coincidence or not, they decided to give an honorary doctorate to ... Teddy Kollek, the Mayor of Jerusalem. If we were indirectly responsible for his degree, given on that hotly disputed second day of Shavuos, we have few regrets. Since Kollek stayed in America for the following few weeks, he was out of the country when we called his office at the end of our annual summer visit to Jerusalem. That, in turn, led to our fateful meeting with his deputy mayor, Yosef Gadish (page 340-346), the establishment of the first Bostoner *shul* in Israel, and the start of the flourishing Bostoner community of Har Nof (a neighborhood of Jerusalem). In a way, our efforts for Shavuos that year were well repaid; but that's another story.

୶ A Cynical Sukkos

Actually some of the worst discrimination religious Jewish students faced in trying to observe Jewish holidays was not at Harvard or M.I.T., but at Brandeis, a supposedly Jewish-oriented university! Brandeis is now quite sensitive to the needs of its religious students, but that was much less the case during the 1950s. In those days, Brandeis was headed by Dr. Abe Sachar, a talented fundraiser who built up Brandeis "with his ten fingers," by soliciting contributions from the Jewish community at large.

The university opened with great fanfare and speeches about education and Jewish values but, nonetheless, one year their academic calendar showed classes scheduled for the second day of Sukkos. Brandeis' religious Jewish students, forbidden by Jewish law to work on that day, would be missing out on classes, notetaking, homework, etc. Jewish students were once again faced with a choice between violating the tenets of their faith or putting themselves at a disadvantage. Although not well enough to personally attend, I organized a delegation of distinguished Boston rabbis to discuss the matter with Dr.

Sachar. "How could Brandeis, a Jewish university, do this to its Jewish students? How could they desecrate a Jewish holy day less than a week after Yom Kippur?"

"We are *not* a Jewish university," Dr. Sachar corrected his distinguished visitors. "We are a Jewish-*sponsored* university," which in this context meant: Jewish money, yes; Jewish holidays, no.

"Well," said the delegation, "by observing only one day of Sukkos, aren't you actually favoring the Reform Jewish position and your Reform Jewish students, who observe only one day, over their Orthodox and Conservative counterparts, who observe two?"

This was a more serious matter. Dr. Sachar was himself a Reform clergyman, and he had to be sure that he could not be accused of favoritism. He thought awhile and then told the waiting delegation: "Well, if that is what's bothering you, we could hold classes on *both* days of Sukkos, so everything would be equal!" That was Brandeis' thoughtful "solution" to their own students' plea for spiritual recognition and sensitivity.

Brandeis had to learn the hard way, as did that whole generation, that cutting corners religiously will not help maintain Jewish identity, not even within their own lowered criteria. Fundraising and loose "affiliation," rather than committed observance, just isn't enough. Today Brandeis organizes well-funded studies, meetings and institutes to investigate the "erosion of Jewish identity." How could American Jewish identity erode with "Jewish-sponsored" universities there to guard it? One hardly knows whether to laugh or to cry.

Shoftim

Judges and policemen you shall appoint
In all your gates.
(Deut. 16:18)

The existence of laws, the appointment of judges to apply them and the commissioning of policemen to enforce them are essential to any well-regulated society. The establishment of a legal system (dinim) is one of the Sheva Mitzvos Bnei Noach, the seven commandments obligatory even on non-Jews. The Rabbis were under no illusions as to what would happen to a society — especially a non-Jewish society — once law and order broke down. Even during the dreadful days of Roman domination, R' Chanina S'gan HaKohanim said, "Pray for the welfare of the government, for without it men would devour each other alive (Avos 3:2)!"

Indeed, Jews have always had great respect for civil (non-Jewish) legal systems, as long as their laws were nondiscriminatory and were fairly applied. This attitude is codified in the Talmudic insistence that: "The law of the land is the law," in the case of such nonreligious matters as taxation, commerce ... and traffic!

Driven

As a young man, I was probably the first Chassidic Rebbe to have a driver's license. While we were getting started in Boston this was a necessity; and once I had my license, I soon found myself the official "sponsor" for other members of our extended family who also wanted one. The sponsor had to accompany the new candidate to his driving test in his (the sponsor's) car, and — most important and nerve wracking of all — the sponsor had to sit in the back of the car throughout the exam.

One relative, who was particularly learned and usually quite self-assured, became very nervous as the time for his test drew near. At the test site, a policeman in full uniform got into the front seat, while my relative got behind the wheel. I sat in the back seat waiting on pins and needles for the next move he was going to make. Actually, I kept on waiting, because he made no move at all!

There were no problems with how to park the car or signal a turn. No matter what he pushed or pulled, the car just wouldn't move. He fiddled with the key, turned the steering wheel, pushed the gas pedal and tried all kinds of interesting procedures but to no avail. The policeman in the front seat kept looking more and more uncomfortable. There we all sat ... and sat.

Suddenly I realized what the problem was; the car was still in neutral! Cars just don't move in neutral, and my relative, frantic at this point, was striking out before he even got started. His goose would be cooked anyway if I didn't try something fast, so I whispered, *"Daled."* This is the fourth letter of the Hebrew alphabet, the equivalent of the English letter D and a sure reminder to put the car in "DRIVE!" The policeman turned around and snapped, "No coaching from the rear," but my relative already had the car in gear and, with a lurch, off it went.

The test went pretty well after that, and the policeman became more relaxed and friendly. Finally, it was all over. The policeman took out his pad and gave my relative his long-awaited pink slip, which allowed him to drive for 30 days while his permanent license was being processed. Everyone breathed a sigh of relief.

I got back in the driver's seat — I had seen enough of his driving — and took off. The policeman, now off duty, got into his own car and followed closely behind. Still jittery from the previous tension and very anxious to leave, I accidentally misgauged the road ahead. The car barreled off the road onto the sidewalk at the first sharp right turn, thumped back off the sidewalk onto the road and kept on going, while the policeman sat there with his jaw wide open.

It was easy to imagine his thoughts: "What am I letting on the roads? Never mind the new driver, what about that sponsor?!"

Despite its humorous side, this story has a serious moral as well. If that is how nervous a person can become while preparing for a trivial exam with trivial consequences — at worst a few months' delay in getting a pink slip of paper — how much more nervous should we be while preparing for that great examination before the Heavenly Court in the World to Come.

❦

It's hard to think of drivers and policemen without recalling the story of one of Boston's more colorful *chazanim*, a Holocaust survivor who found his way to Boston in the 1950s. He had never had a driver's license, but he was very anxious to get one. That accomplished, he really "took off," enjoying the feeling of one with full rights to use the roads of Boston and its environs. He was, in fact, somewhat reckless, and would proudly tell one story after another about his driving adventures. His favorite story was about how he was once stopped by a policeman who "was a real *chacham* (wise man)."

"I drove through a stop sign," he said, "and this policeman pulled me over and said, 'Do you realize that you drove through that stop sign at 60 miles an hour? Do you know what you could have done to yourself?' I gave him the only excuse that came to mind: 'I'm sorry, officer, but I am a clergyman rushing to a funeral.'"

"'Oh,' he said, 'what time's the funeral?' Well, his question really shook me up, because I had to coordinate the current time with how long it would take to reach the funeral chapel and so on. I was too nervous to think straight, and was really in a fine fix. I slowly tried to pick up my arm to sneak a look at my watch, to figure out what time it was."

"The policeman caught me trying to look at my watch and smiled. He told me, 'Rabbi, unless you want to go to your *own* funeral, you had better be more careful next time!' That policeman was a real *chacham* all right."

Quite true; and that policeman's well-meant advice could apply to "moving violations" of Jewish law as well. *Ki heim chayeinu v'orech yameinu*, the Torah is quite literally "our life and length of days," and we ignore its stop signs at our own risk.

This week's parshah not only emphasizes the importance of honest leadership and impartial justice, it also emphasizes that designing and maintaining a proper system for choosing communal leaders is man's responsibility ("Judges and policemen you shall appoint"). Although no man-made system is perfect, Americans are strong believers in democratic elections as the best of all practical options.

The Rebbe's connections with the American political system and its leaders are well known. Although he has always tried to stay above the fray, he is all too aware of how helpful politicians with a sensitivity to Jewish concerns can be when properly approached. Thus, while one should not "put his trust in princes," neither should one forget or denigrate the important role that good leaders, even secular leaders, can play in promoting Jewish causes.

~ On Politics

It has often been said that religion and politics don't mix, and that is generally good advice. However, although "politicking" for specific candidates would seem a bad idea for religious leaders — unless strong principles are at stake — one cannot ignore the fact that religious Jews are members of a broader community and must ensure that

Many of Boston's Jewish leaders joined the Rebbe and U.S. Senator (later President) John F. Kennedy during the latter's 1959 visit to New England Chassidic Center. Also shown (from L to R): R' Isaac Simon and R' Isaiah Wohlgemuth (Maimonides School), R' Akiva Stefansky, R' Abraham Rose (Head of the Boston bais din), R' Meir Strassfeld, R' Lippa Solomon (Dorchester), Israel Schon and Jack Rosenberg

society is sensitive to their needs. In a democracy, such as the United States or Israel, this can require taking a stand on general issues and even voting, just like any other member of the body politic.

As a child, perhaps because I was always surrounded by adults, I was fascinated by politics. Father was relatively apolitical until the 1928 presidential race between Al Smith and Herbert Hoover, which raised an issue that bothered him deeply. Al Smith was a Catholic, and this was harped on mercilessly by many of the opposition. Father felt that it was unconscionable that religion had become an issue and, for the first time in his life, he registered to vote in an American election. This was unheard of for a Chassidic Rebbe in those days, and the election officials had to come to the house to register him privately.

As the great day drew near, "election fever" gripped the New England Chassidic Center. Excited political discussions were on everyone's lips. Father officially came out in favor of Al Smith, the

The Rebbe still maintains close relations with major political figures. Here he is hosting Benjamin Netanyahu, the current prime minister of Israel.

Democratic candidate, a particularly brave thing to do in Massachusetts which was then — before Tip O'Neil and the Kennedys — a very Republican State. Smith lost, of course, but Senator David I. Walsh, who was also on the Democratic ticket, did not. He became a good friend of my father's and, at Father's request, did many favors for Jews trying to leave Europe during World War II. That politicians could literally help save Jewish lives was a lesson not soon forgotten.

We returned to Boston in 1944, just in time to find a young Jack Kennedy running for congressman in our district. Although I didn't believe in giving public political endorsements, I did let Jack's representatives know that we were basically "in his corner." Our tacit support was repeated in 1948 and again in 1952, when Kennedy ran for the Senate. In 1960 Kennedy insisted on coming over to my office at the New England Chassidic Center to personally thank me for supporting his 1958 campaign. Our relationship continued even after he became president; and he was always very gracious whenever we asked him for help.

Joined in a common purpose (from R to L), the Rebbe, R' Eliezer Shach and R' Yehudah Adas present the Chassidic, Litvish and Sephardi Torah perspectives (respectively) at a political rally in Israel.

In 1962 Larry O'Brien called from the White House to solicit help for Ted Kennedy, Jack's younger brother, in his senatorial race. As he put it, "There isn't one Kennedy sign on all Blue Hill Avenue." Again, I felt it inappropriate to publicly endorse a candidate; but we did develop a good personal relationship with Ted, who is still our senator. Ted has also graciously been of help to the Boston Jewish community.

I have long since outgrown my childhood fascination with politics and frankly don't much care for it. However, I do feel a personal debt of gratitude for the consideration and help offered by public figures to the Jewish community and individual Jews. *Hakaras hatov* is a basic Jewish precept, if politics is not.

Ki Seitzei

When a man marries a new wife
He is exempt from the army and all things,
He shall stay home for a year
And cheer the wife he has taken.
(Deuteronomy 24:5)

This week's parshah deals with marriage and its military exemptions, with divorce, remarriage, false charges of unfaithfulness, true charges of unfaithfulness, adultery, assault, incest, the attractive captive (yefas toar), the rights of the widow, the laws of levirate marriage (yibum) and its refusal (chalitzah). In short, it deals with just about every aspect of marriage except the one the Rebbe is asked about most frequently: "Where can I find my bashert (destined mate)?"

There is no standard "one size fits all" answer. People differ, their needs and opportunities differ. That's why we ask Hashem to handle it all as He sees fit, at a sha'ah tovah u'mutzlachas, a good and successful time. Sometimes people seem to know right away, some seem to take a little longer and some ... set new records.

❧ Slow to Go

Rabbis, as a matter of course, often counsel couples planning to become married. Since most of my marriageable visitors are of college age or just beyond, I was somewhat surprised, one day in the '50s, to see a much older first-time couple approach my desk. They were in their late 40s or early 50s; and they had been seeing each other for 15 years or so at last count! The gentleman, a confirmed bachelor, still wasn't enthusiastic about getting married; but his prospective bride of a decade-and-a-half was getting impatient. The Rebbetzin invited them over for Shabbos several times and started trying to change his attitude. Eventually he announced that he was ready to take the plunge.

The great day arrived at our Dorchester *shul*, and the wedding began amidst great *simchah*, a *simchah* all the greater for being 15 years in coming. The congregation was happy; the *kallah* was happy; everyone was in a particularly jovial mood.

Just before walking down the aisle to the *chuppah*, I happened to turn to the *chassan* and noticed that he was particularly somber. I questioned him with my eyes, and he replied somewhat nervously, "Rebbe...this is the saddest day of my life!"

❧

That's certainly a comment one (fortunately) doesn't hear too often; but, even when the "happy couple" are indeed happy, their wedding ceremony can be anything but predictable. Luckily, it is the happy married life which follows that really counts.

❧ The Wayward Glass

A wedding is both a serious and a happy occasion, and both emotions must be kept in balance. Perhaps the clearest example of this is the custom of breaking a glass under the *chuppah* (marriage canopy) at the ceremony's end. It reminds us that, as long as our *Bais HaMikdash* is in ruins, our joy can never be truly complete.

Many years ago, I arrived at a wedding hall and began going over the usual checklist with the family: *Kesubah*? Yes. *Kittel*? Yes. Wine? Yes. Glass? No ... no one had thought to get a glass for the *chassan* to break under the *chuppah*. "No problem," said the *chassan*, as he sent someone to get a glass from the caterer. Now, although glasses and plates usually break all too easily, somehow whenever a caterer provides a glass to a *chassan* it turns out to be almost indestructible. The same seems true of the plate they give the two mothers to break at the *tenaim* ceremony.

The glass finally arrived, but the *chassan* still needed a bag to put it in, otherwise there would be broken glass flying all over the place. Time was almost up, and all that anyone could find at the last minute was a large brown paper grocery bag. The music played solemnly, and the *chassan's* parents slowly escorted their son down the aisle. Next the *kallah* and her parents slowly walked down the aisle towards the waiting *chuppah*. They were followed by a distinguished-looking man with the very undistinguished-looking brown paper grocery bag.

Unfortunately the *kallah*, a lovely young lady, had one slight but crucial flaw: She was a "giggler." She took one look at the incongruous scene and began laughing.

The Rebbe at the mitzvah tantz, one of the most mystical and unique parts of a Bostoner wedding celebration. The kallah (bride) is holding the other end of the long white sash.

Devarim ⬥ 329

The whole solemn assemblage, who couldn't see the bag, sat looking attentively towards the *chuppah*, where the *kallah* was, by now, laughing hysterically. It wasn't your everyday sort of wedding.

Things eventually calmed down. The *kallah* caught her breath, and the rest of the ceremony went smoothly, at least until the time came for the *chassan* to break the glass. Someone put the paper bag on the floor. The *chassan* stood up straight and stamped his foot on the bag; the glass didn't break. He stamped again, this time much harder. Still nothing. Finally, he stamped straight down with all his might, and the glass shot out of the bag!

It zoomed across the entire room, and the *kallah* started giggling uncontrollably all over again! This time, however, everybody was laughing with her, almost rolling in the aisles.

Finally, the wayward glass was found, brought back and duly broken. The *simchah* turned out just fine, as did the marriage. The *kallah* is now, by the way, a great-grandmother and, *Baruch Hashem*, still laughing!

> *If you come across a bird's nest ...*
> *You must first drive away the mother*
> *And only then may you take the young.*
> *(Deuteronomy 22:6,7)*

*S*hiluach HaKan, sending the mother bird away from the nest, is one of the very few mitzvos whose reward is explicitly stated in the Torah: "It will be good for you and you will live long." Why such a special reward for so simple a mitzvah? Our Sages note that the same reward is promised for honoring one's father and mother (Deuteronomy 5:16), suggesting an implied respect for the "mother-principle" of the world. On a deeper level, they see the mitzvah as a hint not to probe too deeply into the Divine mysteries: one may take the "young birds" (the secrets of the Torah below a certain level) but must leave the "mother" (speculations on still higher levels) alone. Kindness to the humblest levels of existence and humility before the highest — these are two complementary roots of the command.

In practice, it is now quite difficult for city dwellers to perform this mitzvah properly, which makes it somewhat rare and all the more precious. The Rebbe likes to tell the story of how he was able to do this special mitzvah, albeit a bit more dramatically than he had expected.

ଈ *Shiluach HaKan*

One night, during a visit to *Eretz Yisrael* in the early '80s, we were staying with a long-time friend, Lazer Moses, and his family in Bayit Vegan, a religious suburb of Jerusalem. It was 11 o'clock at night when a young *yeshivah bachur* rang the bell. He explained that he "specialized" in helping people do the *mitzvah* of *shiluach hakan*, sending the mother bird away before taking her eggs.

Opportunities to do this *mitzvah* are quite rare because of all the special conditions that must be met. It must be done with a non-domesticated bird of a kosher species, which must actually be sitting on its eggs in a nest. The nest must be in a place not owned by anyone (*makom hefker*); and one must actively "send" — push or shove rather than frighten — the bird away. Finally, one must take and use the eggs.

This young man had found just such a nest in an abandoned hut outside a *shul* in the Bais Yisrael neighborhood of Jerusalem, and had come all the way out to Bayit Vegan to offer me the *mitzvah*. Despite the hour, I was deeply excited by an opportunity to perform this very special *mitzvah*. Immediately changing my plans for the evening, I bundled up and followed the young man into the cold, dark Jerusalem night. Reb Lazar drove us in his car and, by the time we arrived, a small crowd had already gathered.

The crowd and the wall were quite visible; but where were the bird and the nest? The young man silently pointed up into the blackness, but I couldn't see a thing. The nest was at least 15 feet straight up.

How was I supposed to get up there? Our guide brought over a tall, old-fashioned straight ladder and carefully set it up against the wall.

Here I was, at nearly midnight, ready to climb a rickety old ladder up into the darkness to try to find a bird that no one could see. Determined to succeed, I had already started up the ladder when the young man gave me a stick to carry as well, Why? Because the preferred method was to sneak up on the bird and then tap her with the stick to make her fly away.

Miraculously, I somehow managed to climb up the ladder, stick in hand, and found the nest. There, in the semidarkness, was the bird and her precious cargo of eggs. I held my breath. She stayed in place until I lightly struck her with the stick and then she flew away.

Gingerly taking the two eggs and dropping the stick, I headed back down the ladder. By now nearly the whole neighborhood was outside watching the Bostoner Rebbe trying to climb up and down the ladder without breaking the eggs or anything else more vulnerable. Mission accomplished! We were all so happy we broke into a *rikud* (dance) right there at midnight, with everyone joining in. It was a very special occasion. When it finally ended, I gave the *bachur* a hug, an enthusiastic *yasher koach* and a suitable donation.

Once home, I had to figure out how to use the two little blue eggs. They were too small for omelets, so we bought a little silver container with two compartments and used them as a decoration in the glass breakfront in my Boston office, where they are until this day.

Ki Savo

I have removed all the sacred [tithes] from my house,
And given them to the Levite, proselyte, orphan and
widow ...
(Deuteronomy 26:13)

The Tribe of Levi was not given one of the 12 tribal portions into which the Land of Israel was divided. Instead they served the nation as a whole, as functionaries in the Bais HaMikdash and as teachers. Rather than the large agricultural regions of other tribes, the Levites received a series of small cities spread throughout the land, and ma'aser, a 10th of the nation's crop. This tithe was given every year, whereas another 10th of the crop was given to the poor every third and sixth year of the seven-year Sabbatical (shemittah) cycle. Thus, from the earliest times, Jewish landowners found themselves in a maximal 20 percent Biblical "tax bracket" — low by current standards — that taught them the necessity of supporting both scholars and the needy, i.e., both communal responsibility and social responsibility.

The idea that three identical-looking Jews might serve different communal and religious functions — Kohen, Levi and Yisrael — is an important one. A community ultimately derives its strength not from repetitive uniformity, but from focusing its diverse talents on a single objective. This division of labor is true in a family as well. Each member is unique and complementary to every other member and is, therefore, irreplaceable. Being different does not mean being inferior, it means being special. Serving Hashem in the Torah's prescribed way, fulfilling one's special role, is always something to do with pride.

❦ The Aliyah

Each Bostoner Shabbaton during the '60s brought 100 or so college students to Brookline. They stayed with local families, and came together for Shabbos meals and lecture programs at the *shul*. There was also time for a lively question-and-answer session after each talk. These spontaneous questions were quite interesting, and the speakers tried to give answers that were equally direct and spontaneous.

One young student asked: "Rebbe, why can't women have an *aliyah* (be called to the Torah)? Isn't that discrimination?"

"You're not alone," I told her. "Although I'm the Rebbe, when it comes to reading the Torah they discriminate against me too!"

"How's that?"

"Simple. Usually *rabbanim* and *roshei yeshivah* are called up for *shelishi* (the third *aliyah*) and Chassidic *rebbes* are usually called up for *shishi* (the sixth *aliyah*). Never in my life, however, have I ever received either *shelishi* or *shishi*! Usually *rebbes* are called up for the reading of the *Aseres HaDibros* (Ten Commandments) and the *Shiras HaYam* (Song of Moses). I never receive one of those special honors. Is that fair?"

"I guess not; but since it's your *shul*, why can't you get whatever *aliyah* you want?"

"Because I am a *Levi*, and *Leviim* only get the second of the seven *aliyos*. But do you think that a *Levi* feels any less important because of what he can't have? Not at all. It's a great privilege to be a *Levi*. He has a special role to play, one different from that of a *Yisrael* who can have *shelishi*. A cardiac surgeon cannot perform neurosurgery and a neurosurgeon cannot do cardiac surgery, but that is not a negative reflection on either of them. Both specialize in different things, that's all. You too have a special role in life, one not affected in the slightest by your not getting an *aliyah*."

She nodded in agreement. One can't be oneself by trying to be someone else. Women have an exceptionally important role to play in Jewish life, and should be proud of what is uniquely theirs. Worrying about what is unique to others is no way to get ahead.

ୠ

Look down from ... Heaven
And bless Your people Israel.
(Deuteronomy 26:15)

All blessings, including one's livelihood, come from Hashem, yet one has to work for them (Genesis 3:19). Having the right mix of hishtadlus (effort) and bitachon (trust) is no simple matter. It is also not easy to adopt the right attitude toward our own success and that of our neighbors. The Rebbe first heard the following two stories from an old Alexanderer Chassid, a Holocaust survivor, and he calls them both "right on the mark."

ୠ *Double Trouble*

A certain *Chassid* came to R' Yitzchak Danziger, the Alexanderer Rebbe, and asked him for a *brachah*. He was opening a grocery store in his hometown and hoped that it would prosper. The Rebbe gave him a *berachah* for success. When he saw the *Chassid* a year later, he asked him how his business was doing.

"I'm all right," said the *Chassid*, "but the fellow with the grocery store across the street is doing tremendous business. I wish I could do as well as he does."

The Rebbe gave him another *brachah* but, a year later, the scene repeated itself. "I'm doing better, but the fellow across the street is really taking off." The Rebbe gave him another *brachah*, but to no

Devarim ୠ 335

avail. Another year, another report: "I'm doing better, but that fellow across the street ..."

Finally the Alexanderer Rebbe told him, "Look, I think I've found your problem. Hashem gave you a good head, but only one head, for one business. What you are trying to do is to run *two* businesses: yours and your neighbor's!"

The Lottery Ticket

A poor *Chassid* once went to the Alexanderer Rebbe to ask for help. He needed money to marry off his children and he wanted the Rebbe to give him a *brachah* to win the lottery. The Rebbe first asked him, "Can you win the lottery without buying a lottery ticket?"

"No. You need a ticket to enter."

"If so," said the Rebbe, "go out and buy a lottery ticket, and may you be successful."

"Good. I'll go right out and buy 10 tickets!"

"Wait," said the Rebbe. "If Hashem wants you to win, you only need one ticket. If He doesn't want you to win, buying 100 won't help. Still, you must remember: If you don't buy a ticket, you can't win at all."

That's a good lesson when it comes to *hishtadlus,* making an effort to improve one's lot. A person who believes that his own efforts alone suffice, without Hashem's help, is an *apikores*. But a person who believes that he can just sit back with his feet up and wait is fooling himself. Hashem prefers to clothe His miracles in the garb of the natural order and you have to work — to buy your lottery ticket, if you will — to let the miracle happen.

Hashem will bring you ...
To a nation you have not known,
You and your fathers.
(Deuteronomy 28:36)

Verses 15-68 of this week's parshah, the most terrifying in the Torah, describe in graphic detail the curses and punishments that are the natural consequence of breaking the Torah's covenant between Hashem and the Jewish people. But from the sins and their punishment we can also learn the cure. If our Temple was destroyed because of sinas chinam (baseless hatred), we can repair it through ahavas chinam (unconditional love). If the curses of this week's parshah result, "because you did not serve Hashem your G-d with joy and a good heart" (Deuteronomy 28:47), then we can negate such curses by treating the mitzvos as a joy rather than as a burden. Indeed, this is the way of Chassidus pioneered by the Baal Shem Tov, to serve Hashem with joy at all times.

Meanwhile, we still live in a world of exile. We often face hostility and we must struggle to maintain our self-respect; but that in itself is often enough to prevail. These were lessons the Rebbe learned from his experiences of the incredible anti-Semitism Polish Jews endured in the European exile of the late 1920s.

∞ The Conductor

In 1929 our family traveled with Father to the health spa of Karlsbad. Our hope was that the hot mineral springs would improve his failing health. We traveled by train from Lemberg, Poland, to Czechoslovakia. We took over a small compartment and the trip began smoothly. Unfortunately, the conductor was a "double" anti-Semite, an ethnic German from the Sudetenland region of Poland. Apparently it bothered him to see a Jewish family enjoying a trip on his train. He came around and collected the tickets from Father but, after he punched them, he surreptitiously did not give one of them back.

The next time he came around, he told us that one of our tickets was missing and that we would have to get off at the next stop. Although Father was quite sick, he tried to protest. Of course we had all of our tickets; the conductor himself had checked them just a short while before! It was too bad, the conductor insisted, we would have to get off. He promptly forced our whole family off the train somewhere in the middle of Poland. Since our tickets were only for a specific train at a specific time, they were now completely useless.

Perhaps Polish Jews, subdued by centuries of victimization, would have accepted the situation silently, but we were American citizens, who took the supposed impartiality of Polish law seriously. Father went to the local stationmaster and complained. We showed him our tickets. Their numbers ran from 91 to 97; only number 93 was missing. Luckily our tormentor had forgotten to protect himself by taking our last-numbered ticket! Since the tickets were sold from a book in order, the glaring gap in the middle gave him away.

We bought new tickets, but Father sent in a strong complaint to the railroad company. They had evicted a sick American rabbi and his family, including young children, through deliberate and malicious fraud on the part of their conductor. Father told us that he had decided to fight this issue for a very important reason: The conductor had looked at him, at his traditional Jewish dress, and thought that we were Polish Jews, *hefker* (ownerless property), people he could mistreat at will. The conductor hadn't dreamed that we were actually Americans, who would protest to the railroad and to our own government if necessary (Poland was very dependent on U.S. aid for its existence between the wars). Father felt that he had to make sure that this conductor wouldn't mistreat other, really helpless, Jews this way.

We did finally receive an answer from the railroad's office in Prague. They claimed to have fired the conductor, and Father was happy that at least this one *sonei Yisrael* (enemy of the Jews) had met his downfall.

Nitzavim

From there [exile] Hashem your G-d will gather you,
From there He will take you ... and bring you
To the land your fathers inherited
And you will inherit it.
And He will do good to you, and multiply you
[Even] more than your fathers.
(Deuteronomy 30:4-5)

To live in Eretz Yisrael has been the dream of Jews through the centuries, and the Rebbe's father tried time and time again to return to live in the Holy Land. The Rebbe inherited his dream and, Baruch Hashem, was allowed to see its fulfillment. In that sense, he indeed received "more than his fathers." But as the next verse makes clear, the real purpose of the physical aliyah (ascent) is to provide the preconditions for a spiritual aliyah: "so you can love Hashem your G-d with all your heart."

This is the Torah approach to aliyah: In contrast, secular Zionism stops partway. Terach, Avraham's father, had the same problem; he left Ur, but he got stuck in Haran. To use a physical analogy, an aliyah in an airplane that stopped halfway across the Atlantic would accomplish nothing lasting — although it would certainly make waves!

Thus, a physical aliyah without a spiritual aliyah does not suffice. Still, the building of Eretz Yisrael is itself a great zechus (merit) and even some secular Zionists, who still retain their pintele

Yid, their innermost spark of Torah Jewishness intact, can rise to the occasion when necessary. One such *pintele Yid* helped the Rebbe and the Bostoner community make an *aliyah* in every sense of the term.

❧ *Boston Comes to Har Nof*

Father had long dreamed of building an American religious community in Israel. In the mid-1980s, it was my turn to dream. Of course, a development on the scale of Father's plans for Shuafat was out of the question, but we began to look around for some spot we could call our own. There were several possibilities in Jerusalem — Ramot Polin, Talpiot Mizrach, even Geulah — and several beyond; but we decided on Har Nof, at the western entrance of Jerusalem. The neighborhood was just getting started, and Boston became Har Nof's first organized community.

At first it was difficult to convince our American friends to come (although the few people who took our advice did, *Baruch Hashem*, quite well!). Eventually things began to happen. The Mishab Construction Company agreed to build two 16-apartment buildings for us on what is now Hakablan Street. We were to help them sell their apartments and, in exchange, the company agreed to let us buy(!) an apartment or two to use as a *shul*. Although we would have to pay for the apartments, the company would at least write agreements guaranteeing the *shul's* existence into the contracts for all subsequent buyers and neighbors. We could also build a *mikveh* in one of the building's bomb shelters. It was that or nothing.

Having just about clinched this "great deal" for Bostoner *Chassidus*, we prepared to go back to the States. The day before departure, I decided to call Jerusalem's long-time mayor, Teddy Kollek, who had expressed interest in helping us. I wanted to inform him of our progress to date. His secretary said that Kollek was abroad, so instead she referred my call to the Deputy Mayor of Jerusalem, Yosef Gadish. In fact, Kollek had once told me, "If you ever need anything, go see Gadish."

Although I had once met Gadish at a *Sheva Berachos* celebration, I wasn't certain that he would remember me. Gadish was one of Israel's old Labor Socialists and their political party (Mapai) was not exactly religious. Nonetheless, when he came on the line, he gave me a hearty "*Shalom Aleichem*" and asked how he could help.

I explained that it was merely a courtesy call, just touching base before our departure. "Oh," he said, "what a great honor to speak with you. You know, I really need to see you!"

"The plane leaves tomorrow afternoon. I really can't see anyone just now."

"So what?" he said. "I really must see you. I could see you tonight. I would come to you myself, but I have a lot of meetings."

All the while I couldn't help but think: Why did I have to call? It would take at least an hour to see him, and now every minute counted.

It was hopeless. He wouldn't stop. He had read an article about us recently, I had helped a friend of his through ROFEH, and so on. He really must see me. Why on earth had I made that call?

Having little choice, I finally arrived at his office. Gadish stood up to greet me. He was short, slim and suntanned, and wore a short-sleeved white shirt and no *yarmulke*. After the usual opening pleasantries, he asked, "So what's going on with your *kiryah* (community building project)?" Despite my disappointment, I tried to put the best face on our proposed deal with Mishab.

"Fine, but what about the *shul*? Do you have a *shul*?"

"Not exactly. We will have a place to *daven*, but not a real *shul*."

"O.K. So I will give you a *shul*! True, the city usually doesn't build *shuls*; but Har Nof is different. I saw to that. We have already built four *shuls*, and each one cost us $150,000. Give me a third of that, and whichever *shul* you choose is yours! Not only that but, with the money you and the other *shuls* give me, I will build a fifth *shul*."

I was amazed. It sounded too good to be true. There was, however, still one problem: There had to be a *mikveh* on site. Many rebbes and their *Chassidim* immerse in a *mikveh* every day before prayers and other special *mitzvos*. Father had always insisted that his *shul* have a *mikveh*. Come what may, a Bostoner *shul* had to have a *mikveh*.

Gadish couldn't believe it. "A *mikveh*? It won't fit! The concrete shells of the buildings are already completed. There is no room for a *mikveh*."

"We don't need a big *mikveh*, like a woman's *mikveh*, only a very small one for men. In fact, it could be very small, as long as the various water pipes, fittings and drains fit in." Gadish was still doubtful; but he picked up the telephone and called his chief engineer.

"Hello. Gadish speaking....Is there enough room in one of those Har Nof *shuls* for a *mikveh*?"

"No!"

"Well, anyway, I want you to go out tomorrow morning with the Admor from Boston and see if you can't find space for a small *mikveh* somewhere."

So the next morning, only hours before departure, we went with the engineer to the building site and started checking things out. I was interested in the upper of two *shuls* that had been built side by side on a hill. The *shul* was even more near completion than expected; Boston could hold its first High Holiday services there two months later! We were very excited; but where could one put a *mikveh*?

Place after place proved impossible. Finally I suggested a small space under the stairs. "Well," said the engineer, "if that's all the space you need, I have a better spot for you, over there between the retaining wall and the building." Later he found a somewhat larger spot; so those who complain about how small our *mikveh* is now should realize how much smaller it could have been!

Finally all systems were "go," but how could Gadish be reached? He had told me that he was going to be jumping from meeting to meeting all day. He had suggested four telephone numbers for starters; but none of them answered and Gadish wasn't at home either. In fact, his wife answered in exasperation, "I wish I knew where he was myself!" And there was so little time left!

Undaunted, good friends of ours, the Singers, went down to City Hall. They split the building between them and went from office to office asking, "Where is Gadish? Where is Gadish?" Finally, they found him walking around on an upper floor of the building.

"The Bostoner Rebbe is ready to sign."

"Great!"

"When? Where?"

"Now. Here!"

Gadish ran off to have someone draw up all the necessary documents, while the Singers called with the good news. A friend, Lazer Moses, quickly got his car and we dashed over to City Hall in record time.

Jerusalem Deputy Mayor Yosef Gadish at his desk, signing the papers establishing the Bostoner shul in Har Nof

Despite the rush, I made sure to bring along an extra *yarmulke*. This was an important occasion, signing the papers for a Bostoner *shul* in Har Nof, the culmination of so many efforts to establish Bostoner *Chassidus* in *Eretz Yisrael*. Gadish should at least wear a *yarmulke* for the occasion. So in we came. Gadish brought over the papers and sat down with a wide smile.

When Moshe Singer handed Gadish the *yarmulke*, he — to our disappointment — politely but firmly said, "No."

Then he got up from behind his desk. He slowly walked over to a closet, opened it up, pulled out his own *yarmulke* and put it on! Then he took me over to his own chair and said, "I want you to sit here." I protested, but he insisted, so I sat down and signed.

After it was over, we were very, very happy. I remarked, "It's such a special occasion, *chaval* (pity) we didn't think to bring along a *l'chaim*." Gadish said, "*Rega*, wait a minute!" and ran out the

Beis Medrash Givat Pinchas is located on a hillside, flanked by a long set of public stairs officially named Maalot HaAdmor MiBoston, in honor of the Rebbe's father.

door. He soon returned with a bottle of whiskey.

Then he said, "But what will we do for cups?"

I remembered how Father would never trust the utensils of the people he visited, lest they hadn't been *toiveled* (immersed) in a *mikveh*. His *gabbai* carried a small silver cup in his pocket to use for *l'chaims* and similar occasions. Whenever the *gabbai* forgot the cup, Father would improvise highly original substitutes. Once he hollowed out an apple to make an impromptu cup; once he used a large bottle cap.

"No problem," I said. "Just take off the bottle's over-sized cap and fill it." That done, I made a *brachah* and said, "L'chaim." Then I handed him the *sherayim*, the whiskey remaining in the improvised cup. Much to my surprise, Gadish also made a *brachah* before drinking. Then we all said, "L'chaim" to each other. Gadish was very moved. He hugged me and said in Hebrew, "I love you." He may have been a *Mapai-nik*, but he had a real *Yiddishe neshamah*.

The *shul*, once completed, was named *Givat Pinchas* in memory of my father. Later, when the city officially renamed the steps leading up the hill past our *shul Maalot HaAdmor MiBoston*, Gadish personally came to the ceremony to pay his respects and we gave him a little Jerusalem-stone model of the *shul*. He was an elderly gentleman, and he passed away from a stroke not long thereafter, on the 8th of Kislev, the day of my father's *yahrzeit*. This seemed appropriate, since he had helped realize Father's dream of a permanent Bostoner community in Jerusalem.

Gadish's funeral was an interesting one. There were all his secular friends in their uniform — a suntan, a short-sleeved white shirt and no *yarmulke*. And there, following the bier, was a Chassidic rebbe, in *his* uniform, a long black coat and wide-brimmed black hat. The members of the Jerusalem *Chevra Kaddisha* (Burial Society), riding in the hearse, looked out the back window and couldn't believe what they saw. What was the Bostoner Rebbe, of all people, doing at Yosef Gadish's funeral? But I believe very strongly in *hakaros hatov*, repaying the good others do, and acted accordingly.

After the funeral, I returned to Har Nof and went straight into

Living in Israel also allows the Rebbe to daven at the Kosel with his followers.

the Boston Kollel, which was learning Torah in the *shul* that Gadish had helped build. I announced that the *kollel* was to learn *Mishnayos* in his memory for the full year of mourning; and arranged for someone to say *Kaddish* for him.

Both Har Nof and *Givat Pinchas* have, *Baruch Hashem*, continued to grow. The *shul* has been expanded twice (at private expense), and a third expansion is underway. *Givat Pinchas* holds eight separate prayer services every morning. The first Torah class starts at 5:15 a.m. and the *shul* is open for learning until after midnight. And that is how Father's original plans for a *Givat Pinchas* neighborhood in 1934 came to life as a Har Nof neighborhood in 1983.

Vayeilech

Be strong and courageous, be not afraid ...
For Hashem your G-d walks with you,
He will not fail you and will not forsake you.
(Deuteronomy 31:6)

Life does not always run smoothly, and people face many problems — some of their own making and some due to others — over the course of time. One must always believe, however, that no matter how difficult things have become Hashem can and will help (although not always in the way one expects). That doesn't mean that a person can sit back passively and relax. Quite the contrary. This week's parshah tells us that we must strengthen ourselves through Torah and mitzvos, seize our opportunities for teshuvah and growth, and pursue them courageously.

The inner strength we develop through our own efforts helps bring the subsequent, all-important Divine aid. "Open for Me an opening the size of the eye of a needle," says Hashem, "and I will open for you doors the size of the Temple gates." In fact, Rashi interprets the last line of our verse as, "[Hashem] will not give you weakness, which would cause you to be forsaken by Him."

The Rebbe has met a lot of people, many in a great deal of trouble, but those with courage and faith have usually been able to elicit the Divine help they needed to turn their life around.

ॐ *The Road Back*

There was a troubled young Boston college student, "David," who had been through a rough time. After he started having problems, he began failing courses and eventually dropped out of school. There he was, finished in his 20s, aimlessly "commuting" between friends in Boston and New York. On one of the young man's flights he happened to sit next to a young girl from Brandeis. He told her his life story, and she suggested that he talk to the Bostoner Rebbe.

The fellow spent a few Shabbosos with us, and started becoming more interested in religious observance. He developed new self-confidence and soon began looking for a job. His first one or two didn't work out so well; but he finally "found himself" while working for a carrier-pigeon message-delivery service! He seemed to have a way with the pigeons, and the monthly paychecks helped him survive. He soon became a regular at the New England Chassidic Center, and was quite helpful to the Rebbetzin and my mother as well.

Our Friday night *tish* brings together quite a collection of people from all over the world. At one such *tish*, he happened to sit next to a special visitor, Prof. Moshe Jammer, dean of Bar-Ilan University in Israel. Prof. Jammer's father had been a prominent lawyer in Germany, but he left for Palestine when Hitler came to power. When Father brought our family to Israel in 1934, Prof. Jammer's father *davened* and *duchened* in our *shul* in Yerushalayim. He also helped Father buy a large piece of land in Shuafat, just outside the city, to be used for Father's planned Kiryat Boston settlement. Prof. Jammer himself was a world-famous scientist, whose books had been translated into most Western languages, plus Russian and Chinese.

During the meal Prof. Jammer and the young man began talking, and it was apparent that they got along particularly well. After Shabbos, I called Prof. Jammer into my study to talk things over. He thought that he had met a particularly nice young man, and I thoroughly agreed, although I had to tell him that our "nice young man" had a difficult past. I then reminded Prof. Jammer that he had once jokingly offered to accept my sons as students at Bar-Ilan. Since my sons had no intention of going to college (all three are Chassidic rabbis), why not take this fellow instead? "By all means," he said. "Tell him to send us an application."

The rest is history. This young man was soon learning at Bar-Ilan, where he won a special prize for excellence in his work. He later became an instructor at the university, married and raised a lovely family. Tragically, he died at a very young age but, by then, he had made his life a true success in every way.

※

> *And Moshe wrote this Torah and gave it to*
> *The Priests, the sons of Levi who carried*
> *The Ark of the Covenant of Hashem,*
> *And to all the elders (ziknei) of Israel.*
> *(Deuteronomy 31:9)*

The Jewish people is unique because of its distinctive relationship to the Torah and to the Torah way of life. This has been the source of our strength and spiritual sustenance throughout the generations. This verse identifies two groups of people whose efforts on behalf of the Torah deserve special mention.

As the Sages of the Talmud (Kiddushin 32) note, the term *zakein* (elder) "refers only to one who has acquired [Torah] wisdom." Thus the *ziknei Yisrael* of this verse are those scholars who learn Torah day and night and whose dedication to learning is our people's glory. "The Priests who carried the Ark" physically supported the gold-covered Ark which contained the stone tablets given at Sinai and the Torah scroll Moshe wrote in the Plains of Moav.

In our day, the supporters of the Ark represent the other great approach to serving Torah: supporting scholars, yeshivos and Torah study. This group also deserves credit for adding to our people's accomplishments. Indeed, they are mentioned first, because without their support it is difficult for scholarship to flourish.

❧ Three Parables

Har Nof, our spring and summer home in Jerusalem, is built on the sides of a steep hill. Thus, most of the apartment houses we pass *en route* to *shul* are surrounded by small lawns and gardens 20 feet or so below street level. One winter, one of the local residents built a balcony which required his cutting off the entire top of a nearby tree. He placed his decorative trophy up on the sidewalk, which happened to be about the same level as the top of a nearby fruit tree, and there they stood — two equally barren, leafless trees — all winter.

Once I walked past them with a *Chassid* of mine who remarked: "These two trees are '*mussar* trees'; they teach us an important lesson. The one on the left [the severed top] is now barren and the one on the right is now barren. That's because it is still winter. But in the springtime, the one resting on the sidewalk, which has no roots, will remain barren, while the one with roots in the soil will bring forth leaves, blossoms and fruits."

His point was that throughout our Exile (the winter), all Jews, whether or not their roots are sunk in the rich loam of Torah, seem to fare equally. Only in the Messianic Age (the springtime) will the difference between the life choices of the two become apparent. Then Torah-true Jews will bring forth their spiritual fruit, while those without Torah roots will not.

Sparrows were perching on the barren branches and I told my friend a different story about trees and birds: The leaves on the trees were happy. They enjoyed the nourishment provided by their roots, had a marvelous view and fluttered cheerfully all day in the breeze. One day, some sparrows came by and perched on a branch. Some of the leaves began to reconsider their lot and became jealous. Why were they stuck there all day? Why couldn't they leave and fly off as free as the bird?

Their jealousy mounted day after day, until a storm came, and a powerful wind swept those very leaves off their tree into the air. Their dream had come true! Upward they soared in the wind as they called out to each other, "This is wonderful! Now we are just like everyone else, the birds and the bees. Look how high we have risen, how free we are. This is the life!"

And then the wind stopped blowing and the leaves fell all the way down, below the birds, below the trees, to the ground. There they lay helpless in the mud, never to rise again. So too, those who leave our tradition, with all its restraints and supports, can fly high "like everyone else," but only for so long. Enduring spiritual heights are achieved only by remaining attached to the Tree of Life.

Those were two important, if sobering, parables. We continued our walk to *shul* in silence, each wrapped in our own thoughts.

The incident stuck in the *Chassid's* mind, because he didn't quite understand. What was lacking in his parable that prompted the Rebbe to offer another one? The weeks passed, spring came and Har Nof was clothed in green. Again we walked to *shul* together and again we passed our "*mussar* trees." True, the living, rooted tree was covered with a handsome cloak of green leaves, but so was the severed one! A honeysuckle vine had climbed up the wall and draped itself over the bare branches, covering them completely with leaves and flowers.

"You see," I told him, "even a tree without roots [a Jew without Torah] has an opportunity to bear fruit in some way, if it supports those who do."

> *And so Moshe wrote this song*
> *On that day and taught it*
> *To the Children of Israel.*
> *(Deuteronomy 31:22)*

It is typical of the Torah, and Hashem's great love for the Jewish people, that even when Hashem wanted to warn and rebuke the Jewish people through Moshe, He did so with a song. For song has the ability to move the heart, to rebuke with love, to involve the whole person and to teach him as well.

❧ *All for a Song*

I heard several beautiful "Chassidic" stories about *Misnagdim* from R' Yosef Dov Ber Soloveitchik, a great Torah scholar who lived in Boston. One concerned his grandfather, the *Bais HaLevi*, R' Yosef Dov (Yosha Ber) Soloveitchik, who once went to visit R' Yankele Gesundheit, the Rav of Warsaw. They were having a pleasant conversation in the living room when suddenly they heard the Jewish maid in the kitchen singing.

Since it is forbidden for Jewish men to hear women (other than family members) sing, R' Gesundheit jumped up, very embarrassed, and headed for the kitchen. Next R' Yosha Ber jumped up, caught his host by the arm, and steered him out of the house, straight into the street outside!

The Warsaw Rav was completely baffled, but R' Yosha Ber explained: "Your kitchen maid works all day. She has a rough job and a rough life, and apparently the only pleasure she has is singing. The *halachah* forbids us to listen to her singing, but is that any reason for us to take away her joy? It's better for us to go outside than to make her stop."

Ha'azinu

My doctrine shall fall as rain,
My speech drop as dew
As the showers on the tender [young] grass.
(Deuteronomy 32:2)

Parshas Ha'azinu, the final song of the Torah, is a beautiful progression of poetic metaphors and vivid images describing the greatness of Hashem, the consequences of sin and the need for repentance.

The Torah is compared to water. Just as water brings life to the earth, covering it with vegetation, the Torah has the power to spiritually inspire others, especially the young, the tender young grass referred to in the pasuk. The effects of Torah on our youth should never be underestimated, as the following story shows.

❧ *Chassidus on the Freedom Trail*

Boston's Freedom Trail connects a set of well-known landmarks associated with the American Revolution. It is traveled by thousands of tourists each year. At the New England Chassidic Center in Brookline, we also get our share of international visitors, but not nearly on the same scale.

One day, during the late '70s, we received a rather unusual letter from El Al Airlines, Israel's national carrier. They wanted to know if we could host a group of 80 French children from Lyon, who were touring America. They would be spending just one day in Boston, and someone had suggested they walk the Freedom Trail and then spend some time in a "Jewish religious setting." Could our community help?

El Al's proposal seemed strange. The group didn't seem religious, so who wanted the "religious setting"? And what were we supposed to do with them? Then there were all the logistical considerations. How could we talk to them, if they spoke only French? Was the Chassidic Center supposed to serve them refreshments or a full lunch? How would they get to Brookline and back? Who would pay for it all?

All of these questions were eventually answered and, on the scheduled day, all 80 children showed up at the Center's doorstep. They seemed nice enough but, look as one might, none of them seemed the type that would be particularly interested in a "Jewish religious setting."

They filed into our big *sukkah* dining room, and I spoke to them before, after and during lunch. Fortunately they had brought along a translator, so language was no problem. All the while we kept looking for some special reaction, some special rationale for their visit, but discovered nothing. They were amicable, apparently quite content, and left a few hours later.

I still don't know who made the New England Chassidic Center a "Freedom Trail" detour or why; but a few weeks later we got a call from the people who had organized the whole tour. They said that, of all the places the children had visited in America, their trip to the New England Chassidic Center had made the biggest impression!

The Rock, His work is perfect,
For all His ways are justice.
(Deuteronomy 32:4)

On Yom Kippur after Kol Nidrei we say, "We are like clay in the hands of the potter ... like glass in the hands of the glazier." However, the Rebbe never quite appreciated how apt the analogy was, until he once met a sculptress.

❧ Sculpt Yourself!

A certain young lady once sent us a letter that joyfully reported, "Baruch Hashem, I'm now living in Israel, and am engaged to a fine *yeshivah bachur*. We are both very happy. I am not sure that the Rebbe will remember me, but when I spent my first Shabbos with you, in the early '80s, you found some time to talk to me on Shabbos morning after *Kiddush*. When you asked what I do, I said that I was a sculptress. So you told me: 'Fine. Why don't you sculpt yourself?' Your words made a powerful impression, and I started trying to follow them as soon as I left your office, and I'm trying still."

This illustrates an important lesson in how to reach people. When I was young and just starting out, I sometimes tried to "prepare" for a meeting with someone. Once, when a philosophy student was coming, I tried to organize my thoughts on philosophy in order to grapple with his "big questions" on meaning and existence. After he arrived, however, I quickly realized that philosophy was the last

These days a Rebbe never knows what problems will come through his door; but he must be ready to handle each one with compassion, insight and common sense.

Devarim ❧ 355

thing he wanted to talk about — he had all his college friends and professors for that. He wanted to hear *Devar Hashem*, the Word of G-d. I soon learned that you have to be ready with *yourself*, to offer what you yourself have, not what somebody else has or brings with him. You must be open, honest and spontaneous.

That's what happened here. I knew nothing about sculpture — she was the first and last sculptress I ever met — but I did know how to be open to her feelings and my single impulsive remark, the remark that Hashem had put into my open mind, changed her life. That's what the Sages meant when they said: "Words that come from the heart enter the heart."

※

Remember the days of old,
Consider the years of each generation.
(Deuteronomy 32:7)

Remembrance is important, but we must know what to remember. Even concerning those tragedies closest to our own time, such as the Holocaust, are we to remember the pain or the self-sacrifice, what its victims died for or what they lived for?

❧ The Interview

Gideon Hausner, the main prosecuting attorney in the Eichmann trial, came to Boston in the early '80s to give a lecture on his experiences. One of the Boston radio stations heard that he was in town and asked him to speak on one of their radio programs on Friday night. At 10 a.m. that Friday morning, one of our friends called to tell me about it. He pointed out that Hausner would be talking about the Holocaust while desecrating Shabbos.

That would surely desecrate the memory of what the many righteous victims of the Holocaust stood for.

Since Hausner was not in Boston very often, and since this program had been planned for some time, I was skeptical about what could be done at the very last minute; but I agreed to try. It was painful enough to hear the Holocaust discussed as cold history even on a weekday, but to have such a program broadcast on Shabbos, in direct violation of Torah law, would be a real *chillul Hashem*.

I called the producer and explained how the planned program would be painful to the religious Jewish community, many of whom were Holocaust survivors or close relatives. He said that the speaker, who is Jewish and Israeli, hadn't objected, so how could the station have known? I explained everyone understood that the station had acted in good faith, but despite the speaker's lack of objection, the local religious community did object. The producer thought it over and decided, despite the late hour, to shift the program to Saturday night. This was but one example of how one can constructively develop the sensitivity of the general community to authentic Jewish values.

※

> *When the Most High gave nations their portion,*
> *When He separated the children of men,*
> *He set the borders of the nations,*
> *According to the number of the Children of Israel.*
> *(Deuteronomy 32:8)*

The 70 Biblical nations of the world correspond in number to the 70 souls of Jacob's household who went down to Egypt. Since the descent into Egypt was the first exile of the entire Jewish people, this correspondence would seem to have a message for our people in all its subsequent wanderings among the nations. Wherever a Jew may go, in whichever nation he may find himself, the potential to live a Torah-true Jewish life already exists there.

Devarim ※ 357

❧ A Mikveh in Nepal

In our age of modern transportation, religious Jews can end up anywhere in the world. As a result, Chassidic rebbes can get some pretty unusual questions. For example, one day in the late '70s a Harvard student called the Chassidic Center after his sister and brother-in-law had sent him an urgent cable. They were involved in a six-month engineering project in Nepal, and they wanted to know how to construct their own *mikveh*!

Of course, I had to tell them that, even for engineers, building a *mikveh* is not a simple matter. Halachically, it is a very complex, expert undertaking; not the kind of thing to attempt for a six months' stay. Instead, I sent someone to Harvard's Weidner Library to pore over the atlases and locate rivers near Kathmandu that meet the special conditions required for immersion. It was important to identify the river's sources, particularly how much was spring water and how much was rain water.

He came back with all kinds of information on Nepalese geography and we soon found a river halachically appropriate for use. Fortunately, the Kathmandu Valley has rather nice weather all year long, so their problem was solved. While other people scaled the nearby Himalayas, this couple scaled spiritual peaks all their own. Torah observance knows no geographical bounds.

VeZos HaBerachah

Although He (Hashem) loved the peoples,
All your holy ones are in Your hand.
They submit themselves at Your feet,
Bearing Your words.
(Deuteronomy 33:3)

The Torah begins with blessings — "And Hashem blessed them saying: Be fruitful and multiply, fill the waters and seas (Genesis 1:22)" — and it ends with blessings. The Torah is full of blessings — Avraham's blessings, Yitzchak's blessings, Yaakov's blessings, Moshe's blessings — all of them ultimately Hashem's blessing.

To bring blessings down to this world, the "pipes" that connect Heaven and Earth must be in order. What are these conduits of Divine blessing? The hearts of those rare individuals who truly "submit themselves at Your feet, bearing Your words." For such Jews the Torah is never completed. An unbroken ring joins the Torah's last letter (lamed) with its first letter (bais). What is this word that leads us once again back to the beginning? Lamed-bais, lev, the heart.

During the first half of this century, Eastern Europe produced a certain type of Jew who instinctively, without fuss or fanfare, devoted his entire heart to serving Hashem — not only such great scholars as the Chofetz Chaim and the Brisker Rav, but even simple "ordinary" Yidden, whose hearts were alive with Torah. There were thousands of them. Here are but two examples.

❧ Clean Hands

We have no way to begin to appreciate the simple piety of many an "ordinary" *Yid* in Europe before the First World War. We once heard this story from the father of Dr. Harry Meiselman, the brother-in-law of R' Yosef Dov Ber Soloveitchik.

There was a Jew in Jassy, Rumania, who learned every day with a *chavrusah* (study partner) early in the morning before heading to work. One morning the *chavrusah* waited and waited in *shul*, but his friend did not arrive. Finally he left the *shul* and began searching the still-dark streets.

He found his friend sitting on the stoop of a building, apparently unable to move. He went over to ask what was the matter, and his friend explained: "I felt very tired while walking to *shul*, so I sat down on this stoop to rest. I soon fell asleep and now I can't get up because I don't have *negel-vasser* to wash my hands." This washing is required by Jewish law immediately after awakening and, despite all the obvious extenuating circumstances, his friend refused to budge without it. His *chavrusah* brought him some water, he washed his hands, and then they both walked back to *shul*.

That was the level of an ordinary Jew in those days.

❧ On Devotion

Mr. Mordechai Stauber was a European Jew, with all that implies. After the war he married a young lady from Boston and settled in our community. He became very devoted to the *shul* and, throughout the early '80s, he was a confirmed "regular" at our Friday night *tish*. Actually there was no formal *tish* in those days, but a few special people used to drop by every Friday night anyway, to help make a *minyan* for *bentching* (special additions are said only with a *minyan*).

Boston weather, especially in the winter, can be cold, stormy and generally quite unpleasant, but come Friday night, Mr. Stauber would tell his wife, a fine *chassidiste*, "I've got to go now to the Rebbe's *tish*." If she objected, "But it's so awful out," he would just say, "Then even more so. If *I* don't go, who will help the Rebbe make his *minyan*?" Sometimes it was one rationale, sometimes another, but he always came.

Once there was a big *simchah* in town, and all the out-of-town guests stayed at or near the Chassidic Center. This was the perfect opportunity for Mrs. Stauber to opine, "Well, at least you won't have to go tonight. The Rebbe has a *minyan* now for sure." "Oh," he said, "tonight I really have to go. All these people came from New York. How would it look if Boston people didn't come to the *tish*!" That was how he always looked at things.

Then one morning Reb Mordechai suddenly passed away. I remember thinking how different Friday nights would be without him. It was then that we began thinking more seriously than ever about moving to *Eretz Yisrael*.

༺

> *And Hashem showed [Moshe] the whole land,*
> *[Even from] Gilad to Dan ... and all the land of Judah*
> *To the furthest sea [yam acharon].*
> *(Deut. 34:1-2)*
>
> *Read not yam acharon but yom acharon, the furthest day.*
> *Hashem showed him all the events that would befall*
> *Israel*
> *until the Resurrection of the Dead.*
> *(Rashi)*

Now, at the end of the journey, Moshe views the ends of the land and the end of time. Indeed, the width and breadth of the Land of Israel is the history of the Jewish people. As Rashi relates, Moshe was able to see in the land itself its subsequent peace and ruin, the battles of Yehoshua, the victories of King David, the Temple of King Solomon, its destruction and rebuilding, age after age, ebb and flow.

Just as Hashem is eternal and outside of time, so is the Torah eternal and the Jewish people eternal. Thus, say our Sages, "Hashem, Israel and Torah are all one," not only united with each other, but each a unity for whom the past and future are equally alive. Thus we live even now with Avraham, Yitzchak and Yaakov. We learn even now with Rava and Abaye, not only figuratively but literally. The curtains separating the worlds and ages are thin indeed.

Moshe saw through the veil. And we too, by purifying our lives with Torah, can carry on our ancestors' work in this world. We need but see.

❧ The Kaddish

Ever since the time of the Ari HaKadosh, visiting the tomb of the *Tanna* Rabbi Shimon bar Yochai (the author of the *Zohar*) on Lag B'Omer has been an important custom. At the turn of the century, however, when Father was a young man in Jerusalem, the trip to Meron, where the tomb is located, was no simple matter. Forget about buses, hotels and paved roads. He had to hire a donkey (a few special characters hired camels) and had to stay with supposedly "trustworthy" Arab families overnight along the way. He was safe as long as he was a guest, but once he left it could be another matter.

Preparations started soon after Pesach. Since the trip was a long one, there were leisurely stopovers in Teveriah (Tiberias) and other special places along the way. One year, when Father was about 21, he had a strange dream *en route* to Meron. It was a year after his father, R' Shmuel Shmelke, had passed away, and he saw his father quite clearly standing in front of him. His father told him, "Say *Kaddish*." He woke up very upset and concerned, since his father was a *tzaddik* and one doesn't say *Kaddish* for even a *rasha* (evildoer) for more than 12 months (in practice, one says *Kaddish* for a parent exactly 11 months). How, then, could his father order him to recite it?

The ideals and spirit of R' Pinchas Dovid, the first Bostoner Rebbe, animate his yahrzeit seudah at Bais Medrash Givat Pinchas in Jerusalem.

The dream was far too real to ignore, but he couldn't bring himself to say *Kaddish* three weeks after his father's year of mourning was over; so he continued on to consult with the wise men of Teveriah. Each gave him a different answer, none of which seemed satisfactory. Finally, he went on to Tzfas (Safed), in the Galilean Hills near Meron, and asked the elders of Tzfas about it. They didn't feel that they had the answer, and one of them advised him, "Why don't you go back to Yerushalayim and consult with your uncle, the *tzaddik*, R' Dovid'l Biederman?"

So Father rode his donkey all the way back to Yerushalayim. Reb Dovid'l quietly listened to the story of the dream and R' Shmuel Shmelke's strange command. Then he told Father, "Why don't you go and ask him yourself?" In other words, why don't you go to your father's grave on *Har HaZeisim* (the Mount of Olives) and ask him what he meant.

R' Dovid'l's word was enough for Father, so he made his way to *Har HaZeisim*. He rested his arm on his father's *kever* (grave) and began to *daven*. He suddenly felt that his father was actually in front of him. It was not just imagination, because Father was a very practical, no-nonsense sort of person.

His father told him, "Why don't you understand what I mean? I want

The legacy continues: the Rebbe reciting Tehillim at the tziun of his father, R' Pinchas Dovid. To the right is the kever of R' Shmuel Shmelke, where R' Pinchas Dovid had a vision of his father.

you to say *Kaddish* for my mother." R' Shmuel Shmelke's mother's *yahrzeit* was the day after Lag B'Omer and, until his death, he had said *Kaddish* for her every year. Now he wanted his son to take over this responsibility.

Why hadn't R' Shmuel Shmelke asked his son to do this for the first *yahrzeit* after his passing? My father felt that, since his grandmother's *yahrzeit* was only two months after R' Shmuel Shmelke's passing, his father's *neshamah* had not yet reached its proper resting place. Thus, until sufficient time had passed, it was unable to transmit messages back to this world (an idea with support in certain Jewish mystical sources).

From that time onwards, Father faithfully observed the *yahrzeit* of his grandmother, just as he did for his own parents. He *davened Maariv* for the *amud* on the Friday night before, he *davened Mussaf* Shabbos morning and he kept all the other associated customs, just as his father would have done.

May the memory of the righteous be for a blessing, and may their merit protect us and all of Israel until the coming of *Mashiach* speedily and in our days.

Genealogy

The Rebbe's Father's Family

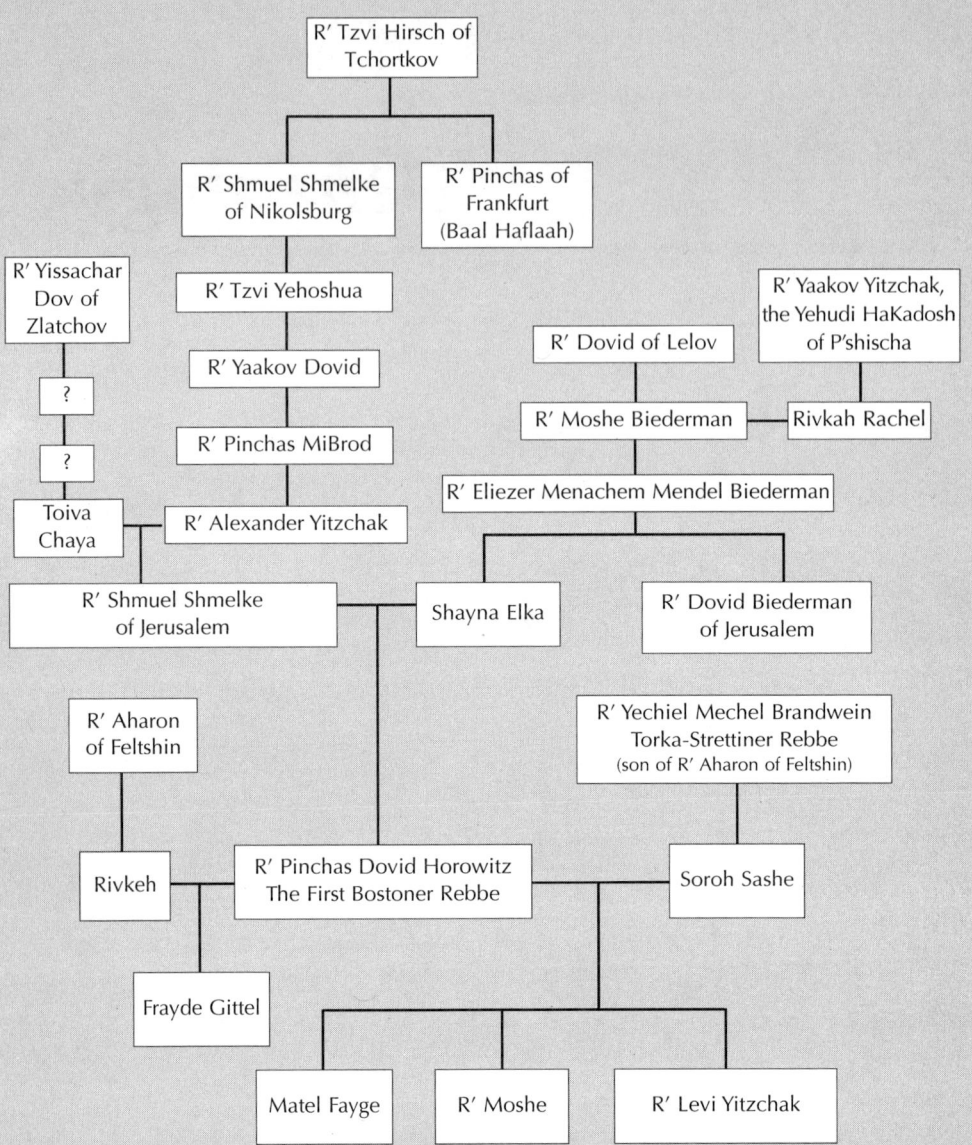

The Family Horowitz

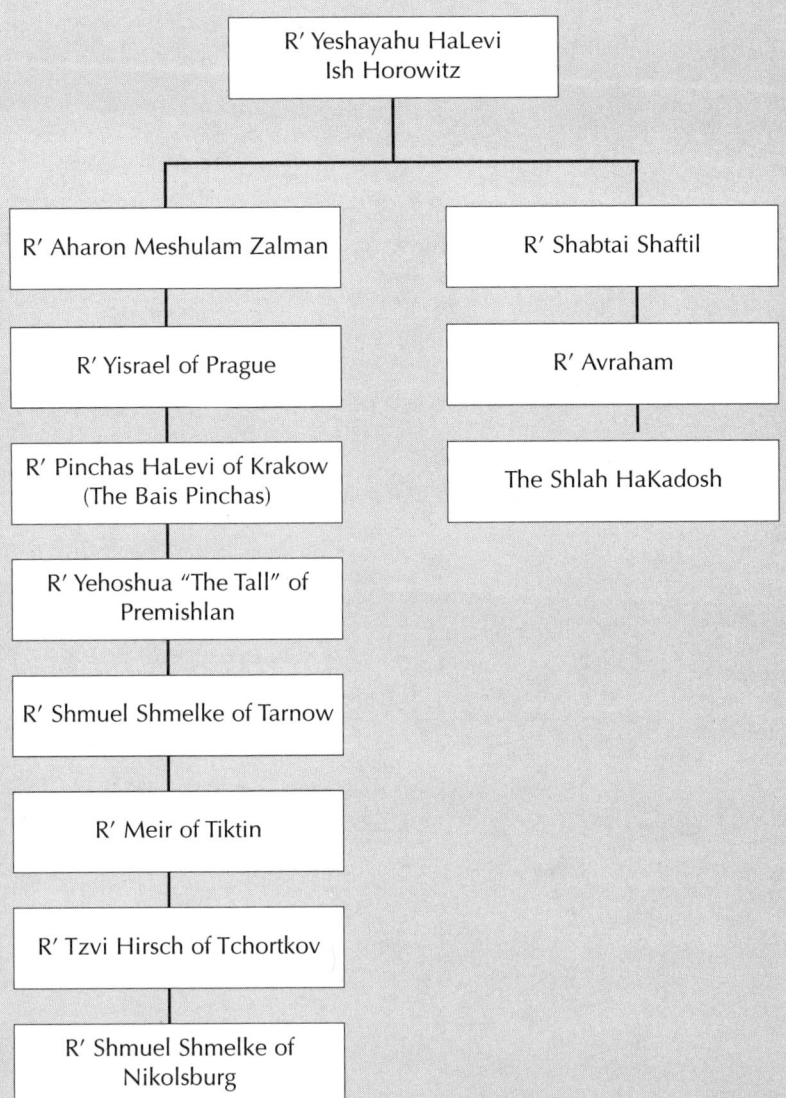

Genealogy 367

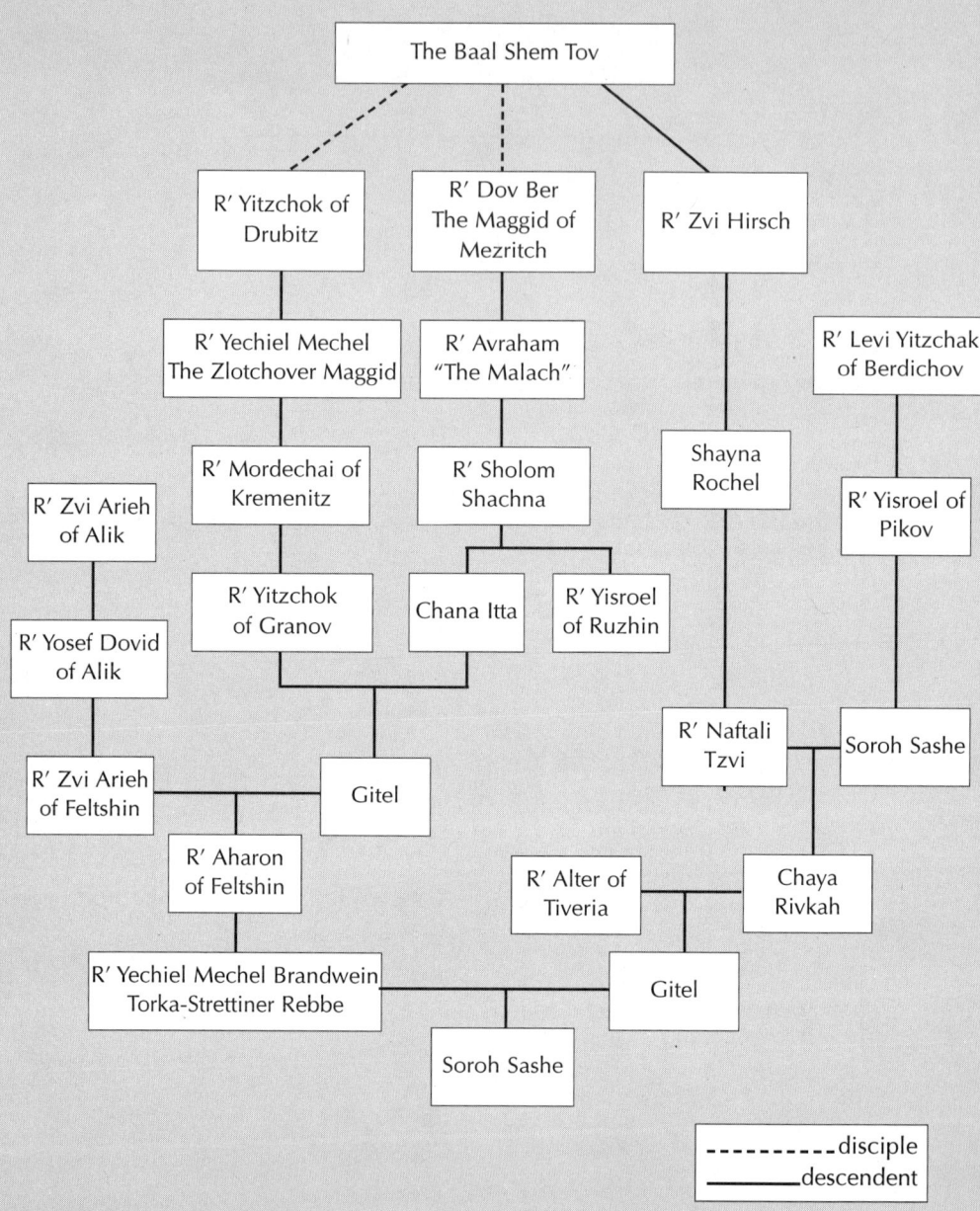

Chronology

A Bostoner Chronology

1876 — R' Pinchas Dovid Horowitz, *zt"l*, born in the Old *Yishuv* of Jerusalem.
1906 — R' Pinchas Dovid marries Soroh Sashe, daughter of the Torka-Strettiner Rebbe.
1914 — Stranded in Europe at the outbreak of World War I, R' Pinchas Dovid finds himself headed for America.
1915 — R' Pinchas Dovid moves from New York to Boston's West End, becoming the first Bostoner Rebbe.
1920 — Rebbetzin Soroh Sashe and her 12-year-old son, Reb Moshe, *zt"l*, leave Jerusalem for Boston.
1921 — R' Levi Yitzchak Horowitz, *Shlita*, the current Bostoner Rebbe of Boston, is born.
1929 — Family's first attempt to return to Israel. Visits to Karlsbad and Poland.
1932 — Family goes to Zydatchov, Poland, for Reb Moshe's marriage.
1934 — R' Pinchas Dovid and his family move to Israel in time for the Rebbe's Bar Mitzvah. The Rebbe attends Yeshivah Torah V'Yirah. The family returns to Boston when their economic support collapses.
1938 — Rebbe attends Yeshivah Torah Vodaath in New York City.
1939 — The family moves to Williamsburg, where the ailing R' Pinchas Dovid establishes the Bostoner dynasty of New York.

1941 — R' Moshe Horowitz becomes the Bostoner Rebbe of New York after his father's passing.

1942 — The Rebbe (R' Levi Yitzchak Horowitz) marries Raichel Horowitz, daughter of R' Naftali Horowitz, zt"l, and stepdaughter of R' Meir Leifer, the Nadvorna-Clevelander Rebbe.

1944 — The Rebbe's oldest son, Pinchas Dovid, is born — soon to be followed by Mayer Alter, Shayna Gittel, Naftali Yehuda and Toba Leah (all are now rebbes and rebbetzins).

1944 — Recently married, and only 23, R' Levi Yitzchak moves back to Boston to become the Bostoner Rebbe of Boston. Most of his flock are over 70! The Rebbe and Rebbetzin soon move to the "Jewish" suburb of Dorchester (61 Columbia Road). They are joined by his mother, Rebbetzin Soroh Sashe, his sister, Rebbetzin Faigie Thumin (now the Altstadter Rebbetzin), and Mr. Singer.

1946 — Rebbe takes the first postwar freighter to Israel to re-inter his father's remains on the Mount of Olives.

1949 — Rebbe establishes the ROFEH medical support organization.

1961 — Rebbe moves to Brookline (1710 Beacon Street) where the New England Chassidic Center is still located.

1963 — Rebbe holds his first major Shabbaton for local college students, the beginning of a major *kiruv* effort among Boston's college students.

1974 — Rebbe becomes a member of the Presidium of Agudath Israel of America.

1983 — Givat Pinchas, the Bostoner Shul in the Har Nof suburb of Jerusalem, is dedicated.

1984 — After annual visits from 1967 on, the Rebbe decides to spend half of each year in Har Nof, Jerusalem.

1988 — The Rebbe becomes a member of the Council of Torah Sages of Agudath Israel in Israel.

1994 — The Rebbe and Rebbetzin celebrate the 50th anniversary of the reestablishment of Bostoner Chassidus in Boston.

1996 — Publication of the Rebbetzin's biography (Mesorah/ArtScroll).

1997 — Third expansion of the Bostoner Shul in Har Nof.

Glossary

Glossary

aliyah — being called up for the reading of part of the weekly Torah portion
Am Yisrael — the Jewish People
amud — prayer stand (used by *chazan*)
apikores — heretic
aron — synagogue cabinet housing the Torah scrolls
auftzulochus — despite it all
aveilus — mourning
avodah — lit. work; worship, religiously purposeful work
bachur (pl. bachurim) — a young man
baal teshuvah — lit. penitent; person who has become observant
Bais Hamikdash — The Holy Temple
Bais Yaakov — network of strictly religious Jewish girls' schools
bais midrash — house of learning, where Torah is studied
balabatim — lit. householders; members of the community
balabusta — capable housewife
Bar Mitzvah — 13-year-old male who is now formally subject to the Torah's commandments; a festive celebration marking this milestone
Baruch Hashem — Thank G-d
bechor — firstborn male (human or animal)
behamah — cattle
bekeshe — knee-length black frock
bentching — recital of the Grace After Meals
beshert — predestined; esp. Divinely-destined mate
b'ezras Hashem — with G-d's help
bitachon — faith, trust, esp. in G–d
bitul — nullification
blatt — a folio page
bor — pit, esp. a storage pit for rain water, adjacent to a *mikveh* used for immersion, from which the latter receives its purifying properties

brachah — blessing
bris milah — circumcision
bushah — embarassment
chacham — sage; wise man
chalaf — slaughtering knife
chametz — leavened food
charedi — strictly religious
chashuv — important
chassan — groom
chassanah — wedding
Chassid (f. **Chassidiste**) — follower of a Chassidic Rebbe
Chassidism — Jewish religious movement started by R' Yisroel Baal Shem Tov (late 1700s)
chavrusah — study partner
chazakah — presumptive claim
chazan — prayer leader
cheder — Torah school for young boys
chelek — share, portion
chesed — kindness
Chevra Kadisha — burial society
chevrah — group, organization, friends
chillul Hashem — desecration of the Divine Name (through impropriety)
chizuk — strengthening
cholov Yisroel — Jewish-supervised milk
chumrah — religious stringency
chuppah — marriage canopy
chutz la'aretz — diaspora, outside *Eretz Yisrael*
daled amos — lit. four cubits; the diameter of a person's personal "domain"
dam bris — lit. blood of the covenant; blood resulting from circumcision
daven — pray
din — judgment, law
drashah — exposition of Torah insights
duchen — the formal recitation of the Priestly Blessing by *Kohanim*
eishes chayil — woman of valor
Eliyahu HaNavi — Elijah the Prophet
Eretz Yisrael — the Land of Israel
Erev Shabbos — the day before the Sabbath (i.e., Friday)
fleishig — food containing meat (which cannot be eaten with milk)
freilach — joyous
frum — religiously observant
gabbai — senior functionary for a Rebbe
galus — exile
ganef — thief
gass — street
gebrochts — *matzah* that has come into contact with water
gedolim — great sages; religious leaders
gelt — money
Gemara — the major part of the Talmud, consisting of discussions on the text of the Mishnah

get — writ of religious divorce
gevaldig — wonderful
gevalt — Woe!
gevirim — rich men
glatt — smooth, esp. smooth lungs, without adhesions; i.e., strictly kosher
goy — non-Jew
grammen — witty improvised verses
hachnasos kallah — fund for needy brides
hakafos — circular processions, esp. with Torah scrolls on the holiday of Simchas Torah
hakaros hatov — expressing gratitude for favors received
halachah — Jewish Law
hargashah — feeling, sensitivity
Har Hazeisim — Mount of Olives in Jerusalem
Hashem — G-d
hashgachah — religious supervision (to ensure food is kosher)
Havdalah — ceremony marking the end of the Sabbath
hechsher — kashrus certification
hefker — ownerless property
heimishe — homey, familiar; unpretentious
hesped — eulogy
hishtadlus — effort
Kabbalah — the Jewish mystical tradition
Kaddish — prayer recited by the chazzan, by mourners, and on the anniversary of the death of a close relative
kallah — bride
kana'i — zealot
kapelia — town band and chorus
kasher — to make kosher
kashrus — state of being kosher
kavanah — intent; concentration
kavod — honor
kavyachol — as it were
kedushah — holiness
kesubah — marriage contract
kevurah — burial
Kiddush — the benediction over wine at Sabbath and festival meals
Kiddush Hashem — Santification of the Name through proper behavior
kinus — convocation, assembly
kinyan — legal aquisition
klop — bang, slap
kneidlach — matzo balls, usually served in soup
Kohen Gadol — High Priest
Kol Nidrei — lit. all vows; the prayer initiating Yom Kippur
kollel (pl. **kollelim**) — study group composed of mature, married students
korban — sacrifice
Kosel — wall, esp. Western Wall of the Temple Mount in Jerusalem
kosher — ritually fit (esp. foods)
kugel — baked dish, usually made from noodles or grated potatoes

kvetchen — complaints; tearful musical flourishes
kvitel — small note handed to a Rebbe, containing the petitioner's name, mother's name and request
lamdan — well-versed scholar
l'chaim — "To life!" the quintessential Jewish toast
Lechah Dodi — hymn sung to welcome the Sabbath
lokshen — noodles
Ma'ariv — the evening prayer service
ma'aser — tithes; to separate the same
madreigah — level
maggid — teller of inspirational stories (often as part of a sermon); preacher
mamzer — product of an adulterous or incestuous relationship
Mapai — secular, socialist Israeli political party
matzah — unleavened bread (used on Passover)
mazel tov — good luck!; congratulations
mechalel — desecrate
mechitzah — partition, esp. the partition separating men and women in the synagogue
mekarev — to bring near (to Judaism)
Melaveh Malkah — Saturday evening meal to "escort" the departing Sabbath
menahel — executive director; manager
mesader kiddushin — one who officiates at a wedding ceremony
meshulach — charity collector
mesiras nefesh — self-sacrifice
mesivta — high school
mezuzah — small scroll placed on the right doorpost
midah (pl. **middos**) — character traits
mikveh (pl. **mikvaos**)— ritual bath
milchig — food containing milk (which cannot be eaten with meat)
Minchah — the afternoon prayer
minhag — custom
minyan — quorum of 10 men (needed for communal prayer)
Misheberach — prayer for well being
Mishpachah — Jewish legal code (compiled by the Tannaim, *circa* 200 B.C.E.-200 C.E.)
mishpocha — family
Mitzraim — Egypt
mitzvah (pl. **mitzvos**)— righteous deed
Motza'ei Shabbos — Saturday night
muktzah — object which may not be used on Shabbos
mum — blemish, esp. one which disqualifies a priest or sacrifice

mussar — moral and ethical teachings intended to improve one's character traits
narishkeit — childishness, folly
neshamah — soul
niggun — melody (with or without words)
olam — world
parnasah — livelihood, income
parshah — weekly Torah portion
pasuk — verse
Pesach — Festival of Passover (occurs in Spring)
peyos — side-curls worn by Chassidic boys and men
Pirkei Avos — "Chapters of the Fathers," a popular section of the Mishnah
pintele Yid — the innermost spark of Jewishness inside each Jew
posek — expert on religious law
poshuteh Yid — a plain, simple Jew
Purim — cheerful Jewish holiday (occurs in early Spring)
pushkah — charity box
rabbanim — rabbis
rachmanus — mercy
rasha — wicked person
Rav — rabbi
Rebbe — Chassidic rabbi and leader
Rebbetzin — wife of a Rav or Rebbe
rechov — street
refuah — cure
Ribono Shel Olam — L-rd of the Worlds (an epithet for Hashem)
ROFEH — Bostoner Rebbe's health services support organization
Rosh Hashanah — Jewish New Year (occurs in early Fall)
Rosh Yeshivah — Head of a yeshivah
sandek — the participant honored to hold the baby at a bris
seder — festive meal on the first night of Pesach
seudah — festive meal
Seudas Mitzvah — a festive meal to celebrate the performance of a mitzva
Shabbos — the Jewish Sabbath
Shabbosdik — appropriate for the Sabbath
shaliach — messenger; representative
Shalom Aleichem — "Peace to you," traditional Jewish greeting
shalom bayis — matrimonial harmony
Shalosh Seudos — the third Sabbath meal (usually late afternoon)
shammash — assistant to a Rebbe; beadle
shechitah — slaughtering (in accordance with *halachah*)
shecht — to slaughter (in accordance with *halachah*)

sherayim — lit. leftovers; portions of the food from a Rebbe's plate distributed among his followers
Sheva Brachos — seven blessings recited for new bride and groom
Sheva Mitzvos — seven *mitzvos* given to all mankind
shidduch — matrimonial match; meeting a potential mate
Shiras Hayam — The Song of the Sea
shiur — lecture
shivah — the first week of mourning
shlachthaus — slaughterhouse
shlep — carry
shmuess — lit. conversation; an informal *shiur* concentrating on the self-improvement of one's character traits
shochet — slaughterer
shofar — ram's horn sounded on Rosh Hashanah
shomer Shabbos — Sabbath observer
shtetl — small Jewish village in Eastern Europe
shuckle — sway in prayer
shul — synagogue
Shulchan Aruch — the Code of Jewish law, compiled by R' Joseph Caro (completed 1555 C.E.)
siddur — prayer book
simchah — joy, happiness; happy occasion
Simchas Torah — holiday which immediately follows Sukkos
siyum — celebration over the completion of a portion of the Talmud
smichah — rabbinic ordination
Sukkos — Festival of Booths, a seven-day Jewish holiday starting five days after Yom Kippur
ta'am — taste
tabak — tobacco, esp. snuff
taharah — ritual purity
tahor — ritually pure
tekios — *shofar* blasts
tallis (pl. **talleisim**) — fringed garment worn in prayer
talmid chacham — outstanding scholar
Talmud — codification and discussion of the corpus of Jewish law
tamei — ritually impure, unclean
Tanna — a Rabbi of the time of the Mishnah
tefillah — prayer
tefillin — small leather boxes containing Torah passages written on parchment
Tehillim — Psalms
tekias shofar — blowing the *shofar*
teletzke — an older calf
tenaim — lit. conditions; financial and other agreements regarding marriage
teshuvah — repentance
tevilah — immersion in a *mikveh*

tish — lit. table; Chassidic gathering at the Rebbe's meal
Tishah b'Av — Ninth of Av, a Jewish fast day commemorating the destruction of both Temples and other tragedies (occurs in mid-summer)
Torah — the Five Books of Moses
treif — not kosher
tumah — ritually impure, unclean; the opposite of *taharah*
tzaddik — saintly person
tzedakah — charity
tzidkus — righteousness
tziun — marker, esp. a grave marker
vort — lit. word; a celebration announcing a couple's intention to marry
yahrzeit — anniversary of death
Yam Suf — Sea of Reeds
yarmulke — skullcap
yasher koach — "May you be strengthened," a blessing to someone doing a meritorious deed
Yerushalayim — Jerusalem
yeshivah — school for advanced religious studies
yichud — a man and woman being alone together (usually forbidden)
yichus — familial descent (and reputation)
Yid — (pl. **Yidden**) Jew,
Yiddish — a Jewish-German dialect
Yiddishkeit — Judaism
yiras Shamayim — fear of Heaven
yishuv — settlement; community
Yom Kippur — the Day of Atonement
yom tov — holiday
yunger mahn — young man
zecher le-churban — to commemorate the destruction of the Holy Temple
zivug — destined mate
zmiros — Sabbath songs
zt"l — acronym for *zecher tzaddik livrachah*, may the memory of the righteous be for a blessing

This volume is part of
THE ARTSCROLLSERIES®
an ongoing project of
translations, commentaries and expositions
on Scripture, Mishnah, Talmud, Halachah,
liturgy, history, the classic Rabbinic writings,
biographies, and thought.

For a brochure of current publications
visit your local Hebrew bookseller
or contact the publisher:

Mesorah Publications, ltd

4401 Second Avenue
Brooklyn, New York 11232
(718) 921-9000